NFB Kids: Portrayals of Children
by the National Film Board
of Canada, 1939-89

Studies in Childhood and Family in Canada

Studies in Childhood and Family in Canada is a multidisciplinary series devoted to new perspectives on these subjects as they evolve. The series features studies that focus on the intersections of age, class, race, gender, and region as they contribute to a Canadian understanding of childhood and family, both historically and currently.

Series Editor:
Cynthia Comacchio
Department of History
Wilfrid Laurier University

Send manuscripts to:
Brian Henderson, Director
Wilfrid Laurier University Press
75 University Avenue West
Waterloo, Ontario, Canada, N2L 3C5

NFB Kids: Portrayals of Children by the National Film Board of Canada, 1939-89

Brian J. Low

Studies in Childhood and Family in Canada

Wilfrid Laurier University Press

This book has been published with the help of a grant from the Humanities and Social Sciences Federation of Canada, using funds provided by the Social Sciences and Humanities Research Council of Canada. We acknowledge the financial support of the Government of Canada through the Book Publishing Industry Development Program for our publishing activities.

National Library of Canada Cataloguing in Publication Data

Low, Brian John, 1950-
        NFB kids: portrayals of children by the National Film Board of Canada, 1939-1989

(Studies in childhood and family in Canada)
Includes bibliographical references and index.
ISBN 0-88920-386-5

1. Children in motion pictures—History. 2. National Film Board of Canada—History. 3. Motion pictures—Social aspects—Canada. 4. Motion pictures—Canada—History I. Title II. Series.

HQ792.C3L68 2002   791.43′652054′0971   C2001-903197-1

© 2002 Wilfrid Laurier University Press
        Waterloo, Ontario   N2L 3C5
        www.wlupress.wlu.ca

Cover design by Leslie Macredie using an NFB photograph from page 67 of this book.

All photographs credited to the National Film Board: Photo Library of the National Film Board of Canada, © National Film Board of Canada, 2002. All rights reserved.

The author and publisher have made every reasonable effort to obtain permission to reproduce the secondary material in this book. Any corrections or omissions brought to the attention of the Press will be incorporated in subsequent printings.

Printed in Canada

Contents

Children in a Cinematic Society

> Hence, by a simple juxtaposition of a series of preserved images and a commentary relating the story vividly, a chapter of contemporary history is recreated.
> — Marjory McKay, "The Motion Picture: A Mirror of Time," *NFB Annual Report, 1958-1959*

Imagine a society that exists solely in cinema, inhabiting urban, suburban, and rural scenes in more than eight thousand films, a society preserved for a half-century in film emulsion (the cinematic equivalent of amber) and so well preserved that every individual and every family, every group, social organization, and institution, every sight, sound, and movement, every social relationship and social practice, every social issue, social goal, and social transformation exists still. Such a society exists; it is preserved by the archives of the National Film Board of Canada (NFB).[1]

Since its genesis in 1939, this society in celluloid has been amassing an evolving cinematic representation of Canadian society, its patterns of social development anchored physically, socially, and intellectually to the socio-historical development of Canadian society and the state. In fact, "NFB society" has inherited much of the coherency of post-1930s Canadian social history and accurately mirrors a myriad of the nation's wartime and postwar social courses.

Notes to chapter 1 are on p. 235.

During the war years alone, more than three hundred films of "ordinary" Canadian men, women, and children were produced by the NFB, depicting citizens in the "intimate drama of their everyday lives," to employ the descriptive hyperbole of the founder of the Film Board, John Grierson. Over the decades that followed, thousands of Canadians were filmed within the social contexts in which real Canadians lived their lives, in urban, suburban, and rural environments, at home or at work, while serving social purposes that would constantly evolve over the National Film Board's first half-century. Of diverse regional, cultural, and economic backgrounds, these "Film Board Canadians" now fill the frames of thousands of miles of film preserved by the NFB archives, eternally engaged in the resolution of their social needs and in the pursuit of their social goals.

It is thus somewhat remarkable that broad surveys of the NFB film archives have seldom been conducted by historians for the portrayals of the peoples of Canada they contain. That is, while reflecting critically upon the institution, its films, and filmmakers, rarely have historians of the NFB made the subjects of their studies the actual subjects of the Film Board itself.[2] This book addresses the omission. It is an intellectual, cinematographic, and social history of the cinematic portrayals of Canadian children that were produced by the National Film Board of Canada from 1939-89, a study of transitions in the imagery and narrative of "NFB kids" within their families, schools, and communities.

NFB Kids charts a new direction both in the historiography of the NFB and cinema, exploring the formation and progressive development of a society in cinema, through a historical examination of three eras of NFB children: wartime, postwar, and post-1960s. The study describes the children themselves, and the physical and functional characteristics of social structures in which they appear[3]; it records social relations and practices revealed by the children's movement and dialogue within those structures; and it determines, whenever possible, the social ends for which the portrayals were produced. It documents transitions in the portrayals of children by the NFB and offers an explanation for those changes based upon action within the films and the activities at the National Film Board, as well as contemporary events within Canadian society and the Canadian state. Ultimately, *NFB Kids* links transitions in postwar NFB childhood to the transience of NFB society after the late 1960s.

The Children

Who are the children found in the microsociety created by the archival film collection of the NFB?[4] The question requires an answer both for the children as images and as real beings, both in terms of the contexts in which they appear and the contexts from which they appeared.

Of the more than eight thousand films catalogued by the NFB, more than seven hundred contain portrayals of children significant enough to warrant mention in the catalogue synopses. Among these portraits are to be found representations of the population of Canadian children at large in terms of age, gender, class, ethnicity, and regional diversity.[5] The children are found in films sponsored by a variety of federal, provincial, and municipal government departments, as well as in films sponsored by public and private institutions, public service groups, and agencies. They have been filmed on both black and white and colour sound stock. Some portraits are animated renderings of children in various media, but the majority are motion picture images of real infants, children, and adolescents. The children are both paid actors and unpaid non-actors (the great majority are non-actors) and they appear within the context of an array of structures and in a variety of documentary film types: public service and personal expression, cinéma direct, docu-drama, and alternative drama.

As with the adults who appear in NFB productions, the infants, youth, and adolescents who appear in the films acting the roles of Canadian children are, for the most part, Canadians. In fact, the long-standing practice of the Film Board has been to cast non-actors who are involved in some way with a film project as the "stars" of the film itself. Hence, the schoolchildren in a film about a rural New Brunswick school are quite likely the very children of that school acting in roles assigned to them by a NFB director; a Saskatchewan farm family portrayed at a dinner table are likely a Saskatchewan farm family; and a family of lighthouse keepers in British Columbia are most probably the very keepers of that lighthouse. This practice of employing the actual subjects of a film to play themselves, however, is far removed from being a hard-and-fast standard. Depending upon a film's subject and the film technique chosen for its treatment, local non-actors, professional actors, or a combination of the two may be used for a production. However, whether actors or non-actors, locals or not, invariably in a film about Canadian children, the children before the cameras are actually Canadians.

Second, the social issues addressed are equally Canadian ones. Whether it is a lecture on the benefits of providing nursery schools for

Canadian mothers at work in wartime industries or on the nutritional requirements of their children; whether a lesson in overcoming recalcitrance to a Manitoba health care plan or in reducing community resistance to progressive education in British Columbia; whether issues of dental health in rural Ontario or issues of mental health in Toronto; the rights of skateboarders in Montreal suburbs or the problems of mobility faced by wheelchair-bound children in Nova Scotia; whether assessing the emotional damage inflicted upon children by domineering mothers, or the damage caused children by fathers who abuse them; whether political issues of the day or of the past; whether issues of culture or region; issues of gender or age; environmental issues, safety issues, labour or recreational issues—whether or not Film Board issues are exclusively Canadian, all the issues of "NFB society" tend to be inclusively so and are seldom presented outside of a Canadian context.

A third significant link between children in NFB society and Canadian society is intellectual, and found in the conception, organization, and production of the films themselves. Since 1945, all NFB commissioners of film have been Canadian. Likewise, the majority of NFB filmmakers since the early 1940s have been selected from the educational, intellectual, and artistic communities of Canada. Thus, the filters of social thought and praxis through which most NFB films have been conceived and produced were, in the main, fashioned from Canadian sensibilities and meant for Canadian sensibilities.[6]

Finally, while individual National Film Board portraits of children vary as to the degree of accuracy with which they portray any particular Canadian social scenario or structure, when arranged diachronically, the entire body of portrayals accurately describes a myriad of Canadian social courses. When "real" Canadians go to war against fascism, "NFB Canadians" are at war with fascism; when Canadian families flock to the suburbs, "NFB families" move to the suburbs as well; when shirt fashions change for Canadian boys, the changes are paralleled by the very same trends with "NFB boys"; when educational practices are being transformed in Canadian schools, "NFB teachers" are at the forefront of the pedagogical changes. Unmistakably, the socio-historical development of NFB society is firmly anchored to that of Canada's. Indeed, the coherency of the social history of NFB portrayals may be wholly attributed to its congruency with the social history of Canada, since there is no unifying vision behind the NFB archival film collection beyond the mandate of the National Film Board "to interpret Canada to Canadians."[7]

A sampling of some of the biannual NFB catalogue synopses over the period of this study illustrates just how diverse the cinematic representations of Canadian childhood are—and just how markedly the texture of childhood in NFB society changes over the decades. The children described in the catalogues of the 1940s, for example, are taken to baby clinics, are inoculated, and eat nourishing lunches prepared by their mothers. They become sick from drinking unsanitary well water. They folk dance, become cadets, cut willow whistles, and sing in choirs. They visit dentists and go to nursery schools. They play on swings in a city park and watch ducks glide by on a pond. They play table tennis with their parents, attend summer camps, play marbles, softball, and lacrosse. They hike and ski and sing "Alouette" at their high school graduation party. They join army or navy cadets. They learn to play musical instruments. They watch films and listen to the radio. They cruise in boats and go blueberry picking with their families. They collect pennies and nickels to help needy children of the world. They join junior warden clubs and plant trees in deforested areas. As residents in hospitals for sick children, they suffer from spastics, polio, tuberculosis, and heart conditions. They act in amateur theatre productions, commemorate the freeing of American negro slaves, wake up early on a Saskatchewan farm, or ride in the hood of their mother's parka. They get a nickel for every cod that their father catches. They join a 4H club, are members of the safety patrol, tour a natural history museum, and try their hand at art in the park.

The children described in the catalogues of the 1950s are more adventurous and more sophisticated. They learn techniques of poise, posture, and good grooming. They play Little League baseball, fall behind in their studies, and attend summer school. They hitchhike on a highway, caddy at a golf course. They undergo moral dilemmas, vacation with their family at Banff National Park, leap into the path of an oncoming car. They are adopted. They learn to be conscientious teenaged drivers, play ice hockey at the tiny "atom" level, wear a kilt and play the bagpipes. They are accused of destructive behaviour and are denied the use of a community centre, join an "angel choir" for a Christmas concert, experience the problems of adolescent emotional adjustment, wander alone on downtown streets at night, and are unhappy about their protruding teeth. They confirm their faith at a Bar Mitzvah, grow up in Vancouver's "Chinatown," go to the Stanley Park Zoo, or sit on a sidewalk in Montreal and watch the Saint Jean Baptiste parade. They learn the techniques of textile manufacture to equip them for a lifetime occupation; they learn English as an immigrant, or learn to drive a hotrod. They learn to play an instrument by the Carl Orff method, watch their grandfather build a wooden chair, study the world's great music. They travel on an immigrant train; they move from a squalid tenement into a low-rental housing project. They are rushed to a poison control centre, are born in an igloo, are treated for strabismus, ride into a logging camp on a big white horse, or sit on Santa's knee at a downtown department store.

By the early 1960s, children are appearing in the catalogues in ever increasing numbers and cast in ever bolder narratives. They are found saving a family of beavers, clowning in a corner coke palace, grasping simple arithmetic relationships using Cuisenaire rods, and cheating on a test. They walk miles to a library in a prairie community. They sit in a circle in a kindergarten class. They spend a week at Camp Mohawk, cut their hair to answer a "Boy Wanted" sign at a saddleshop, tease the animals at a zoo, and swim in a lake at the home of a computer scientist. They tour the Pacific National Exhibition, go to school at a Hutterite colony, and get a taste of the life of a cowboy on a trail ride. They shriek and sob as they watch Paul Anka sing. They go on a bird-banding expedition, experience sibling rivalry, become a pregnant teenager, and use the same racial slurs in public that their parents use in private. They "borrow" a parked motorcycle, spin, jump, and dance on figure skates, and wear the sweater of a famous hockey team. They display inventions at a science fair, or they take part in a soccer seminar. They travel three thousand miles by train on a cross-Canada cultural exchange; they go along for the ride on their parents' second honeymoon.

In the catalogues of the later 1960s, children fly kites and play with war toys. They are part of a noisy motorcycle gang, dance in a bra and mini-skirt at a beach party, or neck with a boyfriend while babysitting. They move into a new neighbourhood while their family is falling apart, catch their first fish, skip rope, tell secrets, or settle a score at recess time. They block Yorkville avenue with hundreds of other young people. They play badminton or volleyball, do a highland dance at the only Gaelic college in the world, enjoy an afternoon of skirling pipes and swinging kilts. They undergo puberty, are the single child of a single mother, or one of five children of a deserted mother on welfare. They step-dance to an accordion on Fogo Island, stage their own act for the television screen. They experiment in freewheeling dramatic expression, roleplay being a teacher teaching teachers in a role reversal, or make a film about themselves and their world: a world of sit-ins, love-ins, and animated discussions. They skateboard down a steep hill with a friend on their shoulders. They witness the effect on their families of strains from the outside. They talk about the world as they see it: authority, drugs, social conflict and sex.

In the catalogue synopses of the early 1970s, the children's experiences vary widely. They vacation at their grandparents' cottage in Ontario, live an isolated life with lighthouse keepers on a coastal island in British Columbia, or are residents in a home for emotionally disturbed children. They are drawn out of the silent world of the deaf through technology; they attend public school despite having Spinabifida, live an active life although they can barely distinguish light from shadow. They learn mathematics from an 8mm single concept film loop; they play the drums, write on the blackboard, and drive a car with their feet. They are paperboys who toss some of their newspapers with neat precision and others with deliberate carelessness; they deliver pizzas with a pull wagon, ferret out golf balls from the rough and sell them to passing golfers. They go on a tour of national parks, face a tough initiation at a Catholic boys' school, or look for a chemical solution to almost everything.

Later in the decade, children appear in films organizing themselves to clean the countryside, while others engage in anarchy at a summer recreation centre. They are one of seven children of a welfare mother, or they are protected by their mother from both welfare agents and their father. They deal with parents who abused them, recover in a hospital from venereal infection, come across an unexploded bomb in a field. They suffer the effects of industrial pollution, torment a substitute teacher, or rubber raft with their parents down the Fraser River. They spend time in the burn unit of the Halifax hospital; they buy a gift for their destitute mother. They discuss morality, sexuality, and birth control. They offer spontaneous views on God, the beginning of life, or what happens to one's spirit when one dies. They join with a thousand other children to play ukeleles at a dockyard.

Surveying catalogues printed during the early 1980s, one notices the preponderance of children now dealing with especially unique or troubling situations. They are the children of Krishna parents, children afflicted with scoliosis or curvature of the spine, children who attempt suicide when their parents don't trust them. One group of schoolchildren initiates a project to learn about garbage and its impact on the environment. Children fight for their life against leukemia. There is a child whose mother is a truck driver at an iron ore company, another whose mother is a veterinarian. There are teenaged boys who talk candidly about masculinity, live with an autistic or a schizophrenic brother, are moulded into leaders at Ridley College. Girls recall the kinds of pressures that they grew up with; they play ringette, want to race in a soapbox derby. They inform their mother that for six years they have been forced to have sex with their dad or with their stepfather. One foster child commits suicide.

Ukelele scene from *Ready When You Are* (1975). NFB, S-13882.

In the second half of the 1980s, they are battered, neglected and sexually abused; they keep the family going despite the absence of an alcoholic father. They confide to friends about family members who watch or touch them; they hope for family reconciliation after divorce. They discuss the factors that influence their career choices: sex-role stereotyping, fear of failure, self-image, marriage, motherhood, and family expectations. They break into homes and steal; they learn how to act with dignity in court. They struggle to get out of juvenile prostitution; they have genetic disorders never documented before, and they learn about the use of a condom. They deal with the pain of parental separation, find out about how the technological revolution will affect their career. They march against cruise missile testing over Canada; they discuss what to do if a stranger, a neighbour, or someone living in the same house

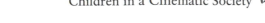

makes a request that "doesn't feel right." They make their dreams come true with the help of their friends.

They are a forest of images, the children in the cinematic society. Over the half-century span of this study, they have filled the frames of hundreds of miles of film and formed an immense social history recorded in motion pictures. But how is their history to be studied? Historiographies of childhood or film are not particularly illustrative of a tenable approach to such research. In the historiography of childhood, for example, very little has been done with motion picture portraiture of children. This is a somewhat surprising situation since the contemporary foundations of the field are, to a large degree, based upon images. In his seminal work, *Centuries of Childhood* (1962), Philippe Ariès developed a new perspective into the development of bourgeois society in Western Europe by observing transformations in children's portraits in the iconography of the late Middle-Ages and the Renaissance. Hence, one might anticipate that changes in cinematic portrayals of children in Western cinemas would likewise reveal novel insights into the evolution of Western societies during the century of the motion picture, a century appropriately dubbed "the century of the child."[8] However, with the exception of Neil Postman, who observed in *The Disappearance of Childhood* (1982) that children are often portrayed in contemporary media in the manner of thirteenth and fourteenth century paintings (i.e., as miniature adults) there is little academic commentary in this body of literature about the social history of images of children in film.

Even in the historiography that makes cinematographic portrayals its subject, there are numerous studies of adult portrayals—women in film, American Indians in film, blacks in film—but few studies of children.[9] Nor is the larger body of literature about film theory and film history particularly illustrative of a research methodology applicable to this task. Work by film theorists tend toward deconstructionist or Freudian semiotics by which to interpret portrayals of film subjects and, while these seem useful within film studies, from a historical perspective they range from being wildly relativistic to being too predictable to be plausible as frameworks for historical explanation. Ever more cautious, mainstream film historiography, for its part, has steered away from longitudinal studies of the subjects of films and toward studies linking cinematic history to issues of censorship and propaganda by the state, as well as to quantitative studies of audiences to determine the popular impact of films, and to considerations of the validity of film as a historical resource. There are, of course, numerous studies of historical events and individuals as they are portrayed in movies and newsreels, and a myriad of diverse studies of the structural history of the cinema itself, but few and inevitably brief are the scholarly historical accounts of the filmed portraits of any cultural, regional, economic, or gender group—and rarer still any historical account of the filmed portraits of children. Indeed, what is most apparent from historical works to date using filmed portraits of children is that very little has been undertaken. This is a somewhat inviting situation given that children have been the subject of cinematographers practically since the invention of the projecting motion picture camera by the Lumière brothers in 1895.[10]

In part, this neglect of cinema portraiture as a subject for social history is due to an uncertainty among historians in general about film as a historical document. Specifically, what does it document? Although they seem seductively attractive as a resource, what physical, social, or intellectual realities of any place or time can be credibly derived from motion pictures? Two streams of cinema historiography have evolved around this question: investigations into the production and reception of larger groups of films (of a genre, an era, an auteur, etc.) and analyses of single films. For both, the mainstream wisdom has been that since "no film escapes fiction," films should be studied primarily for the attitudes that they forward into a society, rather than as credible reflections of that society.[11] *NFB Kids* tackles the issues of external validity with a novel approach to the problem. It juxtaposes images from diachronically arranged bodies of archival NFB films to present an "in-house" history of a cinematic society. This approach circumvents historiographic restrictions concerning what a film may credibly be said to document—it documents the images it preserves. Moreover, it exploits, as never before, the most distinctive attribute of those images: to echo the turn-of-the-century barkers who stood in front of Edison's nickleodeons, "They move!"

Movement and a Social History of NFB Children

Movement is the essence of film; it distinguishes cinematography from all other forms of recorded imagery. Hence, a historian using film documents as a primary resource should utilize whatever is to be found in motion picture movement that escapes other visual documentation—social relations, for example. As E.P. Thompson noted in his classic text, *The Making of the English Working Class* (1968), social relations are best observed within the passage of time: their subtleties by necessity requiring examination in movement. Hence, historically speaking, one may argue that social relations of the past (as well as social practices of the past) may be best observed in films of that past—as only film suspends segments of the passage of time without stopping movement.[12]

Moreover, the relations and practices of childhood as portrayed by the National Film Board of Canada are not restricted solely to observation at twenty-four frames per second. Within the social structures of filmic portrayals—families, their schools and communities—childhood as portrayed by the NFB moves over historical time as well, a feat made possible by the continuous operation of the Film Board cameras since 1939. Film Board children appear within social structures and in a context—a place and a time—and engage in social relations with adults and each other. Replace one reel on the film projector with another, and a second generation of NFB children may be juxtaposed with the first, operating within a similar context, engaged in modified relationships with comparable families, schools, and communities. Thus, childhood as portrayed by the National Film Board, when screened diachronically, may be observed in continual transformation. The eight thousand films in toto in the National Film Board archives capture slices of time for legions of Canadian children, revealing the nature of their social relations and practices through their movement within films and the history of these through their continual reappearance in the film archives.

Conjointly, there is an element of social purpose that distinguishes National Film Board productions from other cinematic genres. From the outset of the documentary film movement in the late 1920s social purpose was joined to film. Documentary films were meant to be (according to Grierson) "creative treatments of actuality," whose primary purpose was to provide knowledge for "moods of resolution," rather than entertainment for "moods of relaxation."[13] Thus, in the narrative of a Film Board production—in the soundtrack or in a mise en scène—one may find, more often than not, an expression of social needs, social goals, or, on occasion, the introduction of a new, ethical principle of social relations. These elements arise within the films due to human activity at the NFB in response to social issues perceived to exist within Canadian society. Hence, while Film Board portrayals may be "creative treatments of actuality," the social purposes they serve can be attributed to changing contemporary perceptions of social realities.

The dynamics among these social elements—the relationships between the social purposes served by NFB portrayals of children and the changing social practices and relations of childhood in the cinematic society—are of central significance to this study, particularly in regard to the introduction of new ethical principles of social relations into Canadian society through NFB productions and subsequent changes in social relations and practices in NFB families, schools, and communities. The study asks how the introduction of new principles of social relations affects both the immediate and later social practices and relations of NFB children, and how are changing social relations of NFB childhood related to later transformations within the cinematic society as a whole?

Cinematographic Children in the Century of the Child

But why study NFB cinematographic portrayals of children rather than adults who are empowered to transform society, and why study NFB portrayals in particular? To begin to answer these questions, recall that the twentieth century was dubbed "the century of the child." What does this designation mean? According to Theresa Richardson in her *The Century of the Child: The Mental Hygiene Movement and Social Policy in the United States and Canada* (1989), it refers to the convergence of medical and scientific interests into the conditions of mass childhood during that century, especially following World War I.[14]

During the "century of the child," medicine and science inquired by direct observation into the physical and mental development of children, a circumstance labelled "the childhood gaze" by Foucault among others.[15] The scientific perspective of this gaze, according to Richardson, was based upon a "positivistic rationalism directed toward controlling social change from positions of authority according to ideals of order and efficiency," while the medical perspective was "a broad based humanism directed toward perfecting the human condition according to equalitarian principles."[16] Providing direction for both perspectives were the philanthropic foundations which funded the childhood gaze with the aim of altering the conditions of mass childhood, and which, coincidentally, harnessed the eyes of motion picture cameras to this purpose.

Lawrence K. Frank was a senior officer of the Laura Spelman Rockefeller Memorial (LSRM), a primary funding body for the childhood gaze in North America. He discussed the implications of possible public reforms emerging from this philanthropic enterprise in his chapter "Childhood and Youth" in the monumental *Recent Social Trends in the United States: Report of the President's Research Committee* (1933):

> As Ellen Key expressed it: "...'holiness of generation.' This consciousness will make the central work of society the new race, its origin, management, and its education; about these all morals, all laws, all social arrangements will be grouped. This will form the point of view from which all other questions will be judged, all other regulations made."[17]

For Frank and other agents of philanthropy, the outstanding outcome of "the childhood gaze" was "the growing belief in the possibility of directing and controlling social life through the care and nurture of children."[18] To a large extent, he reasoned, the social life of tomorrow was already determined by the children of today, since they literally were the future society. "The child is the bridge—biologically and socially—to the future," observed Frank.[19] To build a bridge of a suitable design, however, required some engineering of the social practices of those responsible for the care and nurture of future children, specifically their parents and teachers.

Among agents of philanthropy, such as Frank, there was a growing feeling about the importance of both the home and school for constructing the "new race." In the public schools, predicted Frank, there would be "the assumption...of responsibilities formerly considered the duties of the home and church."[20] And of the home, Frank wrote in 1933, "The attempt to influence the daily life of the home may be regarded as one of the major developments of recent years. It is fairly safe to say that the movement is in its early stages and that its real importance will not be revealed for a decade or two."[21]

Alluding to the means by which "the daily life of the home" would be influenced, Frank noted the significant role played by the mass media in family life, how "the altered relations of parents and children in the small family are becoming a topic of widespread discussion in magazines and journals," and how "those in control of commercial moving pictures and radio broadcasting are influencing the rearing of children."[22] Moreover, Frank noted the considerable attraction of young people to the cinema: "Children are attending moving pictures in large numbers and are apparently receiving a considerable amount of their education thereby, particularly in human relations and more specifically in courtship and marriage."[23]

Almost certainly, the ideas conveyed by Hollywood of the workings of the world from the 1930s to the 1950s, including those concerning human relations, had been subject to ideological management by outside interests. Indeed, in his *Images of American Life: A History of Ideological Management in Schools, Movies, Radio, and Television* (1992), Joel Spring concludes of this golden era of the cinema that "stated simply, the movie industry felt called upon to appease the most vocal and powerful."[24] Whether this included agents of philanthropic foundations or not is unclear, since little research has been undertaken to determine what ideological management, if any, philanthropy wielded over the Hollywood movie and nascent television industries.[25]

What is clear, however, is that motion pictures were, from an early moment, being employed to document the childhood gaze and, from the outset of the postwar baby boom, that documentary films were being made to educate parents about applicable discoveries being made by medicine and science. It is this dual function of film both in the research and the outcome of the childhood gaze that is of interest for this study—the roles films fulfilled as both document and documentary, observer and agent of medicine and science.

In the United States, an illustrative instance of this duality occurred at Yale University's "Clinic of Child Development," a research facility under Arnold Gesell M.D., a psychologist who trained under G. Stanley Hall. In the documentary *Life with Baby* (1946), a *March of Time* film produced for postwar American cinema audiences, Gesell and his staff at the Clinic were filmed as they observed and filmed the behaviour of infants under a "one way vision dome," a device "which conceals from the child those while watching him."[26]

> Here for 35 years a group of child specialists have been diligently at work, charting the behavior patterns of children from every kind of environment in order to establish some standard of development to serve as a yardstick by which parents, teachers and doctors may better understand the child's mental growth. After years of cooperative research and experimentation the various progressive stages of mental growth have been identified.[27]

Following actual film footage shot under the one way vision dome, the *March of Time* documentary records the clinic's walk-in film vault, showing shelves full of film reels, as well as scenes of men and women dressed in white, lab jackets, doing frame-by-frame analyses of the cinematic portrayals of children: "All these and many more stages of child development have been recorded by movie cameras, and the clinic's vaults today contain miles of film. Every foot of this film has been indexed, studied and analyzed by Dr. Gesell and his students."[28]

Gradually thereafter, the film becomes less a document and more a "documentary," its intent—to influence child-rearing practices in American homes—reliant upon the blurring of the distinction between the two functions of the film. By intercutting film documents from the Gesell film vault with "documentary" footage, *Life with Baby* constructs a strong impression of scientific credibility for the work of the Gesell Clinic and especially for the Clinic's research thesis: that all "normal" children develop physically and mentally through observable "natural stages" and socially through observable "normal patterns." In *Life with*

Baby, Gesell states the case succinctly before a group of thoughtful students:

> The mind manifests itself in patterns of behavior, which take on characteristic shapes throughout infancy and childhood. We have identified the behavior patterns which may be used as standards of reference in the clinical diagnosis of child development. When you observe the work of this clinic, you will see how these diagnostic standards are applied.[29]

Applied by the documentary filmmakers, the normative standards as revealed to the researchers by "miles of film" are intended to both impress the cinema audience as to the certitude of the Gesell thesis and the wrongheadedness of believing otherwise. To seal the impression of certain knowledge on the part of the clinic staff, there appears a negative character in the film, an "Aunt Bessy," who fails to understand that "every child develops at its own pace, a fact which amateur experts would do well to understand."[30] The portrayal of Aunt Bessy is a caricature. Elderly, dressed in black from head to toe, heavily made-up, with pencil-thin eyebrows, crooked nose and craggy features, Aunt Bessy looks very much like the wicked witch in the American feature film, *The Wizard of Oz* (1939).

Immediately succeeding this negative stereotyping of "amateur experts" who would contradict the findings of the Gesell Clinic, there is a subtle switch in the narrative script from the "natural stages" of physical and mental development of children to the "normal patterns" of their social development—information shared at a mothers' child study group with parents anxious to "rid themselves of old worries and misconceptions."[31] The attentive parents (both in the film and presumably in the cinema audience) are instructed by a "Miss Janet Learned," an assistant at the Clinic, who, in age, appearance, and demeanour, is a striking contrast to Aunt Bessy.

> Too often parents lacking in knowledge of child development will punish their children for behavior that is entirely normal. During the child's first year of life, most parents are willing to accept his behavior as natural. Nobody punishes a baby for creeping instead of walking. But all too often they do punish him in his second year when he upsets things in the room and doesn't put them back. It is easier for a young child to pull things down than to put them up. After a little more growth he'll enjoy putting things back in their place. Parents punish their four-year-old child for making faces at people. Fortunately, parents who understand the normal stages of growth do not punish

the child for behaving like this. They are better able to guide him and enjoy him because they know that many troublesome phases are simply normal and natural stages in the child's development.[32]

Miss Learned's lecture concerning "normal and natural stages" of social development in childhood is legitimized by the parallel evidence previously supplied about physical and mental development in children and is capped by the film's concluding narration:

> The long and patient study of child behavior made by Dr. Gesell and other workers in the field has made it clear that childhood's greatest need from birth throughout the formative years is for a parental attitude of enlightened understanding. For this understanding with love and care will bring to healthy fruition the budding individuality of the citizen of tomorrow's world.[33]

Many of the documentary techniques employed in *Life with Baby* were developed by filmmakers working under John Grierson in Britain in the 1930s and at the National Film Board of Canada in the 1940s, with similar goals to those of Frank and other agents of philanthropy: to shape the course of society (through the medium of film) or, in typical Griersonian prelection, to "crystallize sentiments in a muddled world and create a will toward civic participation."[34] In National Film Board productions, children were a vital part of these efforts, both in the Grierson years and thereafter, in Grierson's efforts to shape a "cooperative democracy" in Canadian society and the efforts of later NFB documentarians to shape the outcomes of the century of the child.

For this reason alone, the sense that the NFB used children to promote the visions of specific agencies in Canada (most notably Grierson's and those of the Department of National Health and Welfare), it is worthwhile to study the cinematographic portraits of children thus created. But more. Motion picture cameras were enlisted in the childhood gaze to study childhood as well as to influence it. Film had a dual purpose in the century of the child—as observer as well as agent—two distinct uses for cinematography that were developed during the early years of the century, but only one of which, film as agent, for which the National Film Board productions have ever been employed. While the primary intent of NFB cinematic portrayals of children was the promotion of practices and principles expected by childhood experts to produce desirable social outcomes, a subsequent result has been the collection of hundreds of miles of film now available for a new, historical gaze to investigate the outcomes themselves. To paraphrase historian Geoff Eley: "The practitioners have had their say. The historians should now take the stage."[35]

Reconstructing the Social History of a Cinematic Society

The earliest historian of the NFB, Marjory McKay, posited that "the motion picture will always be a mirror of a people's history, even more so in Canada where its documentary character is being preserved."[36] Her supposition that a people's history was preserved in film, that it awaited reconstruction through a simple juxtaposition of images, has inspired the approach of this research both analytically and in manner of presentation. Juxtaposed synchronically (among social structures at any one period of time) and diachronically (within social structures over time), NFB images do, in fact, reflect a people's history, just as McKay suggested—albeit of a cast of people whose society, past and present, exists solely in film emulsion.

To begin the reconstruction, a pool of two hundred and fifty films was selected from a historical collection of NFB catalogues. Films were chosen on the basis of containing significant portrayals of Canadian children which, on the whole, seemed roughly representative of the entire body of children described in the catalogue synopses. Reels were screened, half-decade by half-decade, in blocks of twenty-five films, the first series being 1939-44. Field notes were taken during the initial screenings, and films were occasionally re-examined or transferred to videotape for detailed analysis. The original pool of selections was expanded as particular issues, themes, eras, or contexts warranted further consideration or documentation.[37]

Generally, the earliest childhood portrayals served to determine both the initial forms of family, school, and community structures in which NFB children appear as well as the founding characteristics of the portrayals themselves. The films of this era served also to determine the functional role played by children in Grierson's "democratic education" of Canadians; i.e., how images of children were used to advance his conception of a postwar progressive democracy in Canada. Later reflections (1947-89) contrasted with earlier ones served to determine what changes had occurred in the childhood portraits over the decades; what transitions among the portrayal of families, schools, and communities were accompanying these changes—and why?

As a general rule, explanations for transitions in the portrayals of children were sought both internally, within NFB society, by examining the social dynamics within the films themselves, and externally, by examining contemporaneous activities at the National Film Board of Canada, within Canadian society, or of the Canadian state. In any case, because filmmaking (like history) is a human process, historical explanations for transience among the images were sought first and foremost in the activities of human agents, either acting within the films, working at the National Film Board, or acting upon Canadian society or the Canadian state.

Accompanying this search for human agency, the portrayals of children were analyzed, whenever relevant, in terms of film style, structure, technology, aesthetics, or ideology. Changes in social patterns were also contextualized in relation to changes within Canadian society at large and at the National Film Board in particular—the war years, the cold war, events of the late 1960s, feminism, multiculturalism, the restructuring of the NFB, and the advent of video technology in the 1970s, for example—as well as the comings and goings of fashions and fads.

Philippe Ariès' monumental *Centuries of Childhood* (1962), with its innovative use of iconography, provided the intellectual inspiration for this project while articles by Sol Cohen and monographs by Ellen Herman, *The Romance of American Psychology* (1995), Christopher Lasch, *The Culture of Narcissism* (1978), Esteve Morera, *Gramsci's Historicism* (1990), Douglas Owram, *Born at the Right Time* (1996), and Theresa Richardson, *The Century of the Child* (1989) all bore significantly on the development of the major argument advanced within this book concerning the postwar mental health movement and its impact upon the social lives of the children and adults portrayed in the films.

In addition, a substantial body of secondary literature in related fields, especially histories of childhood, education, family, and film provided ancillary contexts by which to interpret the transience of Canadian social structures reflected in the NFB mirror.[38] Supplemental to these and other secondary sources, screenings of NFB films were accompanied by an extensive examination of primary materials held at the NFB archives, especially production documents, film catalogues, and NFB annual reports. An examination was made of Gallup Polls published in Canada from 1942 to 1989 to explore the relationship between the Gallup results and Canadian society as projected by the National Film Board and, finally, for the third chapter, "*Lessons in Living*," a recorded interview was conducted with some of the children who acted in a 1944 film production on Vancouver Island.

NFB Kids: A Progressive Narrative Emerges

Just as a single NFB portrayal of children imposes its narrative on a spectator through a juxtaposition of cinematic segments, so too does the juxtaposition of a series of portrayals impose a coherent narrative concerning changing patterns of social life in the cinematic society. Before commencing this narrative, however, some contextual information concerning the prehistory, creation and development of the National Film Board of Canada is helpful, if early depictions of NFB society—its ethical principles, social practices, and relations—are to be understood. Consequently, the first section of this book presents the foundation and formative years of the Film Board beginning with a study of its founder, John Grierson. The section examines Grierson as an agent of progressive ethical principles, who adamantly worked the original fabric of NFB society into a progressive weave by exercising sweeping control over his filmmakers, film content, and style. His conceptualization of Canadians as a socially cooperative people inclined less to individualism and nationalism and tending more toward community achievement is a notion still held by many Canadians to be central to the national psyche. This is a stereotype which can be linked to Grierson's engineering of themes embedded in the more than seven hundred films that saturated the population before the end of the war in the first moving, sound images of themselves as a body politic that a significant number of Canadians had ever observed.

Making room for progressivism. NAC, PA 194973.

A progressive subtext to this discourse of social cooperation emerges during an in-depth examination of a single "Griersonian" production of the war years, *Lessons in Living* (1944). Documents related to the production suggest that although the agents who produced, promoted, and even acted in the film appear on the screen to be working towards revitalizing smaller communities by promoting cooperation in educational matters, the evidence supports a dual reading: that an equal aim of the authors of the film was to usurp to the state traditional authority exercised by individual communities over the education of their children.[39] The resulting vision of children increasingly in the service of the progressive state is a recurring one over the next two sections of the study.

Section two continues the examination of the development of NFB society begun by the first section through a juxtaposition of film portrayals of Canadian children from 1946-67, establishing the themes and purposes of the postwar portraits and observing the changes in social practices and social relations pertaining to childhood widely evident by the end of the era. Although drawing broadly upon external contexts for a historical explanation of these changes, an in-house argument develops that the first new ethical principle of significant impact to appear among the portrayals of children after the war was "mental hygiene." This was a progressive concept which, in the guise of "mental health" and "child guidance," was simultaneously penetrating Canadian familial, educational, and community structures virtually unobstructed via government pamphlets, baby books, magazines, newspapers, and radio scripts—as well as through the changing language of educational theorists and practitioners.

This section follows the course of a small shift in adult-child power relations that appears in NFB society shortly after the adoption of hygienist child-rearing practices that clearly originate from the Gesell Clinic at Yale University.[40] Over the next two decades, the gulf of power between adults and children narrows significantly, promoting and advancing the control of children over the events of their social mise en scènes. Over the section, juxtaposed against a broader description of Film Board portraits, the antecedents and after-effects of the postwar mental hygiene/mental health movement are examined as they develop within the archival collection. The section ends with the "new generation" of NFB young people on Yorkville Street in Toronto in the film, *Flowers on a One-way Street* (1967), blocking traffic and flexing their mass, social muscle against traditional authority.

As with the first section, there is a paradox to be pondered at the end of the second section. For rather than "invigorating the family as a social group" or "fostering the spirit of liberty" that is said to animate the individual child (as promised by Gesell for example), both family life and individualism appear to suffer in NFB society. Over the decades following the adoption of mental hygiene principles of child rearing, the rising generation of NFB youth become less and less influenced by the expectations of their individual families and teachers and more and more susceptible to the norms of "the group, the gang, the kids," as their cohorts are described in Film Board productions of the late 1950s and early 1960s.[41]

The final section of the study examines the cinematic mirror following 1967 to observe members of the new generation in adulthood—their families, schools, and communities—and their children. At the same time as the baby-boomers, both men and women, begin appearing in the films in mature roles (including roles as NFB filmmakers), a similar bent toward "democratizing" traditional power relations as was first witnessed in postwar families begins to pervade the cinematic society as a whole. Control over representational voice is yielded to previously voiceless "cultural communities": First Nations peoples, the poor, and minority groups in particular. Soon afterward, Studio D, an autonomous women's studio, becomes established at the Film Board. This section follows the subsequent course of social relations among new generation adults and next generation children as the "new society" progresses into a "state of disequilibrium"—a period of transient and contested power relations.[42] This postmodern reflection of Canadian society is marked by an unabated drift toward child-centered narratives, by the restructuring of traditional social structures and, most notably, by waning roles of leadership for boys and men and, conversely, the ascension to leading roles by NFB girls and women.

This final section concludes by revisiting the first to speculate, at last, upon the origins and implications of shifts in power relationships to be found in the mirror of the NFB. It forwards the view that progressive campaigns advanced by the National Film Board (along with other agencies) into Canadian society during the 1940s and 1950s—particularly those of the mental hygiene movement—had a profound affect upon social relations in the cinematic microsociety through the 1960s to the 1980s.

It suggests that those who conceived of "the century of the child," and those who promoted it, accurately appraised the existing potential to engineer the social conditions of future society by altering mass child rearing and schooling practices but were mistaken (or were misleading) about the outcomes of the practices they prescribed. It concludes that by weakening, rather than "invigorating" or even maintaining the influence of families, schools and communities over the culture of childhood, progressive campaigns of the 1940s and 1950s amplified the influence of the mass media upon a rapidly expanding network of childhood. As a result, in NFB society, the socialization of children over the years of this study becomes more and more directly the prerogative not of families, nor their schools, nor their communities, but of agents empowered to manufacture their social discourse in cinematic imagery.[43]

NFB Kids in the "Mirror of Canada"

Upon first reflection, McKay's assertion that "film constitutes a mirror of a period" appears to be a suspect premise upon which to base a historical study. Indeed, it seems doubtful whether NFB filmmakers could truly "mirror" Canadian society even if they wished to. And yet, on the other hand, used in its classical sense the mirror metaphor precisely characterizes NFB productions. In her outstanding monograph, *The Glass of Form: Mirroring Structures from Chaucer to Skelton* (1991), Anna Torti, a scholar of medieval English literature, takes note of the function of the mirror (*speculum*) as it was used in medieval texts: "The mirror has in fact a double function: it is both positive and negative in showing us what we should be and what we are. In the mirror-image relationship, the mirror has the active role as the means by which the ideal is seen in a transient image."[44] In its classical sense, then, as described by Torti, the mirror provides neither a true image of a subject solely ("what is") nor merely an ideal one ("what ought to be"), but, rather, the movement of the one toward the other—thus proffering both at once. As it was with the medieval *speculum*, so too it is with the NFB documentary.

The portrayals of children by the NFB are both at once images of "what is" in Canadian society and ideals of "what ought to be." A single film has the active role as "the means by which the ideal is seen in a transient image," but moreover, by surveying the entire collection of films, the "what is" may be observed in transience as well. Hence, the archival collection of the National Film Board of Canada does literally constitute "a mirror of a period," just as McKay observed.

The narrative that follows is the mirror reflection, not only of the ideals of "what ought to be" that were introduced into Canadian society through the portrayals of children by the National Film Board of Canada, but also subsequent transitions in images of "what is" within the social structures of the cinematic microsociety: i.e., "NFB society." The narrative proffers a number of insights into Canadian childhood over five decades, the most significant of which is, perhaps, that just as technological science was developing a mass medium of interest to Canadian children, social science was developing a mass susceptibility to it.

Early NFB Society:
The Eyes of Democracy

> Preach to the eye, if you would preach with efficacy. By
> that organ, through the medium of the imagination the
> judgement of the bulk of mankind may be led and
> moulded almost at pleasure.
> — Jeremy Bentham, *Rationale of Judicial Evidence, 1827*

"Why can't we say it and be done with it," remarked John Grierson in
an early-1940 radio broadcast, "the National Film Board will be the
eyes of Canada. It will, through a national use of cinema, see Canada
and see it whole—its people and its purposes."[1] In a nutshell, this is a
fairly precise description of early NFB society—a wartime vision of the
peoples of Canada seen through the unifying lens of the nation's documentary cameras. But as they listened to Grierson on their radios, how
many Canadians could have envisioned that the "whole" of their country was greater than the sum of its existing geographical, political, and
social parts? Certainly, few of them could have imagined that the peoples of Canada were endowed with a national character beyond the
attributes historically ascribed to Canadians.[2] Yet nothing less than a
Canadian public with a "progressive" character, a social dynamic to be
projected upon the nation's motion picture screens, was Grierson's

Notes to chapter 2 are on p. 239.

vision as he spoke over the CBC radio network. Already, his National Film Board was organizing to impress ordinary Canadians with this cinematic sense of their national selves, and, as they listened to their radios, already ordinary men, women, and children like themselves were acting in the roles assigned to them by the National Film Board. Joined together, screenplays and ordinary people, "what ought to be" and "what was," the National Film Board and Canadians would fix in film the founding physical, social, and intellectual patterns of NFB society.

"The Damned Theory": John Grierson and the Sociology of Cinema

It would be fair to say that Grierson, the founder of the British documentary film movement, launched himself into the construction of the National Film Board with vigour and, at the same time and with equal vigour, attempted to launch himself out of it. According to British film historian Nicholas Pronay, Grierson longed to be in Britain to play a major part in the war effort:

> He wanted to be in London. He wanted to be in the centre of the propaganda war, not at its farthest periphery. He signalled his availability to London by stipulating that his appointment [at the Film Board] was to be six months in the first instance and kept on signalling it—but to no avail. No invitation ever came to Grierson from London.[3]

Pronay is correct in his assertion that Grierson wished to resign from the NFB early on in his tenure of the Film Commissionership, but his hypothesis that Grierson's sole ambition was to be in London directly involved in war propaganda is somewhat at odds with a letter written by Grierson to the secretary of the Guggenheim Memorial Foundation during June 1940, asking for funding for a year in which to theorise and write about documentary film:

> I have, as I think you appreciate, been concerned with a theory of education and with the problem of so galvanizing the imagination of democratic citizenship that it would be inspired to efficiency and effectiveness....But pursuing mere war propaganda as I now do, I feel bricked in from saying or doing as much as I might. You will appreciate how limited mere war propaganda can be....It is the idea and its influence that I want further to mature. You can greatly help me to do it.[4]

But no financial help came from the Guggenheim Foundation; Grierson received the bad news in a telegram at the end of July. Nor was any forthcoming from the Carnegie Foundation to which a similar request was relayed, nor from the Rockefeller Foundation. Nor, as Pronay notes, was any lifeline offered by the British Government for Grierson to engage in "mere war propaganda" from a London base. Grierson was "bricked in" at the National Film Board of Canada for the duration of the war.

John Grierson. NFB.

Denied the opportunity to theorize and write about documentary film, Grierson instead began to engineer a massive application of his theory in Canada—the creation and consolidation of a huge propaganda machine meant to "galvanize the imagination" of Canadians toward efficiency and effectiveness. As early as the spring of 1942, in writing the text for a prospective book to be titled *Eyes of Democracy*, he was articulating the role he saw for himself and the NFB: "...to take a country like Canada as an example of what the medium [of film] can do for a nation."[5] Or, as he confided to his friend, Basil Wright, in London: "Perhaps I secretly wish I could put the damned theory into practice on a larger scale."[6]

"The theory" had been evolving in Grierson's mind since his days as a student at the University of Chicago in the mid-1920s. The young Scotsman had been brought to America to study sociology as one of the earliest recipients of a Laura Spelman Rockefeller Memorial (LSRM) Fellowship. Working under the tutelage of some of the foremost progressive intellectuals in the United States, he became immersed in a philosophy of "democratically" imposed social order and stability. Grierson had little difficulty in accepting the principles of the progressive state, having come to America with a philosophical bent toward "absolute idealism."[7] As espoused by the Scottish philosher and historian, Thomas Carlyle, absolute idealism called for the replacement of the governing classes by an elite of "cultivated persons" who would emphasize the highest values at which society must aim—"values which transcended the class values of free enterprise culture."[8] This broad range of values was to be propagated through a comprehensive system of popular education, "which would draw the individual into a rational consensus."[9]

The impetus to the conception of "the theory" was a meeting arranged by his faculty supervisor, the pioneering political scientist, Charles E. Merriam, between Grierson and Walter Lippmann in 1926. Lippmann was editor of the *New York World*, and author of two seminal texts, *Public Opinion* (1922) and *The Phantom Public* (1925). In *Public Opinion*, Lippmann had expressed the view that individuals acted not on direct knowledge but on the mental pictures given to them by others: images for which he coined the term "stereotypes." Stereotypes were pictures people had "of themselves, of others, of their needs, purposes, and relationships."[10] They were "trustworthy pictures of an outside world," and they were "planted there by another human being whom we recognize as authoritative."[11]

Lippmann believed that the mechanics of modern society were beyond the understanding of the average citizen. In his view, it was necessary, therefore, to shape public opinion to ensure the orderly workings of a complex society. Every complicated community, he observed, had sought the assistance of "special men," of augurs, priests, elders.[12] In 1920s society, he believed, there was a need to interpose "some form of expertness between the private citizen and the vast environment in which he is entangled," a need to "introduce into the existing machinery agencies that will hold up a mirror week by week, month by month."[13]

Among the ideas of Walter Lippmann that influenced Grierson, none was more significant than the newspaperman's conviction concerning the propaganda potential of manipulated imagery—i.e., how "photographs have the kind of authority over imagination today, which the printed word had yesterday...they seem utterly real."[14] "In the whole experience of the race," wrote Lippmann in *Public Opinion*, "there has been no aid to visualization comparable to the cinema...the motion picture depicts unfolding events, the outcome of which the audience is breathlessly waiting."[15] He then suggested to Grierson that the yellow press and its popular influence, which had been the focus of Grierson's research, paled in comparison to that of Hollywood's extraordinary mass appeal. He advised Grierson that he might find something useful for his studies in the box-office receipts of the Hollywood studios. In December 1925, Grierson set out on a roundabout route through America to follow Lippmann's advice.

In Hollywood, in June 1926, producer Walter Wanger (himself a colleague of C.E. Merriam during World War I) opened up the box-office files at Famous Players-Lasky to Grierson and offered him a retainer to analyze their productions. Perhaps of most value to Hollywood were Grierson's findings that pictures "could never be too big" for the public's taste and that movies which encouraged people paid off best at the box office: "The single doctrine of the average showman, that it pays him to make people 'feel good'...pays him still better to make them 'feel great.'"[16] Of greater value to Grierson himself, however, especially from his analysis of "westerns," was the opportunity they afforded him to theorize about the sociology of cinema, in particular Hollywood cinema and its relationship to American society.

Grierson theorized that the cinema had its influence on the same "ideological centres to which advertisement endeavours to make its appeal."[17] Because of its persuasive appeal, and because it was truly a "mass medium" ("the one solitary institution on which the masses really depend for imaginative release and daily example") Grierson reasoned that the cinema's "creative possibilities as a guiding force among the needs, desires, and ambitions of emergent democracy [were] obviously enormous."[18] Indeed, noted Grierson, the cinema had "a practical monopoly over the dramatic strata of the common mind in which preferences, sympathies, affections and loyalties, if not actually created are at least crystallized and coloured."[19]

In choosing the American Western as a research sample, Grierson could not fail but observe the importance of Hollywood stars as models for the American public. He noted how the star system was "apposite to individualistic societies like America," how movie stars modeled an ideal of "individualistic socialization within a mass culture."[20] Furthermore, he noted how consistently the "western" genre favoured certain ideals and narratives, and how dependable the resulting patterns of characterization and attitude were within the genre, with the result that every "western" built upon and supported the ideas of all the others. As a result, he found the effect of the Hollywood Western upon cinema audiences to be practically indelible: "the mere horseplay of the woolly west passes into tales of the pioneers."[21]

When he left the United States for Britain in January 1927, the germ of an idea for using cinema as a sociological tool was developing in his mind—an idea he would advance in his work for the British government but which he would not bring to full fruition until he was at last "bricked in" at the National Film Board of Canada. This was the essence of the theory—a cinematic state of mind to discipline the public in the patterns of its imagination. Utilizing films about agriculture, conservation, health, labour, nutrition, the post office, taxation, recreation, rural problems, education, and native and ethnic affairs, he would construct filmic patterns that would enable a progressive Canadian identity of "efficiency and effectiveness" to pass (as had Hollywood westerns for Americans) "into tales of the pioneers."

By the late-1930s, Grierson was certain that a powerful national experience could be kindled through the medium of film—that film was "an instrument of great importance in establishing patterns of a national imagination."[22] Given a carte blanche by the Canadian prime minister, Mackenzie King, to develop the Film Board in a laisser-faire atmosphere, Grierson worked to establish, in his own words, "in relatively short order more of a Ministry of Education than anything else," in which, "the new citizenship of the co-operative state is even now, in spite of the confusion, asking to be articulated."[23] The result would be the burgeoning families, schools, and communities of early NFB society.

NFB Children: The Earliest Years

Largely due to the war effort, few films among the earliest NFB releases contain significant portrayals of Canadian children—and only one, *100,000 Cadets* (1942), could be strictly designated an "NFB documentary" utilizing Canadian children solely. Sponsored by the Canadian Army, the intent of *100,000 Cadets* was to promote enrollment in the army cadet programs at the nation's high schools. During the film, patriotic boys roll up their sleeves to learn airplane identification, rifle drill, and war games. One boy's mother is shown as she "proudly sews stripes to his uniform." At camp on the weekend, hundreds of Canadian boys are filmed drilling under the eye of a lieutenant just back from action. The attractions of being a cadet are made obvious. One boy carries a pipe in his mouth as he practises the skill of bayoneting with a rifle. Others swim, parade in smart-looking uniforms, get paid, or date girls. As the film ends, the faces of cadets are superimposed over a windblown

Union Jack, and the narrator remarks "Next time you write your brother, you can tell him something he'll be proud of."[24]

Other NFB archival films containing significant portrayals of children and released during the earliest years of the Film Board included *Hot Ice* (1940), an ode to ice hockey written and narrated by Morley Callaghan. ("Hockey players grow anywhere the ice comes early.") *Hot Ice*, however, was in truth produced by Frank Badgley and his "Government Motion Picture Bureau," an organization that would be swallowed whole by Grierson and the NFB in June 1941. Likewise, *Iceland on the Prairies* (1941), which includes a portrayal of the children of Gimli, Manitoba, was produced for the NFB by an independent filmmaker, F.R. (Budge) Crawley, while another "Griersonian" documentary with children from the era, *The Children from Overseas* (1940), used Canadian children merely as background characters to document the lives of British evacuee children placed in Canadian homes for the duration of the war.

This neglect of Canadian children as subjects for early NFB productions reflects not only the emphasis of the nascent Film Board to produce films directly related to the war effort but also, more materially, the lack of available "stock shots" (film-library footage) of Canadian children before 1943. By 1943, however, this situation was radically altered as the nation began to prepare for postwar social reconstruction and as Grierson began to act upon his reluctance to produce "mere war propaganda."

Children in NFB Society: 1943-1946

No special role existed in Grierson's post-1942 production plans for children—except in relation to education, for which the Scotsman had a special affection as revealed in a letter written to his brother-in-law, Duncan McLaren, in 1943:

> By the time I'm through it's pretty certain I'll have done something about education that will stick, and that's the main thing. There's a big chance, too, to do something on the social and reconstruction side, out of the information services associated with industrial morale, consumer education and agricultural production. I have gone down all three holes like a triple of terriers, and the dirt will be coming up in a flurry any time now.[25]

Lessons in Living (1944) is illustrative of how films of the era with public school contexts articulated "the new citizenship of the cooperative state." In this "texture-of-life" documentary (which purports to recreate the actual events of a Vancouver Island community) Robert, a boy of thirteen coping with his lack of interest in his formalist, rural school, carves his initials in a desk that also bears his father's monogram. Caught in the act by the school inspector, the boy and his classmates receive a benevolent lecture from the inspector suggesting that they should improve their school and make it a more exciting place to live and work—not by acting alone, as with Robert's act of vandalism, but, rather, by working together as a community. In progressive committees, the children plan their modern school. With the teacher's approval they toss out their desks and bring in tables. They paint the room, bring in plants, a radio, and a library of books. They repair and paint the dilapidated fence around their schoolyard, and install painted exterior window boxes. Robert is in charge of carpentry. On the opening night of their new school, a group of parents are so impressed by what the children have accomplished by "pulling together" they team up to convert a local barn into a community hall.

> From the school it spread out into the homes because, once started, community energy is dynamic. Constantly ahead is a continuing line of objectives, each only a stepping stone to all the rest. This much can be done by cooperation within one community. Soon we can look outward to even greater achievements, through co-operation between groups of communities.[26]

Specifically, the intent of individual early NFB productions such as *Lessons in Living* was the altering of particular conditions; e.g., the conditions of public schooling in rural areas of Canada. But a larger goal in presenting to Canadian audiences a body of texture of life situations resolved through cooperation was the attempt to crystallize an attitude of cooperation among them; i.e., to convince Canadians that an attribute of their national character was to accomplish goals through cooperation that would elude them as individuals. In the film *Before They Are Six* (1943), for example, a young mother, Mrs. Roberts, must work outside her home because "there are more jobs than manpower to perform them."[27] In dealing independently with her need to find child care, she makes arrangements with the landlady to untie her young son from the fencepost in front of her urban flat and take him inside at mealtimes. Scenes of hooliganism and sobbing children betray the folly of this solution. Mrs. Roberts soon learns from the conversations of her workmates of another solution. If they can get twenty mothers together and pool their resources, they can begin a nursery school, a healthy environment where "constructive, cooperative play is encouraged."[28] Individualist mothers who opt out of the scheme are portrayed in an unfriendly light, whereas Mrs. Roberts' decision to join in a daycare is rewarded when, at the end of the film, her little Roy picks up his coat from the floor (a rule learned at the cooperative nursery) and hangs it on a doorhandle.

Pulling together. NAC, PA 194974.

Of American films, Grierson wrote in the 1930s: "I doubt if individual destiny is quite so important and public destiny quite so unimportant as Hollywood would make them appear."[29] That the destiny of individuals in rural Canada was dependent upon public cooperation was demonstrated in films such as *Farm Electrification* (1946), which illustrated how it was possible in a rural area to arrange for a power line to be brought in by cooperative action to serve each farmer. The awe of farm children as they gather around to watch their mother plug in an electric kettle given to her many years ago as a wedding gift screens like parody today. But such films often had immediate public effects:

> In one community, immediately after the film was shown, the audience organized a committee to take action as the film had demonstrated. The following fall the projectionist, who had previously used a gas generator, was gratified to discover that the community hall, as well as many of the surrounding farms, was now attached to a new power line.[30]

In *New Scotland* (1944), the Gaelic residents of Acadia work and sing together as they "shrimp the homespun." In *Better Education-Better Canada* (1945), Ontario high school students not only find "the best vocation for themselves" inside their school, but also "the importance of teamwork and cooperation." For the native *People of the Potlatch* (1944), teamwork counts as well, as does the love of the Union Jack, the song "London Bridge," and sports day, which "today the Indian looks forward to, just as in the old days every Indian looked forward to the potlatch." *Rural Health* (1946) advocates support for the Manitoba Health Plan ("The only question is how soon can we get it?") and shows how a group of women can petition to overturn any opposition made to cooperative health care by recalcitrant men. In *Early Start* (1945), a farm boy learns that one important reason for being in the Junior Farm Club is to be with the group that is in "step with the government," while in *Vitamin B1* (1943), the message for young swimmers is that good aquatic form comes from the muscles of the body working together in coordination with the mind. Even in a film about a school music competition, *A City Sings* (1945), the audience is reminded that the success of a choir comes from its ability to sing together.

One film celebrated accomplishments already achieved by co-operation between groups of communities. *Small Fry* (1946), a prestige film meant for distribution in Canadian theatres, honours the establishment of Family Allowances in August 1944. A "soundtrack mother" reads from her letter of gratitude, with accompanying visuals, explaining how her crippled son now receives medical attention thanks to the $6.00 cheque she receives from the federal government each month. A "soundtrack farmer" reads from his letter explaining how he was putting aside the Family Allowance each month for his children's education. A warning was tacked onto this film, in the form of a compilation of "children of poverty" visuals, reminding the audience that "the difference between us and those not so fortunate as us is our social programmes....The future of the world depends on the kind of people we make our children—for the powers of life and death will be in their hands."[31]

A City Sings (1945). NFB.

Early NFB Society: Internal Distinctiveness and External Otherness

Social cooperation is overwhelmingly the dominant theme in early representations of Canadian children by the National Film Board, but distinctiveness among social groups may also be discerned within wartime NFB society, as well as the conept of "otherness" through cinematic comparisons with other not-so-lucky children, particularly in war-ravaged parts of the world. The latter appeared most often in conjunction with Grierson's crusade to persuade Canadians toward a global point of view, a crusade for which the compilation film—a complex interplay between narration, visuals, and music—was especially effective.

One of the first documentaries of the National Film Board, a compilation as rough as its title, *Youth Is Tomorrow* (1939), contains a narrative that encourages young people to think globally, rather than locally, in order to prepare for the postdepression world.[32] At the other end of the Grierson era, one of the finest compilations of its type, *Tomorrow's Citizens* (1947), remains a powerful evocation of the need to teach "world citizenship" to children.

In *Tomorrow's Citizens*, the stentorian "voice of doom" of Lorne Greene narrates over a Lucio Agostini musical score which "started with a crescendo and went on up from there to the end of the film."[33] Over the ten minutes of the film, a huge collection of mesmerizing stock-shots are rapidly and rhythmically edited in a montage rivalling the work of Eisenstein—politicians, riots, battles, children, students, classrooms, chemistry, atomic blasts (including the famous Bikini Atoll footage, which appears to explode out of a hand-held florence flask) more children, Henry Ford, and the Grand Coulee Dam. "What does the atomic age hold for our children?" asks the voice of doom. "The future threatens catastrophe....New and terrible responsibilities lay on education....World citizenship is so vital to teach to our children...to equip the rising generation, born with science in its blood, to handle a scientific world..." (Nuclear explosions followed by a single, shivering Japanese child) "...The power of life or death is in human hands....The warmth of common citizenship must be taught along with science....No nation now lives to itself alone."[34]

The "internationalization of men's minds," was a crusade Grierson took to Canadian rural and urban audiences and to American audiences as the voice of Canada.[35] A dominant theme of the *Canada Carries On* series for theatrical distribution in Canada, the international perspective was equally in the forefront of the American distribution series, *The World in Action*. Moreover, the 35 millimetre prints used in the series for theatre projectors were often reprinted on 16 millimetre film so they could be taken on rural circuits, even to locations where projectors needed to be powered by gasoline generators. In films such as *Suffer Little Children*(1945) and *Out of the Ruins* (1946), domestic and foreign audiences alike were bombarded with heartrending and shocking visuals of sick and starving Europeans with terror in their eyes: women fighting for bread, or children clawing through garbage piles of worthless paper money in their search for food. These bleak segments of the films were succeeded by two divergent paths. Along one path are the sequences and symbols of hope—Europeans regaining their dignity, replacing their old shoes with new; along the other path, sequences of foreboding—Europeans brooding, bitter, poverty-stricken still. "From the child we helped...we can expect future friendship," the narrator assures us, (compilation of angry eyes) "but from those left wanting...let us hope they meet us as friends."[36]

Grierson's efforts to shape the Canadian public consciousness to look outward to the global community were balanced by inward looking nationalism only in the province of Québec. There the films of L'Office national du film (ONF) examined intimate details of Québec life for an almost exclusively Québec audience.[37] An extensive series of ten minute films, *Les Reportages*, of which there were more than one hundred by 1945, portrayed the land and the people of Québec, the cosmopolitan and the rural, with a film style indisputably distinct from any English-language counterpart. *Les Reportages #102* "Initiation a l'art" (1945) for example, looks at the children who attend a Montreal school of art. The Francophone children, twelve to fourteen-year-olds, are portrayed as affluent, confident, and sophisticated—both talented in, and serious about, their work. The jazz soundtrack on the film is unlike any to be found in English production.

Away from the city, *Conté de mon village* (1946) provided intimate and sympathetic insights into the life of a rural Québec school teacher, including her long hours of lesson preparation, her disputes with parents, and public examination at year's end. Still more inward looking is Alexis Tremblay's film, *Spring on a Québec Farm* (1946). Versioned into English after Québec distribution, the film portrays the details of the filmmaker's family life on their farm in the Saint Lawrence valley: the Tremblay children cutting willow whistles on the way to the stream, the family making soap in vats, having the spring seeds blessed at mass, ploughing the earth by horse, and sowing the seed by the many hands of the Tremblay family.

The independent development and focus of the Québec filmmakers was due, in part, to Grierson's unilingual limitations. From necessity, he employed Québec language advisors and Québec lieutenants, setting in place, from the outset, the structure for a separate Québec unit of production.[38] In addition, Paul Theriault (1978) an early ONF filmmaker, suggests that Scottish nationalism played a part in creating Grierson's sympathy toward the French minority, who, like the Scots, safeguarded their identity and pride against desperate odds. Furthermore, suggests Theriault, Grierson had an affection for "the maverick that French Canada produces in every generation in large numbers—the strong individualist...who isn't chained to the collective process."[39]

Distinct as well are the National Film Board's portrayals of the two indigenous peoples of Canada: the Indian and the Inuit. *People of the Potlatch* (1944) and *Eskimo Summer* (1943) were both directed, in colour, by Laura Bolton.[40] In *People of the Potlatch,* Indian resistance to assimilation appears to linger in the older generation. The elders dress and dance traditionally, while the younger generation wear T-shirts with Union Jack emblems and Lindbergh flying caps, play baseball, and march in brass bands while draped in red, white and blue bunting. As an old chief dances, a narrator intones: "Once he danced as a tribute to his Gods....Now he dances only to recall the old days." However, a group of Indian children intently watching the old chief from the background of the mise en scène, unintentionally belie the narrator's comments—the children appear to be studying the dance.

In contrast to the perception of subtle resistance to assimilation by Indians, the Inuit of *Eskimo Summer,* old and young, are portrayed as eagerly welcoming the culture of Canada, literally meeting it at the boat to help unload the trappings of civilization: tea, tobacco, guns, and building supplies. "The gentle Eskimo is an example of perfect adaption," states the unmistakeable voice of Lorne Greene. On board the ship, an Inuit male goes to work with wrenches in the engine room. "Eskimos make good mechanics," remarks Greene, "and learn about engines quickly." The subtle difference between these two portrayals—the forced impression of Indian allegiance versus the eager cooperation of the Inuit—may have been as much shaped by Grierson's opinion of the two groups as by any reality found by the director, Bolton. In 1944, Grierson helped to compose an article for a London periodical, the *Spectator,* which included these thoughts on Canada's indigenous peoples: "In considering the future populations of the North-West, the Eskimo race would appear to be of considerable importance. The Eskimos, unlike the Indians, are not a dying race, and they show every sign of being able to assimilate some of the ideas and skills of modern Western Civilization."[41]

Both the Indian and the Inuit were portrayed to theatre audiences as being equally irresponsible in their ability to handle money. In *Small Fry,* a film about Family Allowance, the narrator explains that for Indians and "Eskimos," "family allowances comes in cans and packages," implying that neither could be trusted with cheques.[42]

Of all the stereotypes imbedded in the films, the most subtle, perhaps, is that of the "nice" Canadian. Although their thinking may be muddled (especially when they are not thinking cooperatively) the Canadians portrayed in every film are generally thoughtful, generous, cheerful, energetic, imaginative, constructive, and healthy. None could be more exemplary of "Film Board Canadians" than the youths at Betty's graduation party in *Vitamin C* (1943), a film in the *Knife and*

Fork series. At the threshold of adulthood, the youngsters gather around a piano to sing "Alouette" before playing ping-pong. "If it's beauty you want," rhymes the narrator, "don't go out and buy it; just get plenty of Vitamin C in your diet."

Distribution of Early NFB Films

The peoples in the mirror of the National Film Board reflected a national face, a character and a purpose—a mental concept of a "Canadian" —that was significantly different from the characters portrayed in foreign cinemas. Canadians would see themselves as being more social than their American counterparts, somewhat less important as individuals, less inclined to nationalism and more aware of the need to be world citizens as well. Having manufactured these images and the mirror in which they would be reflected, Grierson with the then director of the Wartime Information Board, Herbert Lasch, organized a system of communications to spread the national images "like wildfire across the sky."[43]

School screening: early 1940s. NFB.

A grim fact concerning Grierson's British experience with filmmaking was that he frequently failed to garner that first essential of effective film propaganda—the audience. This despite the fact that, in Britain, Grierson had been an innovative film distributor—as willing to show films in the rear coaches of trains or on continuous film loops at Victoria Station as at the regular venues, such as ciné clubs.[44] In Canada, however, the audience problem was resolved when a way was found to bring the films to the remotest regions of the country, ensuring that the NFB experience would truly be a national one and that the Film Board would be (as Grierson had intended) the eyes of the country as a whole.

Taking advantage of the goodwill he had garnered during his American experience, and by bluff and bluster, Grierson cracked open the theatre markets in Canada and the United States, guaranteeing distribution of the films of the *Canada Carries On* series to three hundred Canadian theatres in the first thirty days of release and nine hundred theatres by the end of the third month.[45] At the box-office, in this the golden era of cinema, English speaking audiences for the *Canada Carries On* series numbered two and a quarter million each month, while another million per month saw French translations. But the Odeon theatres merely serviced a narrow band of the populace near the American border; it was the organization and expansion of an existing network of itinerant "showmen" that truly enabled the Film Board of Canada to consider itself national in scope.

The showmen were the cinematic colleagues of itinerant rural pedlars who rode through circuit territories selling Watkins or Rawleigh products.[46] The advent of motor vehicles, movies, and hand-cranked projectors made it possible to earn a living peddling film entertainment on similar circuits shortly after World War I. By 1939, showmen were being employed by farm machinery companies, as well as by provincial and federal government agencies, to attract crowds with free movies in order to advertise products or disseminate government policies. In January 1942, thirty of these non-theatrical film circuits were organized under the joint auspices of the Wartime Information Board and the National Film Board.[47] Each projectionist was charged with bringing NFB film programs once a month to twenty rural communities, villages and towns without theatres, as well as to an equal number of schools. Attendance, according to NFB figures, averaged 2,200 per week per circuit. By 1945, the number of rural circuits had climbed from the original thirty to ninety-two, a monthly average of 1,700 community and school shows.[48]

In the early days of the rural circuits, the showmen reported that, on their first round, one-half or more of the people in the audience were seeing a sound film for the first time.[49] Illustrative of rural audience naïveté about the medium is this anecdote by C.W. Gray, himself a showman during the war:

In a northern Saskatchewan community the audience was seated on two-by-ten planks set on two-foot blocks of large cordwood down the length of the hall. One of the films showed a train coming straight down the track toward the audience, who had never seen a train before, let alone a movie of one. As the train came closer and closer, and loomed larger and larger on the screen, the audience leaned farther and farther backward. At the climax of the scene every member of the audience tumbled backward, and they and the planks and the firewood slabs crashed resoundingly onto the floor.[50]

The monthly film programmes became widely attended community events throughout rural Canada. It became the practice to combine the movies with basket socials, dances, fund raising, and sports: baseball in the summer or hockey games in the winter. Schools would close in the afternoon and children would hike miles to arrive in a town where the films would be shown.[51] Audiences remained past midnight to discuss the films, the crops, the weather, and the roads. From the outset, non-theatrical films reached nearly a quarter million rural Canadians a month, an average attendance of 250 children at an afternoon showing and 275 adults each evening.[52]

Children in community hall watching film. NAC, PA 169733.

In addition, industrial film circuits were organized to reach nearly 133,000 urban workers each month, while volunteer projectionists covered urban community groups not reached by other circuits—churches, co-ops, hospitals, hotels, libraries, orphanages, women's groups, children's parties, union meetings, veterans' hospitals, seniors' homes, at parks, and even on city streets.[53] By 1945, some 3,112 prints of 761 films were being shown on urban and rural circuits to an average monthly audience of 598,000.[54] Moreover, National Film Board libraries at home drew 400,000 viewers monthly.[55] When added to the three and a quarter million Canadians who were watching the *Canada Carries On* series at the Odeon theatres, nearly four and a quarter million Canadians were exposed each month to their cinematic image in the mirror offered them by John Grierson—this in a country of only eleven and one-half million.[56]

Grierson's Departure: A Chapter Closes

Having brought to maturity "the idea and influence" of the documentary film—indeed, having foreshadowed the influence of television yet to come—Grierson may have felt confident about re-emerging onto the world stage. But fate had a twist in store for him. James Beveridge, one of the early filmmakers trained under Grierson, recalls that the international perspective brought down a certain suspicion of Grierson and his senior director from Britain, Stuart Legg, "an uncertainty concerning their exact focus and motive, and their ideology."[57] Eventually, such suspicions were the undoing of Grierson. Mackenzie King took abrupt and sudden notice when criticism erupted in Parliament from Conservative MP, A.R. Adamson, that the Film Board had "become a propagandist for a type of socialist and foreign philosophy" and was "obviously putting out Soviet propaganda."[58] Although Grierson successfully resisted an attempt by External Affairs to have the Film Board placed under a review committee, his freewheeling and halcyon days were soon brought to an end.[59]

John Grierson resigned from the National Film Board on 10 August 1945. Four weeks later, the Royal Canadian Mounted Police (RCMP) were handed information by Igor Gouzenko, a defector from the Soviet Embassy in Ottawa, implicating the NFB in a spy ring. Although Grierson was never seriously implicated, he became persona non grata to many, including Mackenzie King.[60] In 1946, Grierson attempted to organize a documentary film company based in New York City, "The World Today, Inc.," but the nascent organization collapsed shortly after J. Edgar Hoover, director of the F.B.I., became convinced that Grierson was a communist sympathizer and applied pressure to have his immigration visa revoked. The filmmaker's career never recovered.[61]

John Grierson, however, had often insisted that it was not himself who was of importance, but the documentary idea itself; i.e., film as a sociological instrument for manipulating public opinion. And to judge from the actions of those who held executive sway over the NFB, on this they agreed. For although most NFB personnel anticipated their swift termination following the war, especially in the wake of the Gouzenko allegations, those who held the purse strings evidently judged the efficacy and potential of the NFB worthwhile perpetuating—since the documentary idea, as practised at the National Film Board, survived its founder's fall from grace. The mandarins who kept the NFB functioning after the war did so in part because they shared John Grierson's vision of a progressive democracy in Canada, centrally planned and organized, and, in part, because they shared his faith in the documentary idea to achieve it—that (as Grierson had said all along) "it patently *works*."[62] Indeed, the Film Board had sought and gathered evidence of its own efficacy throughout the war years by ordering special reports from its field representatives concerning selected productions.

One such production was *Lessons in Living*, a film for which sufficient documentation remains to permit a detailed examination of the construction of a rural community in NFB society during the early years of the National Film Board. Given Grierson's interest in education and the interest of the NFB in practical results, *Lessons in Living* is illuminating of the "documentary idea," of Grierson's "educational revolution," of the nature of Canadian progressivism, and of the role played by the NFB—the "eyes of democracy"—in the social refashioning of postwar Canada and Canadian childhood.

3

Lessons in Living: "Deconstruction" of a Rural Community in Early NFB Society

> The community of Lantzville, B.C. is a cross-section of nationalities and industrial groups—farmers, fishermen, lumbermen and railroad workers, with a down-at-heel spirit and a down-at-heel public school.
>
> — NFB Information Sheet, *Lessons in Living*

One morning, early in 1944, the children of Lantzville's two-room elementary school were distracted from their deskwork by a crew of workmen erecting a tower across the roadway. That afternoon, the older boys were excused from their regular classwork and were instructed to dismantle some sections of the fence around the schoolyard and loosen a few of the remaining pickets. They did so with relish. Afterward, all the window boxes were removed from around the schoolhouse and—this to the children's greatest surprise—the Lantzville Community Hall, a converted barn located at the rear of the Vancouver Island school, was loaded with hay and a rough-hewn loft constructed inside it.[1]

The Lantzville school was being prepared as the location for *Lessons in Living*, a National Film Board of Canada production and one of 138

Notes to chapter 3 are on p. 242.

film productions that would be released by the NFB in 1944.[2] Ostensibly, the purpose of each production was to help Canadians in all parts of Canada to understand the ways of living and the problems of Canadians in other parts, in short: to mirror Canada to Canadians.[3] But the reflections were not always the realities that Canadian audiences believed them to be. They were "creative treatments of actuality"—they were "documentaries"—and they were produced not so much to reflect reality as to crystallize public sentiments and manufacture public opinions.[4]

The Lantzville schoolyard. NFB.

Lessons in Living was being produced to manufacture favourable public attitudes for progressive educational practices throughout rural Canada. Distributed nationally for more than a decade, *Lessons in Living* would lead audiences to believe that a poorly maintained and pedagogically static, two-room school had been transformed by progressive action into the very model of what a rural school might be: physically and pedagogically the equal of any urban school in Canada, complete with a gymnasium to serve the school's and community's needs.

Leading the transformation of the community, as documented on film, is an educational expert (the new school inspector) Dr. William Plenderleith, who rouses the village children from their educational slumber with an inspirational classroom speech:

Dr. P.: Just a minute class. Would you like a gym and a library and a workshop?

Class: Yeah - sure do - that would be swell - I wouldn't mind school then, etc.

Dr. P.: Alright, I think you can get them. But you'll have to work for them. I would suggest that you get together and decide what you want; get your parents and the rest of the ratepayers behind the scheme then if everyone agrees you can start to work. You can accomplish almost anything if you pull together. Now, you people, it's up to you to get things rolling.[5]

Lantzville children get things rolling. NFB.

As documented in the film, the Lantzville children rise to Plenderleith's challenge. In cooperative committees, the youngsters plan their modern school. With the teacher's approval, they toss their desks outside and bring in tables. They paint the room and bring in plants, a radio, and a library of books. While Plenderleith organizes provincial funding and school board support for the project, the children repair and paint the dilapidated fence around their schoolyard and install decorated, exterior window boxes. On the "opening night" of their new school, a group of parents are so impressed by what the children have accomplished by "pulling together" they team up to convert a local barn into a community hall.

From the school it spread out into the homes, because once started, community energy is dynamic. Constantly ahead is a continuing line of objectives, each only a stepping stone to all the rest. This much can be done by co-operation within one community. Soon we can look outward to even greater achievements, through co-operation between groups of communities.[6]

On celluloid, progressive education improved both the material and social conditions of life in Lantzville. But in truth, Lantzville school had been proudly kept by the community long before the directors of the film ordered the children to dismantle the fence and remove the flower boxes so that these could be "repaired" and reinstalled for the production. Likewise, the Vancouver Island community had a recreation centre long before the school gym was filled with hay so that "a valueless old barn" could be renovated by cooperative effort into a community hall. Of greater interest to the NFB filmmakers than an accurate portrayal of Lantzville school was that a cinematic "lesson in living" should be conveyed to other towns and villages concerning the utility of progressivism to a rural community—an illusion which, among all the others in the film, may stand as its grandest.[7]

Margo Bate and Lantzville children. NAC, PA 194971.

This chapter is a historical "deconstruction" of *Lessons in Living*—an untangling of the agendas that led to the construction of an NFB rural community in 1944, not by "semiotics," but by the careful uncovering of primary evidence to expose the unseen significance of its cinematic parable of progressivism. As with the film, the chapter begins in Ottawa, Victoria, and Lantzville; but especially in Lantzville where, in early January 1944, an Ottawa-based film unit from the National Film Board of Canada—W.A. Macdonald, Edith Spencer, John Norwood and Hank Lane—checked into the only hotel in town with their sound equipment and cameras, but without a script or a producer. The producer, Dallas Jones, and his script, "#6034, Rural Youth" had been detained in Ottawa for a further week by the Government Film Commissioner, John Grierson, who wished to make additions to the storyline before sending it and Jones to rejoin the group now encamping on Vancouver Island.

The script that the film crew awaited in Lantzville had already undergone significant revisions since Jones had adapted its screenplay from an abridged story he had read in the appendix of the 1942 *Proceedings of the Twentieth Convention of the Canada and Newfoundland Educational Association* (CNEA).[8] The full text of that story, "Kindling New Fires in Smoky Lane: How the School Aroused the Community," had been presented by Leonard Bercuson, an official of the Alberta Department of Education to the CNEA delegates at their convention held at Victoria that year. In his presentation of the story, Bercuson had waxed eloquently over a fable of rural youth imbued with the progressive spirit of democratic cooperation:

> This was the true function of the school. It should be the fountainhead of the community, its laboratory, library and thought centre, dedicated to the service of the whole population. No longer was it to meet the needs of the youth only; no longer was it to foster a cloistered learning that divorced the school from the Community which should give it vibrant life. The curriculum was to have its basis in the problems and activities of the village, town or city in a programme committed to making existence fuller and richer for all.[9]

The children of Smoky Lane, Alberta, according to Bercuson, set out from their village school one afternoon armed with brushes, brooms, soap, and paint to convert "a ramshackle, dilapidated little building on main street" into a community library. "As a final touch the students fashioned lovingly out of sturdy blocks of wood the letters of the words 'Community Library' and mounted them proudly over the door."[10] Inspired by the children's activities, the adults of the village contributed books to the library, and inspired, in turn, by the adults' activities, the province contributed more books. Their lesson learned, the children set out to build a skating rink in the winter, raise funds for the Dominion War Services Campaign in the spring, and later obliged the village council to ban all swine and cattle from the village limits.

> We sought to broaden the horizons of education for those young people; we strove to show them how significant a place the ideal of community service must assume in the scheme of truly worthy living. Because it was our simple faith that education finds its content and its inspiration in the devotion of the community, and that the concept takes on sublimity only as the word community grows broader and broader in its connotation, until it embraces the whole of humanity itself.[11]

Smoky Lane to Lantzville: From Parable to Production

To the delegates at the Victoria CNEA convention, "Kindling New Fires in Smoky Lane: How the School Aroused the Community," was a parable of postwar reconstruction and the role of education in it—a fresh generation of children marching out from their schools to tidy up and improve a corner of the world and thereby inspiring their elders to do the same.[12] To Dallas Jones it was a film opportunity, but one for which he conceived a more believable corner in which the improvements might begin: the children's own school.

"Kindling New Fires in Smoky Lane" was a tale undoubtedly heard by a number of prominent British Columbian educators who were registered at the 1942 CNEA conference at Victoria, among them leading provincial administrators including M.A. Cameron, Dr. S.J. Willis, H.B. King, and G.M. Weir (the former Minister of Education)—as well as Inspector Plenderleith of Nanaimo, to whom Dallas Jones now wrote from Ottawa late in December 1943 to apologize for being delayed in his arrival at Lantzville and to explain further changes to the script:

> Our script has undergone further changes since I last talked to you, these at the suggestion of the Government Film Commissioner. The changes were suggested only a few hours before the unit was ready to entrain here for the West, so the unit will not have a complete revised script with them; however, I am sending one out just as soon as I can get it finished.[13]

"Further changes" was a reference to the changes already made by the producer to his script, "Rural Youth," following his meetings with S.J. Willis and Plenderleith on Vancouver Island in the fall of 1943. Initially, Jones had brought the script to Victoria and to the Deputy Minister of Education, S.J. Willis, since Dr. Willis had been president of the CNEA in 1942 and thus was well aware of the postwar, educational significance of the "Smoky Lane" tale. Willis approved of the producer's ideas for a film on the theme of "Kindling New Fires" and, likewise, he approved of its production in British Columbia. Moreover, the Deputy Minister had a practical idea of his own about the significance of a cinematic rendering of the parable and, in particular, its proclamation that "the word community grows broader and broader in its connotation, until it embraces the whole of humanity itself."[14]

As a delegate at the 1941 convention of the CNEA at Ottawa, Willis, along with the other educational élite of Canada, had been cautioned by the conference keynote speaker, R.C. Wallace, about the necessity to educate the public about progressive changes to their school systems during "the present movement towards larger administrative areas in education."[15] Later that evening, at the CNEA banquet at the Chateau Laurier in Ottawa, the latest vehicle for educating the Canadian public was unveiled as the educators were introduced to Ross McLean, Deputy Film Commissioner of the National Film Board of Canada, who "explained the purpose of the Bureau and illustrated its work by showing some of its newest films."[16]

Now, in the fall of 1943 at Victoria, with an NFB producer before him in his office and the issues surrounding larger administrative areas looming before the Department, the Deputy Minister clearly envisioned the expediency of coupling the Film Board production with the consolidation of rural school districts in the province. He promptly arranged for Dallas Jones to meet with William Plenderleith, who was currently in charge of British Columbia's first, rural-city administrative unit at Nanaimo-Ladysmith.[17]

At this juncture, a note concerning William Plenderleith's career is worth relating. In 1934, Inspector Plenderleith, at age 35, had been in charge of the pioneering effort to create B.C.'s first large unit of school administration in the Peace River area. His report on the experiment, "The Peace River Larger Unit of Administration," became his dissertation for a D.Paed. from the University of Toronto. In his thesis, a work he dedicated to Drs. G.M. Weir and S.J. Willis, Plenderleith argued that decentralization of control in rural school districts was the most significant flaw in British Columbia's educational system.[18] He observed that "the present Public Schools Act gives the local taxpayer practically complete control over the conduct and administration of the local school."[19] Such autonomy, he felt, was detrimental to democratic principles of equality of opportunity in the province.

As long as we have over seven hundred separate autonomous school units—some of which are extremely wealthy, and others pitifully poor—there must remain gross differences in the educational opportunities of our children. Here we find a district with an enriched curriculum; progressive administration and supervision; a teaching staff well-qualified; and buildings that are sanitary, fire-proof and attractive. Yet, in a neighbouring district, we may see housing and equipment that are meagre and unsafe; a traditional curriculum that is poor; administrative and supervisory service that is inadequate or actually lacking; and even a teaching personnel that is relatively inexperienced and untrained.[20]

"In the interests of posterity," Plenderleith concluded, "rural schools must be administered by the provincial government."[21]

But not all of the rural Peace River communities wished their schools administered by the provincial government; and that was the rub for Plenderleith. Some community members perceived a flaw in a democracy organized by outside experts for others to cooperate within:

Now, we [residents] both believe thoroughly in the value of the contribution of experts in all departments of life, but we seem to remember a question propounded by Aristotle in our nearly forgotten classics. In his "Politics" while comparing the respective merits of democratic government and that by experts, he asks, "Which is the better judge of the merits of a house, the expert carpenter who may build it, or the man who expects to use it and for whom it is built?" We think that his answer was not altogether in favour of the expert. And surely it may be that even the rural taxpayer and parent may have a little insight into the practical educational needs and requirements of his children.[22]

Plenderleith made light of community sentiment. "Practically every community in the Peace River area has a distinct individuality which it prefers to keep intact," he wrote.[23] "Too often, the mere mention of abandoning control of the little red school sounds a discordant twang on the heartstrings of memory."[24] But from the communities themselves, residents hammered at the principles of democracy employed by Plenderleith and the department. Wrote one: "The war was supposed to be fought to save democracy. Guess we lost, as Webster's Dictionary defines that word: 'Government by the people.'"[25] While another wrote: "This whole innovation [is] scandalously un-British in character and utterly undemocratic in principle and smacks of Nazi or Fascist Dictatorship."[26] And the headlines of the *Peace River Block News*, November 12, 1935, read: "School Strike Threatened in Peace River: Residents Object to 'Dictatorship' By Inspector Plenderleith."[27]

Plenderleith tackled the insurgency head-on. He advertised a meeting for ratepayers from the districts in which trouble was fomenting and, on 14 December 1935, drew an assembly of 250 people. To the assembled he explained the constitutionality of the larger unit of administration under the British North America Act, then presented an alternate definition of democracy: "The essence of democracy is equality of opportunity."[28] He enlightened the audience about the practical benefits of the scheme, dwelling on a projected $2,800 savings, and promised further benefits if the consolidation proceeded: free medical examination of the children; free preventive treatments including inoculation, vaccination, and goitre prevention; yearly dental services including examination and remedial work; free night schools for adults; free high school tuition for students; subsidized eyeglasses; a travelling library; and "any additional necessary education equipment that will give the children of these districts an equal opportunity for educational development comparable to the best that can be had in the wealthier centres."[29]

> In conclusion, I ask: if you as parents of children, would be willing to sacrifice the interests of your children and the advantages that I have just enumerated by attempting to adhere to a system of administration that has long outworn its usefulness. If you wish to deprive your children of these additional benefits, vote against the system; if you wish your children to receive these benefits, vote for it.[30]

The vote was three to one in favour of cooperation with the Department of Education.

William Plenderleith was now acknowledged as the consolidation "expert" in the Department of Education, and he was called upon to perform the same service in 1937 in the Matsqui-Sumas-Abbotsford Educational Area, before being summoned by Victoria in the summer of 1942 to organize the Nanaimo-Ladysmith Unit: the first rural-city unit of educational administration.[31]

Nanaimo-Ladysmith was to be the final "experiment" in consolidating districts before the Cameron Report of 1946 and provincial consolidation of small districts in toto—and one for which, Plenderleith learned, a "documentary film" would be produced. When Plenderleith was introduced by S.J. Willis to Dallas Jones, the NFB producer in the fall of 1943 there can be little doubt that Plenderleith offered the filmmaker at once some practical advice about writing a script promoting rural-city consolidation. Hence, a story that had begun with children marching out of a rural school imbued with a spirit of community revitalization, now would begin with disgruntled youth trudging to school on a quest for democratic "equal opportunity:"

Boy 1:   Aw, you're making it up.

Boy 2:   But I saw it with my own eyes. They've got a swell gym and workshops with lots of tools and kitchens for the girls and everything.

Boy 3:   Those city kids get everything.

Boy 4:   I wouldn't mind school if we could have all that stuff.[32]

This new beginning would impart a new, and more material, meaning to the original idealism of "Kindling New Fires in Smoky Lane" and a practical message to be read into the film's ending: "Soon we can look outward to even greater achievements, through co-operation between groups of communities."[33] Still, the initiative for community revitalization was to come from inside the school, even if it was for material gain.

Dallas Jones completed the revised script in Ottawa on 22 December 1943 and wrote to Plenderleith the following day to tell him it was finalized. He apologized for his tardiness, set a departure date of 27 December, mentioned the names of the film crew, and assured Plenderleith "We have budgeted for the cost of any materials to redecorate the recreation hall at Lantzville."[34] Of the rewritten script, the producer remarked, "I hope you will like our script when you see it...we leave the village with a healthy progressive spirit of democratic cooperation as they enjoy the improvements they have made and continue to plan more."[35]

> We end our film by pointing to the future of these people. We indicate that cooperation inside the community has been a proven success, but beyond that there is a broader success, their intercommunity cooperation and we lead into the idea of the larger unit of administration and school consolidation. The film ends as it shows the advantages to be had by the larger cooperative effort.[36]

Thus, from Ottawa Station on 27 December 1943, the three man and one woman film crew for Production No. 6043 "Rural Youth" began their five day train journey to Vancouver—but not with the revised script as Dallas Jones had promised. From his Ottawa office on 29 December 1943, the producer wrote to the proprietor of the Lantzville Hotel confirming the arrival of the crew and their equipment on Tuesday, 4 January 1944; then, finally, on 3 January 1944, the producer wrote once again to Plenderleith to explain a further delay:

Our script has undergone further changes since I last talked to you, these at the suggestion of the Government Film Commissioner. The changes were suggested only a few hours before the unit was ready to entrain here for the West, so the unit will not have a complete revised script with them....Hence, the unit will be shooting background and incidental material only until I arrive with the new script on January 15.[37]

The script had been temporarily derailed by John Grierson. Now, the fable of "Smoky Lane" would be altered once again, this time to suit the educational purposes of a Scotsman who claimed to know more about propaganda than anybody alive, outside of Joseph Goebbels.[38]

I have believed that in education was the heart of the matter, but that education needed to be revolutionized altogether if it was to become the instrument of revolutionized democracy I was thinking of...I have had to pretend to a whole lot of powers I didn't have in running my education revolution.[39]

When at last Production No. 6043 emerged from Grierson's Ottawa office, "Kindling New Fires in Smoky Lane," had been refashioned into *Lessons in Living*, a cinematic allegory for building the progressive democratic state through education.

The difference between the script for "Rural Youth" and its Griersonian revision lies in the insertion of an outside educational expert (Dr. Plenderleith) to initiate and direct the reform project. The original script, in which reforms originated within the classroom itself, contradicted the role of the community in the Grierson template of progressive democracy. As Dallas Jones wrote to Plenderleith:

Much of the initiative still has the children as its source, but there is now a great deal more of the organization from the responsible officials in the district throughout the community's improvement. There is a stronger feeling of responsibility toward the provincial school authorities, and the provincial representatives now become a major part of the dynamics of the improvement. This, of course, means you [Plenderleith], even more than the teachers, the school board and the provincial Department of Education. I hope that you will be able to find time to appear in our film and take deserved credit for the work you have done.[40]

The role of "expert" in the Griersonian documentary supplanted that of the Hollywood star. Whether draped in the "Voice of God" soundtrack or portrayed as a benevolent government official, expert intervention between citizens and the reform of their society was an essential premise of the documentary movement, and thus of early NFB society. In the cooperative democracy that Grierson envisioned, experts administered for the public good, and good citizens cooperated. They most certainly did so on film—Grierson saw to it.

Thus, it is in the film, *Lessons in Living*, in which a central character named Robert, left to his own devices, carves his initials on his school desk where his father once carved his. Overhearing the boy being scolded by his teacher for his vandalism, Dr. William Plenderleith, the new school inspector, steps into the classroom and early NFB society:

> Now boys and girls this is a matter that needs some discussion. Bob has carved his initials right where his father once carved his. After we have discussed it you had better decide whether Bob was right or wrong for you are part of the community that owns and supports the school.[41]

Robert is caught carving his initials. NAC, PA 194970.

For his own considerable part of the discussion, Plenderleith lectures the children on the history of the Lantzville school. He tells them that the world around the school has changed, and yet "the school itself has not changed to meet the changed conditions of the modern world."[42]

The school should have changed. Instead of spoiling his desk Bob
should have been spending his time trying to improve it and the
school generally. Really, you're all responsible. You are all part of the
community and the community owns the school. If you want a better
school, you can have it by making it for yourselves. If you want to
carve—and that's not a bad idea Bob—let's work on something
useful.[43]

Plenderleith's intervention, as already noted, results in the collective
refurbishing of Lantzville school and community. As for Bob, his carving
now properly channeled into group objectives, he produces decorative
engravings on the school window boxes and a new "Lantzville" wooden
signboard to mount over the school's main door. Moreover, near the climax of the film, Bob anxiously erases a small smudge of ink from one of
the freshly varnished tabletops in the renovated classroom, clearly a student thoroughly rehabilitated by progressive education.

Like Dallas Jones, John Grierson, of course, looked favourably upon
cooperative, community action in education—but unlike the filmmaker,
the film commissioner had perceived the danger to the progressive state
if small communities could undertake to change educational conditions
independent of their provincial departments of education. By inserting
the government agent into the script to initiate and direct the cooperative action, Grierson suppressed the authority of the small community in
early NFB society. That was the essential difference between the "Smoky
Lane" story told by Leonard Bercuson and the script that Dallas Jones
carried onto the train when at last he embarked for Vancouver Island:
the Smoky Lane story had been written by an individual to glorify community self-revival; the script had been fashioned by progressive agents
who were wary of the concept.

Meanwhile, as the train carrying Dallas Jones and *Lessons in Living*
hurried across Canada, Mr. and Mrs. Collette, the proprietors of the
Lantzville Hotel, helped the two directors, the cameraman, and their
assistant to set up a production headquarters in the hotel.[44] The Col-
lettes had a daughter, Wilma, and a son, Armand, attending Lantzville
School, but neither child can remember the arrival of the film crew, nor
the arrival of the producer. Along with others of their former school-
days, they first recall the construction of the camera tower across the
road from the schoolyard and, secondly, their exuberant efforts to knock
down the fence, which had successfully kept "Enid's cows" away from
the schoolgrounds for a number of years.[45]

The village of Lantzville had been chosen by Dallas Jones after a tour
of inspection with Plenderleith. The NFB producer had originally

expected he would "have to superimpose on one village the experiences of two or three," but in Lantzville he found "every development we wanted."[46] A "local committee" met with Jones and Plenderleith and a bargain was struck: "in return for the cooperation of the people of the village...I [Jones] agreed to pay for the materials for lining the inside walls [of the Lantzville recreational hall] if they would supply labor and any other necessary materials."[47]

> Our part of the project will cost less than $300. I have already passed to the comptroller the invoice for the lumber—approximately $240—and there may be about $60 to be spent on incidentals before we're through. I believe this is a good bargain for us because the cost of building the complete recreation hall set any place else would have been much larger. Only the splendid cooperation of the Lantzville people has kept it as low as it is. And the people of the community are quite happy about it. In return for a great deal of work, which they are doing gladly, they are having a long cherished community hope fulfilled for them.[48]

The formalist classroom. NAC, PA 194975.

The children of Lantzville school were never told the storyline of the film in which they were to act. Although copies of the shooting script were available for the film crew the children were left in the dark as to its theme and purpose, as well. This does not appear to have concerned them, nor their parents—whose concerns revolved instead around the fairness of the filmmakers in choosing which children and adults would be in the film. After the novelty had worn off, some domestic irritations arose, such as washing clothes nightly during the six weeks of production, as the children needed to appear fresh each day in the previous day's attire.[49]

The children were assembled in small groups at various locations in and around the community, including at their desks in the one classroom that had been prepared for both sound and film recording. This room had blankets nailed to its ceiling, from which microphones had been suspended. The children followed orders from one of the directors, who they believe was Edith Spencer, and learned their lines immediately before each shot. One of the children, now in her early sixties, recalled the experience to be among "the best times of her life."[50]

As filming took place in one room, schooling took place in the other, although children in the other room could not be certain they wouldn't be seconded for film work in the first—and indeed, they hoped they would. Occasionally, children from nearby Redgap School were brought over for the shooting as well, and occasionally children were shepherded to country lanes at a distance from Lantzville. Scenes were shot over and over. One child recalled (after he had walked down the same section of gravel road a number of times) the cameraman asking whether the boy realized he had wasted about a thousand feet of film, but mostly the children remember the filmmakers as being gentle and patient with them.[51]

The children remember William Plenderleith better than they remember their own teacher that year—Catherine Mrus—a shadowy figure who stood in the background as shooting proceeded.[52] Some children thought that the actress who played their teacher in the film, Margot Bate (the daughter of Nanaimo mayor, Mark Bate) was their real teacher; she wasn't, but almost all recalled Inspector Plenderleith: "He was real. He was the bogeyman of teachers, who called him 'doctor.'"[53] The schoolboard members were real as well, as were the dozens of parents who volunteered to "put a new ceiling in the hall," or appeared in the school for its "opening night" or at the town meeting with Dr. Plenderleith, where a few even had speaking parts:

> Dr. P.: Yes indeed - the fundamentals of learning - reading, writing and arithmetic - are all important. But modern education is more than intellectual development. It's social development, too. We must give our children a background of shared social experience right here in the school.

Man: We're doing all right in the village and we didn't learn any more than the school's teaching now.

Dr. P.:   But you haven't had to understand people and conditions much outside your own neighbourhood. Your children are going out into a world where every man's a neighbor.

Woman: But how is this new program to let our children know anything about all that?

Dr. P.:   By working together they will learn to understand each other. That's the first step. Then the same principles of tolerant understanding will broaden out into the whole world field of human relations.[54]

The principles of tolerant understanding, like the recreation hall, had actually been in operation in Lantzville for a number of years. What was novel about "this new program" was that Lantzville children were now doing work in school they usually did at home or around their farm. Most prominently, the children recall painting the school. Once begun, their use of paint became dynamic; each painted object only a stepping stone to all the rest, until at last they had painted the piano. The boys actually did make bookcases for the classroom, and the girls did make curtains. A radio-record player and records were donated to the school; and at the end of the project, the old hardwood desktops were sanded and varnished to make souvenir plates of the shooting.[55] Six weeks after they had arrived, the NFB film crew was gone. According to the script for *Lessons in Living*, "formal teaching stopped" in Lantzville School, "in the old sense it would probably never exist again in this room."[56] And for a very brief while, because of the tables, the community followed the script. Regular games nights were held in the classroom and crafts lessons—toy-making and basket weaving—were organized; but for the children themselves, soon after the cameras had left, schooling reverted to a traditional pedagogy. Indeed, the Lantzville children reported that they "loved" their actual "formal" schooling; they had looked forward to going to school, and felt that they were better taught than Lantzville school children in the 1990s.[57]

Post-Production and Distribution: Nanaimo to Nova Scotia

Ironically, *Lessons in Living* never played in Lantzville Community Hall during the twelve years it was included in the NFB catalogues (1945-1957) although it was widely circulated throughout rural British Columbia and Canada.[58] Instead, the Lantzville children who were in the film attended a "Hollywood-style" premiere at the Strand Theatre in Nanaimo on 15 November 1944—a city chosen for the initial screening because "The Film Board directors decided that since the setting was in Nanaimo, that Nanaimo citizens should be given the first opportunity to obtain a preview of the film."[59] At the premiere, Dallas Jones spoke briefly to the press:

> I can honestly say that of all the pictures I have directed, I think that "Lessons in Living" will do more worthwhile and lasting good than any other. It should inspire the parents, teachers and children alike with the dynamics of progressive education and the value of community cooperation especially in rural districts by giving the public a vision of the need and possibilities for community action in connection with educational improvement.[60]

The progressive classroom. Schooling reverted to a formalist pedagogy soon after the cameras had left. NAC, PA 19496.

The children had a somewhat different reaction from the one prescribed by Dallas Jones; recalled one child of his thoughts upon seeing the film: "God! They've been taking pictures for weeks and that's all there is?" Recalled another child: "All that filming and I wasn't even on it!"[61] Two days later, Plenderleith was able to show the film at the Island Area Teachers' Convention held at Nanaimo; although he spoke to the convention about consolidation, no record exists of any reaction Plenderleith may have had to the screening.

Following its premiere, *Lessons in Living* was rapidly distributed throughout the country. The content of the film was simply described in the NFB flyers of 1944:

> How a school project revitalized a community by giving the children a part in community life. The community of Lantzville, B.C. is a cross-section of nationalities and industrial groups—farmers, fishermen, lumbermen and railroad workers, with a down-at-heel spirit and a down-at-heel public school. But school and community changed, and Lessons in Living is the story of their transformation.[62]

Correspondence related to the film indicates that it drew positive reactions from rural audiences wherever it was shown and—indeed—inspired progressive cooperative action as suggested by the film. For example, Thomas Prine, the projectionist on the Prince George, B.C., circuit in August 1945, reported that the school at Horse Creek had been "beautified and improved, both inside and out...a direct result of the showing of this film."[63]

NFB circuit projectionists reported on other cooperative projects inspired by *Lessons in Living* throughout 1945 in "A Special Report," a summary questionnaire sent out to projectionists across the nation. A "prorec" was begun at Naramata and Kaleden in the Okanagan, and a community centre was begun at Clearwater, B.C.; a recreation centre was organized at Ste. Anne, Manitoba, and a community hall was redecorated at Niverville, Manitoba. School improvements were made at North River, The Falls, and Collingwood, Ontario, and at Shawville, Québec, as well. A school was repainted at Morewood, Ontario; school grounds were improved at Whycocomagh, N.S.; and almost everywhere that *Lessons in Living* was combined with the production *Hot Lunch at Noon*, a hot lunch program resulted for a community school.[64] Perhaps an essay written by Betty Boyer, a grade seven student from Miami, Manitoba, best expressed the sentiment that rural audiences took away from the film: "This picture stresses that co-operation is the best means of having a happy and enjoyable community...and I am sure that if this was done in all communities, we would have a happier and better world."[65]

As to the pedagogical issues raised by the film, reactions were mixed. Representative of a critical response was the report of circuit projectionist V. Poloway of Neepawa, Manitoba, who "made a point of interviewing school teachers, principals, school trustees and in one instance a school inspector in order to get their opinions as to the value of the film." The "general consensus" of the educators, according to Poloway, was that the subject matter was "too far-fetched in spots" and "not altogether practical in a one roomed school." "On the other hand some of the ordinary ratepayers, who were living in school districts that have delinquent and incompetent school boards thought the picture was an excellent one for stimulating some action."[66] Also on the favourable side, projectionist Poloway noted, "The talk from the school inspector was very inspiring and was the best part of the film."[67]

Some projectionists took the opportunity of the "Special Report" to compare trends on their circuits with those recorded on the film, such as projectionist J.C. Peck of Sydney Mines, Nova Scotia, who reported, "it may be interesting to learn that the types of desks, large tables with the children grouped around it, is giving away to the individual desk in the Higher Schools in Nova Scotia. In several schools here I have seen the table type discarded for the other type, except in the primarary [sic] grades."[68] Meanwhile, others took the opportunity to extrapolate from the film to their perceptions of curricular trends in general, such as M.J. Krewesky of Circuit "B" in Manitoba: "It...showed the people the modern trend in education, that is, that education should be practical not only theoretical."[69] The final word, in support both of such a trend and the film itself, belonged to Elmer Brownell, the circuit projectionist for Chester Basin, Nova Scotia:

> We need more films like "Lessons in Living." There is a great lack of education in our country even today and most of it is to be blamed on our schools.....The seating arrangements often remind me of cow stanchions in a stable. The child is seated behind a desk and must sit there and work from a text book or on a scribbler, and must not say a word. It doesn't seem right to me. I believe, by keeping the subject before the people we can help to create enough interest to have the curriculum changed to train the child to make a living and be happy. I believe this film did much more for the good of the country than any other one film the N.F.B. have yet produced.[70]

Conclusions

Lessons in Living did do a great deal of good for "the country." However, for the community which cooperated in its production, not all of the outcomes were so beneficial. Among these, the reputation of tiny Lantzville was impugned internationally for the good of the progressive democratic state—as noted by a perceptive film evaluator from the Pennsylvania College for Women, who assessed *Lessons in Living* in

1949 for the Educational Film Library at New York: "A school project involves the whole community of Lantzville, British Columbia and gives new life to the community....Children were given incentives which changed them from trouble makers to cooperative citizens....Shows how a community can be rehabilitated through its public school. Rating: Good.[71]

On the positive side of the balance sheet, Lantzville community gained $240 worth of lumber for its "splendid cooperation" with the National Film Board of Canada and an (admittedly) splendid film for its historical archives. But as the children of the film observed when interviewed, some of the after-effects of the progressive practices promoted by *Lessons in Living*, particularly the rural-urban cooperation to be achieved through school district consolidation, were suspect in the case of Lantzville. All agreed with Ruth Anderson, who played the role of Cindy: "It was an isolated community, and when it became open to the outside it lost its sense of uniqueness."[72] Worse yet in this regard, when the fence came down around Lantzville schoolyard (and "Enid's cows" gained access to the school) a cinematographic camera was on a tower across the roadway to record the resulting illusion of rural community "rehabilitation."

That cinematic record, *Lessons in Living*, was widely circulated throughout rural British Columbia prior to the 1946 Cameron Report and the subsequent consolidation of B.C. school districts from more than eight hundred districts to seventy-five.[73] Although the film was mastered in 35mm film (and was thus suitable for showing in cinemas) all the prints, with the exception of the Nanaimo Strand Theatre copy, were produced in 16mm film suitable for projectors used on rural circuits.[74] *Lessons in Living* was thus built almost exclusively for showing in rural communities—a cinematic "siren's song" to lure unwary B.C. and Canadian communities onto the progressive rocks of consolidation.

As rural audiences watched the film, to judge by the "Special Reports" written by NFB projectionists, they both comprehended and assimilated the main theme of the Lantzville story—that cooperation in educational matters would benefit a community. But they were unaware of vital information that could have tempered the universal appeal of the message. They could not see, for example, that *Lessons in Living* was merely a fictional screenplay set in Lantzville, nor that its "lessons" had been scripted for them in large part by agents of "progressive democracy," such as Grierson, who consciously set in celluloid the appropriate relationship between the state and a rural community's school, and Plenderleith, who viewed cooperation among small communities as a means of diluting the control each held over the education of its children.[75] These things they could not see, in fact, compose the "unseen significance" of *Lessons in Living* exposed by its "deconstruction"—that at the root of the production was a covert aim of the progressive state to consolidate and increase its educational influence over children. It is a goal to keep in sight as the study next turns to the postwar construction of "NFB kids."

4

Fields of Vision: Panoramas of Childhood in the Cinematic Society, 1947-67

> I insist that the photograph is a way to perceive things and not the things themselves. Or better, it is something that invites one to see some other thing or some other things.
> — Roberto Fernandez Retamar, *Cuba: la fotografía de los años 60*

Writing in the NFB Annual Report for 1946-47, Ross McLean, who replaced John Grierson as Government Film Commissioner, summed up film production at the postwar Film Board: "The films of five years ago mirrored the urgencies of Canada at war. The films of today catch the image of Canada facing up to the riddles of readjustment."[1] Considering the "specular" nature of NFB productions, their reflections of both "what is" and "what ought to be," McLean's statement suggests that the NFB mirror was now being adjusted to produce a new image of Canadian society for the postwar period—a contemporary likeness for Canadians to adjust to.

Children played a prominent role in this cinematic readjustment of Canadian society. Following World War II, their images were utilized by

---

Notes to chapter 4 are on p. 246.

the NFB to educate Canadians, adults as well as children, about themselves. They projected information about "what was" and "what ought to be" in regard to their families, schools, and neighbourhoods, about their safety and health, their work and recreation, and about their opinions, attitudes, and social relations. Consequently, as a body of films, the postwar portrayals of children constitute a panoramic record—an unfolding field of visions—of the changing physical, intellectual, and social realities of the peoples of Canada.

Moreover, they document "other things," to borrow a concept from the Cuban poet, Roberto Retamar. As NFB filmmakers strove to recreate the texture of life of postwar Canadian society, they filled their productions with popular patterns of common sense—attitudes, beliefs, and other social constructions—which were so ubiquitous that they were at the same time both before and beyond the field of vision of both the filmmakers and their audiences. Conversely, as they strove to be in the vanguard of social change, they selected certain new things to reflect in the mirror which, at first glance, appear historically obscure, while missing things of genuine importance to Canadian society at large. These ubiquitous and obscure "other things" compel a shift in our focus from acknowledged ways of seeing postwar social history and insist that we perceive other vistas by which to interpret the transience of Canadian society after World War II.

Fields of vision are the foci of this chapter—the "things and not the things themselves" visible in a broad survey of NFB portrayals of children produced from 1947 to 1967. The chapter records the narrative themes of these portraits, the historical contexts in which they were produced, the ostensive purposes for their production, and, perhaps of greatest significance, "other things." The panorama begins with the earliest of postwar images of Canadians "facing up to the riddles of readjustment"—the images of Canadian adults facing up to the birth of their first baby of many to come during the outset of what would come to be known as the "baby boom." To help Canadian mothers unravel the puzzles of pregnancy, birth, and infant care at the outset of an 80 percent rise in fertility rates among Canadian women of the twenty to twenty-four age group, an "NFB baby" was conceived for film as well: "Leonard," in *Mother and Her Child* (1947).[2]

In *Mother and Her Child*, a young businessman who is informed by his new wife of her pregnancy wants to drive her to their doctor's office immediately, telling her, "We want you looked after properly from the beginning." At the clinic, the doctor (who smokes in his office) tells Ruth that many women think that they have a cold when they become

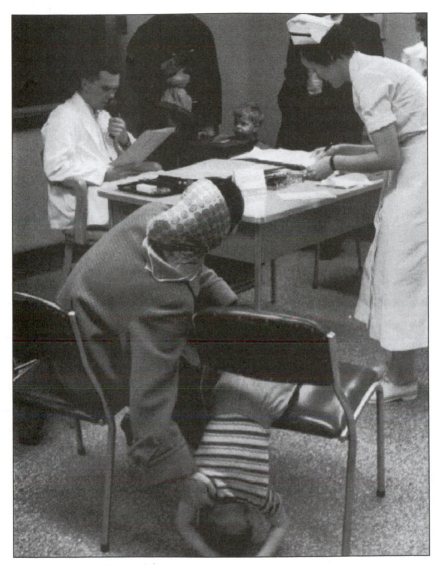

At the clinic in 1950s NFB society.

pregnant: "So take many hot foot baths." Ruth is tested for syphilis, and Paul, her husband, is advised that it is his job to keep Ruth happy and cheerful. "My," says Ruth, returning from the blood test, "I'm beginning to feel important." Several months later, Ruth is hospitalized and chloroformed and her baby, Leonard, is delivered, diapered. The balance of the film, *Mother and Her Child*, contains a great deal of normative information for mothers of infants who are under the age of one year, including the advice that good mothers, like Ruth, should allow dad to sleep when the baby cries out at night.[3]

The same year as Leonard's birth, a five year old by the name of "Johnny" visits the Canadian National Exhibition (CNE) at Toronto in *Johnny at the Fair* (1947). There, he has a good look at the wonders of the postwar society which await Canadian children like Leonard, as they grow up. Hand in hand, through gates festooned with British Union Jacks, Johnny and his parents enter the grounds of the CNE. Once inside the ramparts of "the Ex," however, Johnny strays from his parents' side, lured from their charge by his awe of the exhibits. Although initially alarmed by their son's disappearance ("Where's Johnny?") his parents are not exceedingly anxious. In fact, they are annoyed and, thereafter, as they proceed through the CNE they keep a sharp eye open for their youngster.[4]

Meanwhile, through Johnny's eyes we witness the "pagentry of tomorrow" passing us by—especially the "wonderful" technology of the era, washing machines and other convenience gadgetry. "He's not the first to be baffled by a lady's bonnet," observes the film's narrator, as Johnny quizzically strolls past a young woman who is attired in the latest fashion and is enthusiastic about the latest in kitchenware. The Swedish and French displays at the CNE are featured in the film, followed by displays from "the two new Dominions of the Commonwealth—India and Pakistan." Churning up Lake Ontario are the "Sea Fleas," tiny watercraft whizzing about in group formation. The American boxer Joe Louis is present, and he shakes Johnny's little hand, as does the Canadian prime minister, Mackenzie King. Barbara Ann Scott, the Canadian and World Ice Skating Champion, gives Johnny a kiss and "those screwballs...Olsen and Johnson" appear doing a slapstick routine. Johnny's parents and Johnny eventually meet up at the "Lost Children Building." Comments the film's narrator: "His parents haven't taken in half of what they wanted to see."

These cinematic images of "Leonard" and "Johnny" reflect the immediate postwar readjustment of the NFB mirror in regard to children, an adjustment which maneuvered the "eyes of Canada" away from community-centred, cooperative narratives that had been the hallmark of Griersonian portraits of children, and onto individual children situated within a variety of social contexts. Despite this movement from community to individual, however, most filmmakers continued to produce portrayals of Canadian children who, by their example, would provide a service to real children. Such was the case with the film *Out*

Beyond Town (1948), a fairly typical portrait of a rural Canadian child, which was directed by Evelyn Cherry.

In the film, Paul, an eight-year-old boy, slakes his thirst after collecting firewood on his family's farm by drinking water pumped from an unsafe well outside the farmhouse door. Soon afterward, he is sick and in bed, and, following a visit from the doctor, he is wrapped up in a blanket and carried out to the doctor's car. The seriousness of Paul's illness is conveyed by his elder brother, who stands disconsolately by a tree, scratching a branch in the dust as Paul is driven away to the hospital. The following day, the health inspector arrives and notes all the problems with the farm's water supply. Immediately thereafter, Paul's parents and brother and sister commence a huge cleanup of the sanitation problems on their farm.

"You know, my husband was really humiliated by the remarks of the sanitary engineer," says Mrs. Wilson (Paul's mother), co-narrator of the film, as she cleans and whitewashes the cellar walls and sprays around the doors and windows with DDT. "My, when I think about how the sanitary conditions used to be around here....Paul's illness was a good lesson for us. Thank God we didn't lose him. We know now what cleanliness really means." Upon his return to the farm, Paul is given a kiss by his sister. He runs with his brother to the family tractor, climbs up into the driver's seat and tugs at the steering wheel.[5]

The filmed portrayals of "Paul," "Leonard," and "Johnny" are representative of the first "other thing" of significance to become evident within the NFB's postwar portraits of children: the arbitrary gendering of children's roles to feature boys in community narratives. The practice appears to have been an unconscious one—a consistent, yet independent, choice made by both female and male scriptwriters and directors —and is especially noticeable during the 1940s and 1950s. A rare exception to this narrative rule was the Sydney Newman film, *Inside Newfoundland* (1949), in which the occasion of Newfoundland joining confederation was heralded by a girl, Hazel Greeley.

Inside Newfoundland was an introduction for both adults and children to the rural culture of Canada's tenth province as observed through the "bright eyes" of an "industrious" nine year old, whose Irish-laced accent is so broad as to at first seem incomprehensible (at least to west coast ears). Hazel leaves church and tags alongside her father to the wharf (she's "the apple of his eye"), ever hopeful he'll promise her five cents. "I'll give you a nickel if I get a salmon," answers her father, and then Hazel runs to school, where she and other children sing "God Save Newfoundland" and answer factual questions about their new country.

At the end of the film, Hazel's teacher asks her class, "What can New-foundland send to Canada?" Hazel answers "Fish!"[6]

Hazel's portrayal, although not expansive, is significant in other ways. Among these, whereas most of her cinematic counterparts during this era conveyed information directly to adults to be mediated to children, Hazel's image was constructed to speak directly to children, especially at their schools. Furthermore, her portrayal is bold when compared with most other late-1940s NFB portrayals of children. For the most part, cinematic children of this era are passive individuals in the films in which they act. They are taken to a dentist by their mother to prevent them from becoming "dental cripples" in films such as *Something to Chew On* (1948), or they are part of a team collecting pennies in a classroom project to buy school supplies for children in war-devastated Europe in the film *Pennies from Canada* (1948), or they are cheerful assistants constructing a family rumpus room in *Fitness Is a Family Affair* (1948). With the exception of "Johnny" at the fair and "Hazel" inside Newfoundland, however, children in late-1940s NFB films are most often found in "bit" parts, in a world controlled by the adults around them.

Even so, with the exception of children who are portrayed as troubled by physical or mental illness, the vast majority of them are portrayed as being happy. Indeed, among some of the most "naturalistic" portraits of children of this era, one finds the sentimental images of "childhood lost" so often associated with the period—such as with the happy campers in Ontario summer camps on Georgian Bay as represented in the film *Holiday Island* (1948).

Produced for National Parks Canada, *Holiday Island* surveys a Georgian Bay island for the parents of prospective Canadian and American campers—in particular, Camp Kitikewana near Midland, Ontario, over which both the Union Jack and the Stars and Stripes are flown. The highly structured activities of the young campers compete with the natural beauty of the island for the attention of the movie cameras. Although segregated by sex, all the children at Camp Kitikewana play "feathered Indian," swim, canoe, and take part in nature studies "on the Indian trail" under the friendly tutelage of camp counsellors.[7] And whether wearing straw caps, baseball caps with white piping, Mountie-style scout hats, or sea cadet caps, every child appears to have an enjoyable time on the holiday island.

NFB portrayals of Canadian children were expanding in the late 1940s to include commercial vistas as well as public ones. Typical of this growing commercialization of NFB portraits of Canadian children is the film *From Tee to Green* (1950), a twelve-minute, colour production selling the concept of a golfing vacation in Canada. In the film, a blonde-haired fifteen-year-old boy hitchhikes solo across Canada to caddy at the country's most prestigious golf courses from Newfoundland to British Columbia. The narrative moves at a hectic pace, especially since the boy visits the provinces out of geographic order. From Saint George's Golf Course in Ontario, where he caddies at the Canadian Open, he hitchhikes to Québec, where he wears a beret and carries a French-English dictionary. From there, he is off to New Brunswick and then to Newfoundland, where he learns that Newfoundlanders speak with an Irish accent (and where he learns the "hand mashie" shot). In the final three minutes of the film, he caddies at the Oak Bay Golf Course at Victoria then back to the Rockies, where he watches Bing Crosby play two fairway shots at the Jasper Golf and Country Club.[8] An interesting aspect of the film is that, as with *Johnny at the Fair*, there is the presumption of the child's safety alone, a confidence or naïveté long held in NFB productions.

Happy campers in *Thousand Island Summer* (1960). NFB, 92014.

The expansion of the NFB vision into the field of tourism may have appeared to Ross McLean to be a partial solution to some postwar riddles of readjustment being experienced at the Film Board itself. Soon after the war ended, the NFB suffered large-scale reductions in its size, a steady bleeding of almost two hundred personnel over three years. Compounding this malaise, NFB filmmakers were obliged, by 1949, to operate under the scrutiny of the Royal Canadian Mounted Police (RCMP), who probed their social and political lives for evidence of communist sympathies.[9] But if tourism seemed an ideologically safe subject for film productions by which to keep his personnel employed, the films in fact brought only further censure of the National Film Board and further criticism of McLean himself.

Tourism (never an interest of Grierson's) encroached upon the domain of commercial filmmakers, who lobbied Ottawa vigorously over this intrusion into their livelihoods. Their complaints abounded just as the NFB was being labelled by the Conservative opposition in the Canadian Parliament as a safe haven for communist spies and fellow travellers. Making matters worse, influential newspapers such as the Toronto *Globe and Mail*, the *Montreal Gazette*, the *Ottawa Citizen*, *Le Devoir* and the *Financial Post* were attacking the Film Board for excessive spending. According to Marjory McKay, a senior NFB administrator at the time, "It wasn't a happy place to work now, but if one left for any reason, the obvious conclusion was that one had been fired as a security risk. The employee was damned if he stayed and damned if he left."[10] Early in 1950, McLean himself resigned after it became known that his contract would not be renewed.

An outsider, W. Arthur Irwin, was appointed to replace McLean as Government Film Commissioner. Irwin's appointment was marked by an immediate respite from external attacks on the NFB. Chief editor of *Maclean's* magazine for twenty-four years prior to his NFB position, Irwin had little knowledge of the medium of film, but he possessed exceptional management skills and political savvy.[11] Moreover, his association with the Maclean-Hunter group of magazines meant that the *Financial Post*, a sister publication to *Maclean's*, would cease its crusade against the NFB since "one of their own [was] in place to get to the bottom of the Film Board mess."[12] Of no less importance, Irwin was chosen to head the NFB for his ability to express a cultural vision of Canada at the mid-point of the century. The essence of that vision, that Canada was a young nation, nonthreatening and "born of compromise," was delivered by Irwin in a 1949 speech to an American audience: "[Canada] has shown that a nation can be, can achieve independent identity, can capture freedom to live its own unique life under a sovereignty not unlimited but a sovereignty limited by organic association with other nations for a common purpose."[13]

Under Irwin's supervision, the cinematic mirror of Canada was readjusted, temporarily at least, to exclude commercial fields of vision and to now include, among other things, images of Canadians facing up to cold war exigencies. As Doug Owram observes in his *Born at the Right Time: A History of the Baby-Boom Generation* (1996) "the outbreak of the Korean War in 1950 made the world a fragile place."[14] By the early 1950s, NFB portrayals of children, especially in films intended for children, began reflecting visions of both the opportunities and challenges of a future possessed by the potential for war.

Cadet Holiday (1950) was produced by Sydney Newman to attract high school boys into the cadet movement. At the start of the film, a group of boys are shown parading in kilts at Springfield High School. From these recruits, the narrator notes, twenty will be chosen for the Cadet Corps. Even if a boy is overweight, the narrator comments, he might be chosen for the cadets, "for soon he will be in trim." Those who are chosen as cadets are filmed operating a tank turret and gun. As cadets, the narrative claims, boys learn to handle weapons safely. They learn to drive jeeps and trucks—even tanks, as a wild episode with a boy in an out-of-control tank demonstrates. "All is fun and games in Cadets," the narrator comments as the tank is brought to a halt. "Dad is very proud of his boy." The comment is similar to one delivered during the wartime film, *100,000 Cadets* (1940). At the conclusion of that film, however, it is an older brother in battle who is said to be proud of the cadet. Nor does any flag appear at the end of this latter production.[15]

Peacemaking is the aim of a second, NFB cold war film produced for children that year: *Our Town is the World* (1950). A nine-minute, black and white production produced for the United Nations, a client of the National Film Board since 1946, *Our Town is the World* begins with an assortment of preadolescent children running playfully through a rural town as a male voice announces, "At first the world is our town...on one side of the river 'we,' on the other side 'they.'" One mother says of the children on the other side of the river: "They are a bunch of no goods." In the next scene, the tidily dressed "we" children build a fort on one side of the river, while "they," the far grubbier "no goods," gather on the opposite bank. Ominous music plays whenever "they" are on screen. "We" appear to be the children of a small business class; "they" appear to be of a poorer working class. Soon, a shouting match erupts between the two groups: "Your father is an iceman....Your father sells rotten meat." As the fight becomes physical, one boy falls off a railway bridge and into the river, unnoticed.[16]

The fight carries on into the town where a rock is thrown, breaking a window at the local newspaper office. At that, all of the children, about twenty-five in number, are ordered into the newspaper office by the editor of the local paper. One little boy named George explains how the fighting began. After listening respectfully to George and the others, the newspaper editor shows the children a United Nations poster about human rights. "You all have the same rights," he tells them, but suggests (with a Griersonian echo) that instead of working together, they fought, and that consequently the boy who fell off the bridge nearly drowned. Remorseful, the children from both sides of the river volunteer to pool their resources and buy "Alphie" a $1.29 get-well gift. For his part, the editor vows to write an editorial advocating a new playground for both "we" and "they" children.

One change that Irwin's commissionership did not bring to the portraits of children by the NFB was the predominance of boys' characters in screenplays about the community. If anything, this trend became more entrenched during the early 1950s, with the exception of documentaries produced for adult audiences in which children were typically cast as "extras." In these documentaries, such as the NFB *Eyewitness* series which were intended for Odeon theatres, boys and girls appear on the screen more or less equally.

Each of the *Eyewitness* productions contained four, three-minute, newsreel-type slices of Canadian life which could be screened before a feature film and which, years later, were occasionally used as television fillers. Vignettes of the *Eyewitness* series often show children in community situations, supervised by teachers, team coaches, scout, guide or cadet leaders, police officers, doctors, nurses or other adults. Typical of the newsreels that appeared in the series are the following two from *Eyewitness #29* (1950): *Pied Piper of the 3R's* and *Church of the Open Road*.

Pied Piper of the 3R's (1950) was the first NFB production of the decade to portray indigenous children of Canada. In this vignette, which claims to show an arctic school at Fort Simpson in 1949, a white, middle-aged man dressed in a safari suit and wearing a pith helmet, strolls along a dirt road carrying a sign which reads "School." This itinerant teacher, whose classroom is a circle drawn in the sand, brings an "exciting introduction to the 3R's," announces the film narrator. "Here, Indian pupils learn reading, hygiene, and organized games...Education comes to the land of the muskeg." Although somewhat bewildered by the presence of the NFB camera, the children are eager to do well. The teacher passes around a word, ("Face"), on a large flash card for each to say aloud, and then tosses a large rubber ball from the centre of the circle to each of the laughing students. "Shy and retiring by nature," remarks the narrator of Fort Simpson Indians, "they learn initiative and competition." The children, dressed in dusty frocks and ragged pants, range in age from three to fourteen years old. The film ends with a closeup of an enthusiastic eleven-year-old girl with bright eyes and a cheerful smile, who is identified simply as "Florence."[17]

On the same film, *Eyewitness #29*, there is a clip about Sunday religious services, a topic rarely found in the NFB archival films containing children. *Church of the Open Road* (1950) describes a drive-in movie theatre, a growing venue for family entertainment in the early 1950s, at Britannia Bay in Ontario, which was converted Sundays into a drive-in chapel where families "attend church in the privacy of their own cars."[18] "Each week the congregation changes," quips the film narrator concerning the Sunday drivers. "The congregation on wheels can worship without leaving their cars." The cameras peer through windshields at families and older couples listening happily to the drive-in speakers hooked inside the passenger windows of their cars. The pastor stands at his microphone on a platform in front of a huge drive-in screen, a stiff breeze whipping his robes. A choir is shown at his left, singing into what looks to be an inadequate microphone for the task. Drivers roll down their windows to add to the collection plate. As the film ends, a young boy is shown holding his head against a drive-in speaker still attached to its post, a smile on his face.[19]

NFB Children in the Incunabulum of Television

The image of the boy with his ear glued to a drive-in speaker in *Church of the Open Road* is an apt signifier of the second "other thing" of significance revealed by the postwar portrayals of children by the NFB; i.e., the impact of innovations in audio-visual technology, especially television, upon those images. The telecasting of television signals into Canada coincided with Arthur Irwin's appointment at the Film Board and no less directly redefined fields of vision of and for NFB films—especially in relation to Canadian children. Perhaps as Joyce Nelson, a Canadian media anthropologist, has suggested in her *The Perfect Machine: TV in the Nuclear Age* (1987) the arrival of television redefined much of Canadian culture. Nelson's observation is worth quoting at length:

Rapid changes through this century, escalating during World War II and in the postwar period, have altered every aspect of society, particularly those time-honoured social institutions that once provided some form of stability and containment for the individual: church, family, community, meaningful work, pageantry, the arts....The problem is that these social changes have been accompanied by if not instigated through, a tremendous rise in the power and hegemony of the mass media. The spiritual and social vacuum created by the demise of traditional Western institutions has steadily been filled, not by alternative social arrangements or more viable forms of face-to-face rituals, but by the media themselves, which have rushed in to fill the breach. This is especially true of television, which for millions and millions of people is church-family-community-pageantry-the arts all rolled into one.[20]

Prior to American telecasting into Canada in the early-1950s and telecasts by the Canadian Broadcasting Corporation (CBC) commencing in 1952, postwar audiences for NFB films had actually grown to nine million viewers annually following the war, despite the downsizing of rural circuits. Rural audiences flourished as volunteer film councils took over projectionist duties and communities began operating over 230 film libraries from which films were lent to individuals and hundreds of small groups weekly for entertainment and discussion.[21] In addition, theatrical productions such as the *Canada Carries On* series and (later on) the *Eyewitness* series were being screened in Odeon theatres in urban and semi-rural areas to an audience of more than two million each month.[22]

The theatrical audience count seems credible given that this was the golden age of cinema in Canadian society. Odeon audiences garnered during the war expected, for a while at least, to see a film from the NFB on the theatre screen before an American feature film.[23] While the credibility of the rural figure is less certain, there was clearly a desire in even the most remote of Canadian audience areas for motion picture entertainment and, prior to the establishment of a CBC television network in Canada, the NFB serviced a broad public interest in newsreels and cultural information from a Canadian perspective.

As television signals became available, however, adult audiences dwindled for NFB productions.[24] Television sets were expensive but worth it to Canadian consumers in terms of entertainment, prestige, and sociability. Neighbours would meet to watch television together. People would gather on city sidewalks to watch television images inside storefronts. Indeed, in 1953, so many Canadian men and women regularly stood in front of department store windows and watched the new medium that the Canadian Gallup organization assigned them a separate category in one poll.[25] The eventual impact on NFB film distribution is not difficult to augur. After a rapid rise in telecasts of NFB films from 1950 to 1952, from 1953 onward telecasts of NFB productions declined sharply as a supply of fresh films dried up.[26] Non-theatrical distribution continued to be a mainstay, as reported by Gary Evans in his *In the National Interest* (1991): "In rural Canada, audiences in church basements and community halls continued to enjoy programmes on the monthly circuits as they had in the forties....From 1949 until 1954, there appeared to be healthy annual rises of 10 per cent or more in both non-theatrical and theatrical statistics."[27]

But as television broadcasting expanded into rural areas, it was doubtful that the loyalty of even this audience could be maintained, especially since their numbers, according to Evans, were widely believed by NFB insiders to be "doctored."[28] In truth, with the arrival of television in the 1950s, the audience for the NFB became largely juvenile.[29] In descending order, nationally everywhere but in Québec, where Maurice Duplessis ordered a school boycott of Film Board productions, NFB audiences were comprised of elementary school children first and foremost, then adult community groups, followed by high school students. Thus, portrayals of children blossom in the NFB film archives at the very time that baby-boom children, some 370,000 strong in 1952 alone, according to Owram, were beginning to fill enrolment registers at Canadian public schools.[30]

1950s NFB Films for Canadian School Children

If the first wave of the baby boom produced a strain upon Canadian school systems, just the opposite was true for the National Film Board. The arrival of ever increasing numbers of children at elementary schools from 1952 to 1960 reduced the strain on the institution to find an audience to replace the one being lost to television. By 1953, NFB portrayals of children were frequently intended for classroom audiences of Canadian baby boomers.

Among the most popular of the films for elementary school children of this and succeeding eras were the *Ti-Jean* series, which were based upon French-Canadian folklore. As late as 1990, the *Ti-Jean* series held first place for NFB bookings in Canada among the top two hundred non-theatrical films ever produced by the National Film Board.[31]

The first film of the series, *Ti-Jean Goes Lumbering* (1953) was the second most popular NFB title of all time according to a 1960 survey of audiences. With a viewing audience of over one million school children, *Ti-Jean Goes Lumbering* ranked a close second to *The Loon's Necklace* (1950) and ahead of the RCMP spectacle *Musical Ride* (1955).[32] In the film (directed by Jean Palardy) a kindly grandfather relates to his grandchildren the fable of a French-Canadian boy, Ti-Jean, who possessed superhuman power. Through cinematic special effects, Palardy's little Québecois hero outperforms all the other lumberjacks at whose camp he appears. He carries hundreds of logs in the space of minutes; he eats enough for ten men; he beats them all in their bunkhouse games, and finally disappears into the Québec woods on a huge white horse—a "what ought to be" fantasy to fire the imagination of Canadian school children.[33]

Two other films portraying children of various regions of Canada and released in 1953 likewise proved to be popular fare at Canadian schools: *Angotee: Story of an Eskimo Boy* (1953) and *The Story of Peter and the Potter* (1953). The latter film, according to a 1960 audience survey had been viewed by 800,000 Canadians, most of whom were elementary school children. Titled with childlike lettering, the film begins with a nine-year-old boy, Peter, who comes to town alone to choose a birthday card and present for his mother. "It makes you feel grown up to come alone to the city," remarks the male narrator, again an adult oblivious to the possibility of danger in the city to an unsupervised nine-year-old. Peter buys a card for 15¢ and a bowl for 65¢, which he breaks in a fall on the way home. This leads to his rescue by a thirteen-year-old girl, Annika, who wears a maple leaf crown on her head, and who takes him to her parents, the Deichmans, "the famous Nova Scotia potters."[34] The Deichmans fashion a superior bowl for Peter's mother, a process that Peter and Annika follow over three days, from the working of raw clay to the final firing. A postwar fashion trend among NFB boys first becomes pronounced in the film, *The Story of Peter and the Potter*—the ubiquitous plaid shirt. In the postwar years, plaid long-sleeved shirts on boys in the wintertime and horizontal striped T-shirts in the summertime become one of the most enduring continuities among the NFB depictions of Canadian children.

Of appeal to older students and adults, *Angotee: Story of an Eskimo Boy* was a striking departure from the anthropological gawking evident in earlier films about the Inuit produced by the Film Board. It was an attempt by a director (Douglas Wilson) to structure the childhood and youth of an Inuit boy in a way comprehensible to 1950s audiences.

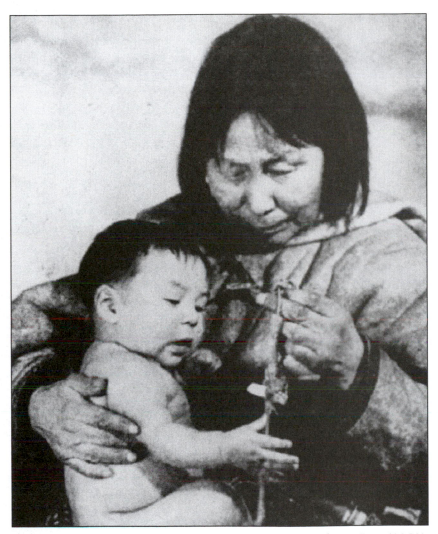

Angotee and Maunee, from *Angotee: Story of an Eskimo Boy* (1953). NFB.

Thus, it creates a narrative that, while anthropologically correct in a number of aspects, ultimately leaves a viewer with the impression that the Inuit in the 1950s had become the suburban descendants of the Inuit fashioned on film in the early 1940s by Laura Bolton.

The narrative begins in an exceptionally roomy and tidy igloo. There, Angotee is born beneath cariboo skins. A close-up of his mother's hand shows her wedding ring. Angotee's birth is attended by his grandmother, Maunee, who is a cigarette chainsmoker. A teenaged Inuit girl, Ookpik, leaves the igloo just prior to the boy's birth since "unmarried girls avoid childbirth." Maunee, the grandmother, names the baby, Angotee, who is delivered naked and is immediately cached inside his mother's parka, to be warmed in authentic Inuit fashion against her body. Angotee is likewise carried this way on a trek with his mother to "Missionary Settlement," where his mother watches a school being built and where, at the Hudson's Bay Company (HBC) store, free food, "Pablum," is provided for Inuit children. "There was a time," remarks the narrator, "that this was not so."[35]

Back at the igloo, Angotee's mother is shown doing her igloo-cleaning. For the first time, Angotee's father appears in the film. "Always time to play with his son," observes the narrator, who declares Angotee to be "ruler of the household." The HBC pablum is served to the boy, but a shot of traditional Inuit mouth feeding is also shown, as is breast feeding under the mother's parka. Angotee is said to be "very fond of the special food from the store" but "Grandma doesn't think much of the stuff." At seven years old, Angotee is again described as "the ruler of his household" by the film narrator yet, when he knocks over a shelf in the igloo, his mother spanks him. "No, no," says his grandmother, Maunee. The narrator points out that spanking is a "white man's habit" picked up from the settlement. "Times and customs have changed but not little boys," says the narrator cheerfully. "His mother knows that he will soon forget his spanking." Angotee's bride-to-be, an unnamed eight-year-old Inuit girl, is shown honing her sewing skills and using her teeth to stretch animal hides. The film ends with Angotee marrying her at age eighteen, in a ceremony performed in Latin at a little, white, Catholic church. All admire his wife's wedding ring in the final scene, suggesting domesticity and suburban values are now the "what is" on the frozen tundra as well.

Some films produced by the NFB took a more eclectic approach to school social studies by integrating topics and finding ways to inspire school teachers to undertake project work and integrate subject areas. Such a film is an early Tom Daly production, *Winter in Canada* (1953), a film designed to introduce children to the workings of the Canadian post office, the geography of Canada, and similarities and differences in Canadian regional cultures. In *Winter in Canada*, a ten-year-old immigrant boy named Peter has come to live in Canada (likely from Western Europe) and resides in a small town in the Ontario Laurentians. At the end of his school day, he and his classmates rush to their lockers, put on their winter coats and toques, and head home to play in the snow. Peter pauses twice on his way home, once to watch an early snowmobile, a "snowplane," tractor across a field, and later to watch boys dressed in Maple Leaf hockey sweaters playing ice hockey on an outdoor rink. Peter's home, an elegant brownstone, is heated by a coal-fired furnace. Peter uses a fountain pen to write a letter to his penpal, Julian, in Cochrane, Alberta.[36]

The film follows the progress of Peter's letter through the postal system and onto a twin-engined CP propeller-driven airplane. The plane flies through a snowstorm and then into open skies, through elliptical time marked by changing aerial shots of the ground below. At his ranch outside of Cochrane, Peter's penpal, Julian, an eleven year old, is shown on horseback. He feeds hay to the cattle and fetches milk from the barn for his mother, who is in the kitchen making a blueberry pie.

Julian's father brings Peter's letter to Julian from the Cochrane Post Office. In the evening, Julian writes a reply to Peter ("I hope Blacky, our steer, will win a prize at the Spring Fair.") His father is shown reading a story to his two daughters, aged four and five. The next day, Julian takes a truck ride with his father to Mt. Norquay Lodge, where he uses a Brownie camera to photograph the Rockies, a snapshot to include in his letter to Peter. As the film ends, Peter is once again shown in his rural, Eastern-Canadian home, playing with his Tinker Toys on the living-room carpet, and anticipating the return letter from Julian. The film ends without Julian's letter being delivered—an open ending which allowed teachers to assign a writing project and an informal ending that would be later popularized by the *What Do You Think?* series.

Social studies films comprise the bulk of NFB productions for school children in the early 1950s, but cinematic children of the era mirrored information about health and safety as well. Curiously, only by the early 1950s were NFB films concerning nutrition for children actually being targeted at audiences of children. While films about nutrition were plentiful during the war years—*Strength for Tomorrow* (1943), *What Makes Us Grow?* (1943), the *Vitamin Films* (1943), *Children First* (1944), and *School Lunches* (1945)—a significant difference between these and the nutrition films of the next decade was that films of the 1940s, for the most part, explained children's nutritional needs to adults (or to high school students, as in the case of *What Makes Us Grow?*) whereas 1950s nutritional films, such as *Food for Freddy* (1953), were aimed directly at school children and only indirectly at their parents.

Food for Freddy, a colour film, begins on a snowy day with a class of grade four students preparing to eat lunch in their classroom. One girl wears a sweatshirt with a print of a skier pressed onto it; another wears a red ribbon in her hair. The children slide their desks together to form lunch tables. One boy, Bobby, drinks pop. "Maybe that's why he hasn't enough energy," remarks the narrator over a shot of a lethargic Bobby. For a class project, the teacher brings caged white rats into the classroom and provides them with different diets. One group of rats drink pop and eat jam sandwiches and cookies. The other group of rats eat cheese and carrot sticks and drink milk. A "Health-O-Meter" scale is used to weigh the two rat groups. The children use "growth charts" to compare the changes in the two groups of rats over four weeks.[37]

Being conscious about vitamins in *Vitamin-Wise* (1943). NFB.

After four weeks, the pop and cookie rats have small, "greedy eyes" and scrawny fur. They are badly tempered, and one has died. The cheese and carrot rats, of course, are thriving. They are plump and friendly, with bright eyes and sleek fur. At home after school, Freddy, who unlike Bobby has a lot of energy, chatters away with his mother in the kitchen, presumably about the classroom experiment. The reason for Freddy's vitality becomes clear as we observe his mother shopping the next day. She pushes both a baby in a carriage and a shopping cart with a huge load of groceries including cheese and vegetables. "She reads labels for grade and weight," the narrator observes with satisfaction.

Back at school, with the rat experiment completed, the "Canada Food Rules" are passed out to each child to take home. Some children are shown packing these in cube-shaped lunchboxes for safekeeping. That evening, Freddy's mother fries liver in a flour coating for dinner for her son and her husband. "Even dad agrees that nutrition has an effect on health," announces the narrator in summing up. Ideally, copies of the Canada Food Rules would have been distributed to school children after watching the film, to be put in their lunchboxes, with the intention that the pamphlet and the children's retelling of the film would persuade mothers to shop for healthy food for their children's lunches.

Government health and safety films had their greatest impact when they were brought to a school by a medical or public official who would answer questions after the screening. Undoubtedly, this was the intent with the pedestrian safety film *Look Alert: Stay Unhurt* (1954), a cinematic lesson delivered to young children by a stern-looking policeman. In the film, a group of children are playing ball when one, a boy named Ted, steps out into the roadway without looking. Several cars come to a screeching halt, and an angry driver says: "Kids that jaywalk should be taken to court." Just at that moment, a policeman appears at the scene and leads young Ted away, past his friends, one wearing a cub scout uniform, into the police car and down to the police station. Once inside his office, the policeman laughs to break the tension and gives Ted a special lesson about traffic safety using a scale model city, complete with plastic cars, that he keeps on his desk. As he pushes around the plastic cars, the policeman describes traffic safety violations involving children. At this point, the scale model dissolves to the scenarios he is describing.[38]

One example of what not to do leaves a young boy, who unwisely tried to cross the road on a yellow light, stranded in the middle of the intersection with cars whizzing by him on either side. The policeman says emphatically: "Roads are for cars." In the next scene, two girls of ten years of age are playing dressup with dolls in carriages. A carriage belonging to one of the girls is wiped out by a car on the road. "They weren't paying attention," warns Ted's policeman. After the scale model demonstrations, some photographs (not shared with the camera) are shown to Ted of accident victims. "All this pain and tragedy," warns the policeman, "all because children were careless." At the policeman's bidding, Ted writes the "3 Safety Rules" on the police station chalkboard : "1) Don't cross except on a green light; 2) Don't play on the street;

3) Don't cross around parked cars." Ted promises to teach all other children these rules and he is released from custody.

Moppet Models (1953): Adult Visions of early-1950s Canadian Childhood

Vignettes showing ambitious young Canadians involved in extracurricular activities were commonly included in the *Eyewitness* series for Canadian movie-goers. A sampling of some early-1950s *Eyewitness* titles captures something of their spirit and central themes: *High School Glider Pilots* (1950), *B.C. Develops Schoolboy Rangers* (1950), *Junior Bengal Lancers* (1951), *Peterboro Ornamental Swimmers* (1951), *Grand Champ Junior Farmers* (1952), *Traffic Cops in Jumpers and Jeans* (1952), *Ball Stars Start Young* (1953), and *Moppet Models* (1953). An earmark of each production was the enthusiasm attributed to Canadian children for whatever junior career activity they were involved in—even the youngest children, "scarcely out of the nursery," in *Moppet Models* from *Eyewitness #52* (1953).

Subtitled "Small Fry Learn to Pose for Pay," the vignette, *Moppet Models*, explores "a school for junior models" in Toronto, where "good grooming and graceful movement is taught" and "personal poise developed." At this school "for boys and girls as young as three or four," the children learn not to be frightened by lights and cameras and to pose for fashion parades and commercial artists. Although left unstated by the film, there is also a level of precociousness being developed within the toddlers that is novel to previous Film Board portrayals. Scenes of adults rushing youngsters into clothes are followed by a parade of "moppets" strolling over a fashion runway. "A real contribution to Toronto's fashion industry is made by Toronto's moppet models," remarks the narrator at the end of the film.[39]

The *Eyewitness* series was the forerunner to the half-hour television newsmagazine series, *On the Spot*, which was produced from 1953 to 1956 for the CBC by the NFB. Often narrated by Fred Davis, who became a perennial CBC television personality, the *On the Spot* series was a televised social studies program for adults which frequently introduced the ethnic cultures of Canada to CBC television viewers. *Chinese Canadians* (1954) was a typical half-hour segment of the series. Filmed in Vancouver, it contains considerable footage of Chinese Canadian children of the era and was the first cinematic portrayal of Asian Canadian children since the wartime depiction, *Of Japanese Descent* (1945).

Davis walks through Vancouver's Chinatown with a noisy hand-held microphone. "There are 40,000 Chinese in Vancouver," his report begins. "Prejudice is on the decline." He dwells for a considerable time at a kindergarten conducted by the "Good Shepherd Mission" in downtown Vancouver. Chinese children (the vast majority are girls) are filmed listening attentively to a white teacher as she reads a story to them. Older Chinese girls—some dressed in blazers with British Columbia crests on their lapels and some wearing saddle shoes—are also filmed at the mission, listening to the *Call of China* program from the Vancouver radio station, CJOR. A children's choir at the mission sings "Praise Him, all the little children." The conductor of the choir, another white woman, joins with the first white teacher to hand out diplomas to the graduating kindergarten class. Ultimately, the narrative of *Chinese Canadians* seems to imply that if prejudice against the Chinese community in Vancouver was in decline, it was because Chinese children were making a transition from an ethnic Chinese culture to one incorporating contemporary Western cultural traits and values.[40]

Chinese Canadians was among the first films approved by the newest Government Film Commissioner, Albert Trueman, who succeeded the retiring Irwin. An academic and another newcomer to the film industry, Trueman had previously served as president at the University of New Brunswick. Curiously, the outgoing commissioner, who had taken the helm of the NFB in stormy seas and then sailed it into calmer waters, steered the Film Board into a fresh political gale just before handing the commissionership to Trueman by originating the screenplay for *Farewell Oak Street* (1953). The film, which dramatizes the construction of public housing at Regent Park in Toronto, has similarities to an early Griersonian production about housing in the slums of Britain, *Housing Problems* (1936), but relies on sympathy for the plight of children, rather than sympathy for other adults in order to deliver its message to Canadian adults concerning the need for public expenditure for government-subsidized housing.

In the film, the squalor of a downtown Toronto tenement is illuminated through the plight of a family of six: a mother and father, a teenaged son and pre-teenaged daughter, and a boy and girl both of primary school age. The narrator, Lorne Greene, is constantly expressing his sincere sympathy with the family's situation: "Keeping clean was an endless and losing battle...the place, not the family was the problem...some of them made the best of a bad lot." Nineteen tenants reside in an old brownstone sharing one bathroom, and they include an older male child molester, who offers the twelve-year-old girl a stick of candy on her way up the stairs to her family's apartment—a filthy, insect-infested flat. Inside the apartment, the family members are surrounded by cracked walls, live beneath bare lightbulbs, and wash with rusty tap water. The four children are compelled to share two single beds. Over shots of industrial development, the narrator laments, "We raise up houses for commerce and machines....There are too many Oak Streets for our rich, resourceful nation!"[41]

A change in mood music announces the change in camera location, which now records the construction of Regent Park: "the nation's first public housing!" Later, the awe-filled tenement family members cautiously wander through their new home. As the mother imagines the curtains she will make for the windows, the father smiles. Just then, the parents are alarmed by the sound of running water. Rushing upstairs, they open a door to the bathroom where they find their eldest son, grinning sheepishly, preparing to be the first to use the new bathtub—a hopeful ending for a fresh beginning. Although *Farewell Oak Street* appears to be an exemplary use of the documentary mirror—"what was" and "what ought to be"—the film was greeted, in fact, by strong negative reaction from the actual residents of Regent Park, who resented the "what was" representation of themselves as "slum dwellers." The member of Parliament for the riding expressed their collective outrage, calling the film offensive to human dignity and demanding its withdrawal from distribution. The new commissioner, Trueman, refused the request.[42]

Early in 1954, however, Trueman began the process of further adjusting the mirror that had been created by Grierson. While in Grierson's mirror, the social held sway over "what ought to be," for Trueman, "the Film Board's role was not to tell the country what was wrong with it."[43] Instead, according to Evans in *In the National Interest*: "Trueman fostered an unwritten policy and priority, the shift from social realism in film to the *art* of film."[44]

> He [Trueman] recalled "Mulholland [then director of production] and many others were burdened with what seemed...an excess of social conscience, a do-the-people-good-whether-they-like-it-or-not complex." He felt that the balance between art film and educational film was not being maintained. He encouraged a new niche: more art and less social propaganda. The change occurred gradually, but perceptibly.[45]

Ironically, the new emphasis on art over education had virtually a crosswise effect on the social content of some films portraying children.

Applying the genre techniques of film noir, for example, on *Night Children* (1956)—a recruiting film for the Ontario Children's Aid Society—advanced the film as a social critique. *Night Children* begins with an eight-year-old girl wandering alone along rain-swept city streets late at night. "The face of the city is the face of its people," remarks the narrator with a typical film noir intonation. The girl is eyed by one man wearing a beret, smiled at by a friendly old man playing an organ grinder, approached by a drunk man in a business suit and asked her name. A fashionably dressed young woman rescues her from the latter and offers to escort her home to her mother. A moody, musical soundtrack plays out the scene to a dark dissolve.[46]

In the next scene, a phone call to the Children's Aid Society (CAS) is received by a cigarette smoking, female social worker on night shift. The young CAS worker puts on her cloth coat and drives to a slum tenement where she finds the girl sitting next to her schizophrenic mother who is lying on a cot, staring up at the ceiling from which paint is peeling. The girl is apprehended by the worker since, "Mother was withdrawn from life." On other cases accompanied by the obligatory oblique shadows, extreme close-ups and the eerie music of the genre, an impression is given to prospective CAS workers of the type of people they are likely to meet—heroin addicts, alcoholics, the emotionally disturbed—and the place where they are most likely to meet them: in downtown slum tenements. The film has a happy ending when the "night child" is returned months later to her now recovering mother. The CAS worker returns to her office above the rainswept city street; she lights another cigarette; she inhales deeply, and waits by the phone.

Film noir, popularized in American detective movies such as *Naked City* (1948), *The Asphalt Jungle* (1950), and *The Big Heat* (1953), was the film art likewise used to portray two adolescents in trouble with the law in the film *The Suspects* (1957), which was part of the made-for-television *Perspectives* series. Despite its opening quotation, "The police force is the most important and greatest good in society"—said to be from Aristotle—the film shows the seamy side of a police station. Much of the acting (overacting) by the male adolescent is done James Dean style. In the film, a sixteen-year-old girl and her boyfriend are taken into custody on "suspicion" (of what is not clear) and the girl is grilled by a Detective Brewster who wears a fedora and a trenchcoat. Detective Brewster turns a bright, goose-neck desk lamp onto the face of the frightened girl. A blinking, neon cafe sign can be seen outside the window. Brewster's rapid-fire questions are accompanied by the sound of a metronome in the background. "Your boyfriend's a crook, and he's no good," he shouts at the girl. He threatens to book her for prostitution unless she "stools" on her boyfriend. Ultimately, the two young people are released (apparently not guilty of "suspicion") and a gentler detective, a mug of hot coffee in his hand, reflects upon the darker side of the business of policing: "Frankly, I don't know if I blame Brewster," he murmurs.[47]

Conflicts between adolescents and adults in NFB portrayals of children first appear in a film entitled *Having Your Say* (1954), one film of the *What Do You Think?* series produced mainly for high school audiences. The *What Do You Think?* films briefly present a conflict situation, then leave the resolution of the conflict to the audience, via a discussion led by a teacher. In *Having Your Say*, an adult group about to use a meeting room find it in disarray and leap to the conclusion that it was the fault of an adolescent group that shares the use of the room. "Teenagers don't appreciate our help," complains one of the adults, and the adolescents are barred from future use of the place. The adolescents in question, a pleasant group of young people, protest their innocence in the matter and make plans to hold a meeting to discuss their arbitrary treatment by the adults. The question that perplexes them is this: should everyone, even the adults who opposed them, be allowed to speak at the meeting? In the end, the answer belonged to the high school students watching the film.[48]

Joe and Roxy (1957)

One adolescent concept that many Canadian adults opposed in the 1950s was that of "going steady." In 1954, 76 percent of Canadian adults polled by CIPO-Gallup said that high school students were too young to go steady.[49] The NFB film *Joe and Roxy* (1957) explained the concept to adult audiences and attempted to account for other intergenerational conflicts, as well. In the film, Joe and Roxy (both seventeen years old) are going steady. The two are like big kids playing house. At the start of the film, with an early rock and roll soundtrack playing in the background, Joe is repairing a toaster while Roxy watches him admiringly. "It's a good thing I'm taking commerce at Tech," she says. "I guess I'm just a rattlebrain." After fixing the toaster, Joe, who is torn between becoming an engineer or an auto mechanic, presents Roxy with a steel ring he has made using his father's tools. "See you tomorrow?" he asks. "Natch," says Roxy, who kisses him quickly on his way out the door. On her way to the kitchen, she hums the tune "On Top of Old Smokey."[50] Roxy's mother, who is a single parent, is upset by the sight of the ring, even after Roxy has explained the difference between "going steady" and "going steadily" to her:

> Mother: Steady, steadily, I don't see the difference.
> Roxy: Ohhhmm well, going steadily you can go out with more than one person if you want to but going steady you can just go out with one.[51]

Her mother, a single parent and possibly the first divorcee portrayed by the NFB, seeks further information from her daughter about the phrase, "going steady."

> Roxy: Oh golly it's not all that complicated; its just going steady. You always have a date when you want one and you know what to expect from the boy so you can relax; so can he. You don't have to put on a big act to impress each other just because you're nervous. You can help each other along.

Over at Joe's house, the teenaged boy has wandered into the basement of his home to talk to his dad, who is operating a lathe. His father appears irked to have his son lay out his struggle whether to be an engineer or a mechanic while he is working. He begins to dissuade Joe from engineering, citing Joe's lack of commitment. With frustration in his voice, he says: "Just do whatever you want." Joe is crestfallen. "Seventeen is a moody time," comments the narrator. "More optimism than doomsaying."

Joe and Roxy attend a technical and commercial high school. The narrator observes, "Mostly it gives them a practical education. They learn to do rather than think." Scenes of shop work (all boys) are followed by those from a typing class (all girls). "It's more valuable to be able to print a poem than to write one," the narrator comments. From typing class, the camera cuts to a physical education class where boys dressed in grey sweatsuits tumble on mats with synchronized precision, followed by an appearance by the cheerleading team: "Some think our schools are too materialistic, too frivolous, too superficial. Perhaps. But they fit our world, meet our tastes. The young don't originate, they imitate. And if our grownup world insists that the way to happier living is to possess a pretty pair of legs or to be popular why blame either student or school?"[52]

The cheerleaders perform the "Team is on the Beam" routine wearing very short, pleated, plaid skirt costumes ("skorts"). The cheer is followed by scenes from the sockhop, at which both Joe and Roxy appear. "On Top of Old Smokey" is the hit song of the dance. Over scenes of dancing—shots of boys with Brylcreem hairstyles and girls with bolero skirts, bobby socks, and saddle shoes—the narrator comments: "The kids, the crowd, the gang, the most important people in the world to themselves."

The next day, Sunday, Joe and Roxy snuggle on a couch at her mother's house with a *Star Weekly Magazine*. The narrator sums up the life philosophy of a teenager circa 1957: "They want all to be orderly and precise; they want all to be predictable. Youth wants a role to play in life. Simple problems, simple solutions, simple actions—a little world in which everyone has a definite place. What will happen to them? Probably the same as happens to most of us."[54]

The importance of being popular among "the group" becomes a recurring theme in late-1950s NFB portrayals of children, especially among adolescents. The phenomenon was conveniently exploited in 1957 by the Canadian Dental Association, which sponsored the NFB production *Putting It Straight* (1957), the first dental film to use a female narrator. The narrative concerns "poor Mary," an eleven-year-old girl who is taunted by her peers because of her crooked teeth. Although not unsympathetic to her daughter's tearful alienation her mother tells her to get used to it because there is nothing that can be done about teeth like hers. The narrator, however, a fashionably dressed woman who has been following Mary at a distance, knows otherwise and likewise forsees that "Today it was her looks, but tomorrow it could be her health affected."[55]

Following an insertion, in which a male narrator provides medical information about the formation of "mouth deformities," the female narrator, with a bright and even smile, boldly approaches the mother and, using a photo album to illustrate her narrative, tells the story of another desperate girl with hopelessly crooked teeth—herself, of course. Astonished by the contrast between the photos in the album and the virtually perfect teeth before her, Mary's mother accepts the moral of the story: "Better late than never to have braces inserted." The mise en scéne dissolves to the near future in which, skipping along with other girls wearing saddle shoes, we now see that Mary has friends—and that her mother has earned the respect of her neighbours.

At this juncture, the composition of NFB neighbourhoods is worthy of a comment. As with the depiction of almost every urban and suburban neighbourhood in NFB films portraying children up to 1957, the neighbourhood culture in *Putting It Straight* is monolithically white, Anglo-Saxon.[56] A million and a half immigrants had come to Canada between 1945 and 1957, many of whom were non-English speaking and, although most of them had settled in urban areas of Canada, their children remained essentially invisible in the neighbourhoods created by the NFB. Rural Canada had been depicted as being culturally diverse almost since the inception of the Film Board (Laura Bolton had filmed *Iceland on the Prairies* early in 1941) but up to 1957, NFB urban and suburban neighbourhoods were depicted to have a uniformly Anglo-Saxon culture. Only after the mid-1950s, and then only occasionally, did the cinematic mirror begin to reflect urban cultural diversity. As the narrator of the film *Bar Mitzvah* (1957) observes, "Ours is a society transplanted from a hundred different homelands. We are slowly learning to appreciate the differences."[57]

In contrast to the portrayal of children in *Chinese Canadians*, in which the differences from "mainstream" Canadian society are overt, and in which viewer appreciation is constructed from the depiction of the willing cooperation of Chinese Canadian children to minimize those differences, in *Bar Mitzvah*, the approach to the portrayal is to represent the differences as being minimal from the outset. Hence, the film begins with that most classic of opening scenes among NFB portraits of children—with Canadian school children, including "Morris Shidowski," running happily out of a Canadian school after dismissal.

Dismissed from public school, however, Shidowski heads not for the hockey rink with his friends, but to the Ottawa Talmud Torah, a Hebrew school where he and others learn "lessons that will make them good citizens as well as good Jews." As Morris studies for his Bar Mitzvah, the camera explores the interior of the Hebrew school. During the Bar Mitzvah, the narrator explains, women may look on as spectators but only the men can participate. Morris waits anxiously, then he sings from the *Torah* and the *Book of the Prophet* before leading the assembled men in a prayer thanking God "for the gift of being a Jew." Through the ceremony, Morris's faith is confirmed; through the NFB film of the ceremony, the social acceptability of religious differences between Canadian Jews and Canadian Gentiles is affirmed.

The film *Bar Mitzvah* preceded a series of NFB immigration films—many of which portray children—which, in the late 1950s, included *A Foreign Language* (1958), a *Candid Eye* film made for the CBC as well as *The Threshold: Immigrant Meets the School* (1959), a drama produced to be screened to new immigrants to Canada.

Sponsored by the Department of Citizenship and Immigration, *The Threshold* portrays the "Mag" family—mom (Anna), dad (Mr. Mag), fifteen-year-old Susie, and eleven-year-old Leo who have emigrated to Canada from Austria. At the outset of the film, the family members, all dressed in their best clothes, walk to school to start the children's first day. The narrator warns: "School will be far more baffling for parents than child." Their son, Leo, is immediately out of place dressed in his lederhosen among the other elementary school children, and his mother, Anna, finds the schoolyard to be a chaotic place. At the high school, Mr. Mag is dismayed by the lack of authority and formalism that exists between students and teachers. He is surprised when Anna's new teacher declines the title "professor" (the film narrator explains that Canadians dislike formal titles). Mr. Mag—who was himself a teacher in Austria— is further upset when his daughter, Susie, is set back a year in her studies due to "language and history differences."[58]

Within a few weeks, the Mag children "are adapting at a furious pace," but the parents are resisting change. Their boy, Leo, is at home in both worlds. He races around the apartment building playing "cowboys" with the neighbourhood children. Their daughter, Susie, who was at first unused to "the slack discipline at the high school....It was too casual for her taste," now sees that "there is a subtle discipline in effect."[59] To her, a Canadian high school teacher "is like a kindly uncle." She is dressing more like her peers who, for the most part, wear tartan skirts and white bobby socks, but not with her parents' knowledge, since it would upset them. In the apartment below the Mags, another Austrian family, the Roccas, have Austrian literature read to them nightly by their father. The Rocca children are on the edge of rebellion, observes the narrator: "Father Rocca has become more Austrian than he ever was in Austria."

That evening, the mother of one of Susie's high school friends knocks at the door of the Mag family apartment. She is part of the "Home and School Association" and asks both parents to come to the next meeting. "The school and home are not separate worlds here," the narrator remarks. Mr. Mag declines, but Anna agrees to come and thus breaks free from her Austrian life at home. She becomes involved in a report card survey that involves her with the community. The school culture that has changed her children affects her as well. She gains in confidence; she even speaks at a public meeting and is applauded. The school, it is clear, is "the threshold" for both young and old to enter into the Canadian mainstream. "Growth and change are constant for this young country," the narrator reminds the Mr. Mags and Father Roccas watching the film, "All Canadians are immigrants or descended from immigrants."[60]

Whereas *The Threshold* was intended for screening by home and school associations to new immigrant parents and was focused on broad outcomes, the aim of the *Candid Eye* production, *A Foreign Language*, was to provide television audiences with knowledge about how immigrants were being Canadianized in public schools. The film, which is innovative for the naturalism that results from the mix of both candid and scripted shots of authentic immigrant children, opens with a roundtable setting of seven youngsters, aged seven to ten, chattering in various languages until they are told to speak English by their teacher.

The children live in Montreal and appear to attend the class on a "pull-out" basis. For the most part, they are portrayed as being highly enthusiastic about the experience. One boy, however, looks sad and confused—and there is a brief, unexplained, shot of a boy sitting out in the school hallway. The class is taught by a stern, but friendly, woman in her mid-fifties. The children are of Italian, Spanish, Greek, Dutch, German, and Asian origin. Canadian food is the focus of their lesson this day. "Canadians like to eat corn," says the teacher. A simple discussion ensues about milk and milk bottles. A Spanish girl is especially outgoing; she corrects a German boy's pronounciation: "curtains...not cortains."[61]

In addition to simple conversations, the children of this group, and a younger group, participate in singing and dancing games. A very young group marches to the tune of "The Battle Hymn of the Republic," and an older group performs the singing game, "Bluebird through my Window." At recess, some boys are filmed throwing trading cards against an outside wall. On one of the cards, there is an image of Sputnik. After recess, a new group, predominantly Asian, discusses synonyms (the three meanings of "spring") and practises responding to "W" questions: "What do you do to help others?...Why do we help?...When do you wash your hair?" The Asian students appear to be most eager of all to do well in the class. At the end of the film, the children put on paper hats stereotypical of their country of origin.

Refocusing on Education in the late 1950s

As George S. Tomkins notes in his *A Common Countenance: Stability and Change in the Canadian Curriculum* (1986) concerning the launch of Sputnik, its immediate effect upon Canadian society was to validate contemporary criticisms of progressive education, such as those raised by Hilda Neatby in her popular work, *So Little for the Mind* (1953).

> Critiques of the alleged soft pedagogy of progressivism came to a head in 1957 with the Russian launching of Sputnik. Shortly, the Gordon Commission on Canada's Economic Prospects was voicing concerns similar to those being expressed in the United States about the

scientific-technological gap between the Soviet Union and North America. As in that country, national shortcomings were laid out at the door of deficient school curricula and related educational neglect.[62]

Technology, as television, had already played a significant part in changing the fields of vision of and for NFB portrayals of children. Now, technology in the shape of a grapefuit circling the planet with a radio beacon compelled the "eyes of Canada" to refocus on education, to reassure Canadians that the development of intellect *was* of primary importance in their public schools. The cinematic outcome, *The Gifted Ones* (1959), is a uniquely progressive vision of intellectual development—a vision of intellect being trained to attend not solely to technological matters, but to social ones as well.

The opening scene of *The Gifted Ones* immediately establishes its link to the Sputnik scare as a chubby, freckled, ten-year-old boy named Drew, wearing a checked shirt and sporting a crew-cut, talks to his teacher about the effects of gravity in space—in particular, about ways of creating an artificial gravity in a spacecraft through magnetism or centrifugal force. The teacher, a kindly, grey-haired woman, sits facing the boy, nodding encouragingly as Drew further extemporizes about the fuel requirements of space travel. At last the film narrator observes, "This is an intellectually gifted child....Children of superior intelligence are among the chief assets of a developing nation."[63]

At issue in the film, *The Gifted Ones*, is whether child prodigies such as Drew should be provided special classes in Canadian schools or whether "they should be left in their regular classes to become the leaders." Scenes from a "regular" class, in which a male teacher holds up a "bad" example of a composition to alter essay writing behaviour, are contrasted to scenes shot in a "special" class. A bell rings, and the children from both classes prepare for recess. In the cloakroom, the camera briefly observes a girl dressed in a sailor suit and a boy in a heavy, black wool coat with metal buckles. "On the playground," proclaims the narrator, "children are simply children."

After recess, the film focuses entirely upon the special class, where a round-table discussion ensues among ten "gifted" students—six girls and four boys. The discussion is chaired by one of the girls, Susan, who wears a distinctive guitar-shaped pin on her sweater. The discussion is watched over by the kindly woman teacher. The children discuss a biographical novel, *Ralph J. Bunche: Fighter for Peace*, by J. Alvin Kugelmass.

Susan:	Will the meeting please come to order. The name of the story is *Ralph Bunche*, by Alvin Kugelmass. So far in the story, we have read about slavery and how the civil war was taken, and then Ralph Bunche was born, and then grandma's care and influence was in the third chapter. Now then the first question is, why did the boy, Ralph, find life confusing?
2nd Girl:	I think one reason he was confused was because the things that the negro cared about and the things that the white people cared about were so different to him and he couldn't see why...
Drew:	When he saw the white people wearing furs and the negro people wearing old potato sacks, he *must* have been confused. [General laughter. Teacher smiles.]
3rd Girl:	I think that why he was confused was he was wondering why these people that had set them free, fought so hard for them, just shoved them out and let them go on their way without even providing them even any room to live in.
2nd Girl:	I don't think that's the best point in this chapter because pennies are half as much worth as love is.
Susan:	And they're the two basic fundamentals of life for the negro and for the white man, too, although the white man doesn't need money, he's already got it. What he needs is a bit of love.[64]

Their teacher, formerly a social studies specialist in a regular classroom, comments about her students in general. "They have a much longer attention span and are avid readers. All have an insatiable curiosity....They are sensitive with a keen sense of humour and are very definitely individualists and are thus interesting to teach." She interviews each student individually. Drew shares a tip about solving mathematical problems: "I put myself in the place of the person who has the problem." In support of special classes for gifted children, the narrator opines:

> In our North American society, there is often a tendency to deplore intellectual development. The word "brain" and its more slangy counterpart "egghead" are terms of scorn or at best grudging respect. A gifted child sometimes finds his intellectual prowess both an advantage and a handicap. If gifted children are given an opportunity to let their minds expand their adult lives may ripen into brilliance.[65]

But a further handicap to the brilliance of their adult lives is neither recognized by the narrator nor by the children themselves. When asked the age-old question about their future careers, the gifted boys can foresee themselves as scientists, pianists, doctors, and lawyers, whereas the gifted girls can envision themselves as teachers, authors, nurses, and actuaries. Despite their brilliance and their disussion about the emancipation of the American "negro," none perceives a cultural limitation operating on their own ambitions.

The Gifted Ones (1959). NFB, 87866.

The same year, at the other end of the intellectual field of vision, the more readily evident career limitations of "mentally retarded" children in Canada, and questions about public responsibility for their education, were the foci of the NFB film *Eternal Children* (1959). Produced by Sally Lindsay as part of the *Frontiers* series for CBC television, the film begins with a nine-year-old boy, Kevin, assembling a five-piece jigsaw puzzle of a "Dutch boy." His completed Dutch boy is decidedly abstract. "Good boy," says his psychologist. "Kevin will never be mentally older than eight," the narrator comments.[66]

Eternal Children distinguishes levels and types of retardation for Canadian television viewers, while gently advocating public support for differentiation of training facilities. The visuals dissolve to the interior of a large institution where one hundred "mentally retarded" children are filmed seated at a mealtime. "There are 160,000 mentally retarded children in Canada," notes the narrator: "Three of every hundred children in Canada is mentally retarded; 16,000 are severely retarded." A child whose head has been enlarged by hydrocephalia is filmed in his institutional bed; his physical appearance is juxtaposed with a shot of a mildly retarded child in a classroom situation: "Mildly retarded children can melt unnoticed into the general population," the narrator suggests.

Since their children had not been accepted into public schools, the narrator explains, some parents had organized their own schools. The balance of the film is a study of educational activities at one such school. The children are shown to be extraordinarily skilful at doing the hula hoop. They perform a humorous action song, "I'm a Texan," and in speech therapy classes they repeat, among other exercises, "I'm a Puffy." One mother admits tearfully, "It [her son's disability] was a terrible disappointment...acceptance is the most important thing." As for the children's future, the narrator suggests that "many will find themselves in specialized institutions of work and recreation," but a psychologist at the end of the film is especially vague about this: "Boys grow up to be men," he says, "and girls grow up to be...?" The ellipsis offered by the psychologist was, no doubt, intended to be ironic in regard to the prospects of girls with lower than average mental ability. But in truth, the irony of his omission was in its prescience concerning girls in general, and the portrayal of girls by the NFB in particular.

Cinematic Children in the "Changing Present"

By 1957, the NFB had moved its production and administrative headquarters from Ottawa to Montreal and named its fifth Film Commissioner, Guy Roberge, to replace Trueman, who had become director of the newly created Canada Council. Roberge, a lawyer and the first French Canadian in the post, had served as counsel to the Massey Royal Commission on National Development in the Arts, Letters and Sciences in the late 1940s and had co-written a chapter of the report dealing with film and the Film Board. According to Evans, with the move to Montreal and the appointment of Roberge, a campaign by the Québec press (especially *Montréal Matin*, *Le Devoir*, and *L'Action Catholique*) to label the NFB as discriminatory in its administration and production practices ceased.[67] The French production wing took material and political advantage of these changes, utilizing advances in technology and film theory to revise the folkloric image of Québec often presented to cinema-goers in the past, both inside and outside the province.

Improved camera technology and television production methods in the late 1950s had opened windows of experimental opportunity for both English and French Canadian filmmakers interested in producing naturalistic portrayals of subjects. But it was the Québec filmmakers who were ultimately best able to synthesize the lighter, more portable cameras and sound equipment with the experience of "Candid Eye" screenplays and the influence of French "new wave" cinema in order to produce a truly innovative genre of documentary film—a form which became known as "cinéma-direct."

Cinéma-direct required no prior written script—only an event to record, multiple hand-held cameras to record it, and production facilities in which to shape the raw images into a narrative. Québecois filmmakers were quick to see its possibilities for fashioning a distinctive Québec documentary style at a particularly momentous time for both French-language production and Québec itself.[68] Typical of an early cinéma-direct production was the film *A Day in June* (1959), a depiction of the St. Jean Baptiste Day parade at Montreal on 24 June 1959. Filmed by, among others, Claude Jutra, *A Day in June* resonates with the tension of past, present, and future. "Above all," as the narrator interprets it, "it is a day for the children. A day to remember. *Je me souviens.*"[69]

Filmed in Eastmancolor with a jazz soundtrack, the central figure of the film is a six-year-old boy who will act out the role of St. Jean, "the prophet of the wilderness," on a float in the parade. In contrast to his formal performance, there is a steady stream of candid shots of Montreal children along the parade route, an urban street on which Québec flags and Canadian Red Ensigns fly. Before the parade, the boy, St. Jean, is observed playing with his lamb; at the same time, another Montreal youngster is observed helping to set up the chairs in the park where the parade will end. St. Jean, the boy, is driven to city hall for photos with the mayor, Jean Drapeau.

All along the route, Red Ensigns are handed out to children sitting on the curbs. Some children sport tinfoil derbies; others wear handkerchiefs knotted over their heads. Oriental and East Indian children are among those filmed at the parade; many children wave the tiny Canadian flags. St. Jean Baptiste, the six year old with the lamb, is continuously blowing kisses from his float. As the crowds disperse in his wake, some enterprising children collect discarded pop bottles for their deposit value. Finally, at the end of the parade route, the tired St. Jean is carried away by his father as the narrator proclaims: "Our tongue, our faith, our history is a living force that nourishes our changing present."[70]

The "changing present" is a recurring theme in the mirror of Canadian childhood of the late 1950s and early 1960s. One film intended for school audiences, *The Chairmaker and the Boys* (1958), is described in a late-1950s NFB catalogue as a portrayal of a bygone craft—a portrait of an artisan in the Margaree Valley of Cape Breton Island. But it is also the last of a very few NFB depictions of a child being spanked. The narrative involves two boys named Duncan (aged eleven) and Bruce (aged ten), who ride a pony to visit Duncan's grandfather, a master chairmaker. "Grandpa likes getting Duncan to help," comments the narrator, as Duncan is sent to open and close a dam below a millpond which powers a mill for the woodworking tools.[71] After lunch, as his grandfather snoozes, Duncan whittles a sailboat and sails it on the millpond. Soon the boys have removed their shirts and jeans and stripped down to their underpants to splash under a waterfall. Foolishly, Bruce climbs down the

The Chairmaker and the Boys (1958). NFB, 88656.

penstock followed by Duncan. (Grandpa said never to go down there.) When his grandfather returns to his mill and cannot find Duncan, he opens the dam himself. The two boys are suddenly in grave danger, and there is high drama as they whistle and yell for help. Duncan manages to get out of the penstock and rushes to close the dam to save Bruce. When his lathe stops, Grandpa realizes that something is wrong, and he returns to the pond to find the two boys wet and exhausted.

Duncan is spanked by his grandfather with a birch board slat—a punishment that ends abruptly when the boy's mother, the chairmaker's daughter, arrives at the mill to fetch Duncan home. The two males, Duncan and his grandfather, hide the fact of the punishment and the circumstances surrounding it from Duncan's mother, keeping the secret of the day's events to themselves. At the end of the film, Duncan has a sore bottom, which he rubs as he walks his pony home.

By the early 1960s, the changing present witnesses novel social issues occupying the lives of children portrayed by the NFB, particularly in films produced for school screenings. The children portrayed begin to act as self-interested agents who attempt to change or contravene existing social attitudes and practices. In *Beaver Dam* (1960), for example, two farm boys, both ten years old, discover a dam built by a family of beavers in a creek. The beavers have been anthropomorphized on the soundtrack so that they sing a little ditty as they work:

> Work will keep you merry;
> work will keep you well;
> so don't get in a tizzy,
> just get busy;
> you'll feel swell.[72]

The pond created by the beavers has flooded the road through the woods used to harvest hay. The farmer, the father of one of the boys, having likewise discovered the beavers, hides in a blind near the dam with a shotgun to rid the farm of the rodents. The boys decide to subvert his efforts and save the beavers since they would like to swim in the pond. They hide in the bushes as well and throw stones into the water whenever a beaver surfaces. A dinner whistle calls the farmer away.

Having thwarted the farmer from killing the beavers, at least until after his lunch, the boys conceive of an environmentally friendly solution to the problem. They break the dam and allow the pond to drain. When the farmer returns, the boys convince him to allow them to keep the creek running free until the haying is completed and then, when the road is no longer needed, to let the beavers rebuild the pond so the boys can have a swimming pool. The father readily agrees. The two boys pitch in to help with the haying, and afterward, in a scene that undoubtedly caused disruption in more than one Canadian classroom in the early 1960s, the two boys go skinny-dipping in the beaver pond.

Just as *Beaver Dam* was introducing the concept of environmental consciousness to Canadian children, another NFB film, *The Saddlemaker* (1961), was introducing the notion of gender discrimination in the world of paid labour. Filmed at High River, Alberta, the narrative follows the dilemma of a fourteen-year-old girl who enjoys horseback riding and needs, but cannot afford, a new saddle. Andrea, dressed in a white stetson, blue shirt, and plaid pants, sees a sign that reads "Boy Wanted" in the shop window of a world-renowned saddlemaker, Mr. Eamer. A quick trip to the barbershop for a short haircut, and "Andrea" becomes "Andy," who obtains the "Boy Wanted" position under false pretences by sweeping the walk in front of Mr. Eamer's shop with his (her) own broom.

None of the male workers in the saddlemaking shop suspect that Andy is, in fact, Andrea since she is capable of doing the work asked of her. The narrator comments, "She can cut leather because it is like cutting cookie dough." Andrea takes her wages in leather rather than in money, in order to craft her own saddle. Following a typical NFB digression—a study of the actual two hundred hours of craftsmanship involved in making a hand-tooled saddle—Andrea acknowledges the skill of her co-workers: "Of course I couldn't get it done in time without all the help the men gave me." And, during a moment of bashfulness, she blushes as one of the men works closely beside her, commenting, "I guess Jim thought I was ashamed to be sewing."[73] At the climax of the film, Andrea is recognized in the shop by the town's middle-aged, female busybody. Her ruse ended, the girl runs out of the shop, leaps onto her horse, and races bareback over the foothills of the Rockies, while being pursued by one of Mr. Eamer's male workers. Although she rides well, she is caught and returned. "She knew that she would never get that saddle now." But she discovers that Mr. Eamer isn't angry at her, nor was he fooled, and, while it does not appear that she will be allowed to continue working in the shop, Mr. Eamer's men finish the saddle for her and even present her with saddlebags.[74]

As with gender attitudes, some aspects of the past appear more resistant to change over time than others. This is especially evident in films concerning recreation for Canadian youngsters, such as in *Thousand Island Summer* (1960), a film which is remarkably similar to the 1948 production, *Holiday Island*. Filmed in Eastmancolor and utilizing a bouncy musical soundtrack, the later production depicts Camp Mohawk, a Kiwanis summer camp on the St. Lawrence River for seventy-five girls.

A Red Ensign flutters on a boat as it ferries the children to the island camp. Most of the girls wear straw boaters and most of those with eyeglasses wear the dark elliptical frames fashionable for girls of the time. In the evening, around the campfire, they play "Indians" and pretend to conjure up the spirits of the indigenous people who once lived there. Next day, a rainstorm sends the campers indoors for "a gay afternoon," during which time they perform skits and dances, notably in the roles of "orientals" for their skits and as Hawaiian "hula girls" for their dances.[75] A Hawaiian motif is also employed in another film of the era concerning recreation, *Boy Meets Band* (1961), in which the boys of a West Vancouver junior high school band, most with brushcuts, and dressed in aloha shirts and Panama hats, perform an outdoor concert at Stanley Park. The film follows the behind-the-scenes organization of the concert and includes a humorous scene of teenaged girls eating Dilly-Bars.[76]

The Rink (1962) NFB, 96910.

A third film on recreation, *The Rink* (1962), is notable both for its depiction of "happy" children and its advances in candid-eye filmmaking—a film so naturalistic that "what ought to be" becomes virtually indistinguishable from "what is." In this depiction of a suburban, outdoor skating rink, a seven-year-old girl laces up her skates; a young father pulls his two infant boys across the ice on a sled; an eight-year-old boy wearing hefty hockey socks skates shakily in front of the camera; children lean over the boards to watch a pickup game of hockey; and two girls in bright blue sweaters "jive" and do the "twist" on ice. The soundtrack is exclusively composed of the popular music of the time. All manner of wobbly ankles are followed about by the camera, including those of an infant who cannot stand at all, but who keeps slipping and falling and laughing.[77]

Indigenous Reflections in the early 1960s

In contrast to the untroubled impressions of mainstream Canadian childhood, there is a body of early-1960s portrayals of children of a more complex social and emotional mix. The most troubling of these are the mirror images of indigenous children. Supplanting the confident visions of the Euro-Canadian rescue of indigenous lives during the 1940s, or myths of assimilation in the 1950s, portrayals of indigenous children in the early 1960s may be characterized as ambivalent, a reflection of frustrated attitudes both before the cameras and behind them.

Among the most patronizing of these reflections is the film *Northern Campus* (1961), which was sponsored by the Department of Northern Affairs and Natural Resources and which was used as a training film for managers of northern resource projects, as well as for northern educators, and for Inuit adolescents chosen to undertake secondary education in the Northwest Territories. "The face of the north country is changing fast," the narration begins. "Minerals and oil are demanded by the world. Training of the young people to manage this is necessary." To illustrate this training, the film follows the case of "Charlie," a boy who is sixteen years old who "was born in an igloo," and who is now "a thousand miles from home" at Sir John Franklin School at Yellowknife.[78]

Charlie's bewildered condition is graphically demonstrated when his classmates must cut the sales tag from his new jeans, since the Inuit boy does not realize that they are neither a practical nor decorative part of his apparel. His old way of life is described as "bad diet, disease, and dirt." At the school, however, Charlie is given "a chance for a life in the new north." He learns practical skills: "dishwashing, tidying up, and keeping things in apple pie order." And although "academic subjects don't yet make much sense to him" and the boy is said to be "handicapped by language" and the "mysteries of arithmetic," the narrator notes that "big machines excite Charlie."[79] Of the Inuit girls at the school, the narrator remarks, "the girls must master the amenities that the white man takes for granted. Most will raise their families in a furnished house." In a final assessment of Inuit youth in the "new north," the narrator observes "most will enter the modern complex world, where the question is not what is the color of your skin, but what can you do with it? All who can do something useful will find their place."

"The place" of indigenous peoples in "the modern complex world" cannot be firmly fixed in the cinematic mirror. Indeed, one conclusion to be drawn from three separate 1964 NFB films about Indians in Canada is that integration may be impossible. Generalizations are made in *Trail Ride* (1964), in which a narrator with a cowboy accent declares, "there ain't no difference between white kids and Indian kids when you got a job to do"[80] and resolutions are proposed, as in the film *Because They Are Different* (1964) in which a seemingly judicious narrator concludes of Indian children, "So people will accept them, they will have to leave the reserves."[81] But, in hindsight, these seem overly simplistic or authoritarian. Perhaps the most instructive comment on Indian children in a "modern complex world" is the least didactic (yet most enlightening)—the cinéma-direct production *People Might Laugh at Us* (1964), which illuminates the vast cultural gulf that would have to be bridged without attempting to bridge it. The film is a portrayal of the Micmac Indians of the Gaspé Peninsula of Québec produced by Jacques Godbout. Indian children are observed at play, running and swinging, amidst a panorama of open fields and desolate outbuildings. There is no soundtrack beyond the natural sounds of the village. The children, aged six to ten years, appear poor, but happy. Their shirts and blouses are torn. Extreme close-up shots juxtapose the children's brown eyes with the eyes of horses. Shots of adults and children clam-digging and basketweaving are followed by a film segment in which the children shyly display paper maché constructions they have built at school which incorporate felt, paper, shells, and tinfoil. The final image is of a shy Micmac girl looking out at the camera from between the clapboards of her house.[82]

Unnarrated soundtracks, such as on *People Might Laugh at Us*, were an innovation that further advanced naturalism in the fields of vision constructed by cinéma-direct. The most renowned use of this device in a film portraying children was in *September 5 at Saint-Henri* (1962)—a film by Godbout, Jutra, Jacques Bobet, Michel Brault, Claude Fournier, and other notables of the ONF, which idealized youth as the romantic symbol of "Amérique française."

People Might Laugh at Us (1964). NFB.

September 5 at Saint-Henri employed twenty-eight filmmakers using "New Wave" techniques to depict "Smokey Valley," an industrial district of Montreal. The genius of the film lies in its masterful mirroring of the moods and relations of an entire working class community so that the seam between "what is" and "what ought to be" virtually disappears. The first children to appear are a group of Catholic school girls, some with braids in their hair, others with ribbons, off to their first day of school. A boy of about eight years passes by the camera, dressed in a horizontally striped T-shirt and vertically striped pants. Indeed, stripes appear to be the "in" fashion among the children of Saint-Henri on 5 September 1962.

September 5 at Saint-Henri (1962) represents a distinctly urban French-Canadian working-class culture. NFB, 101618.

At a barber shop, the camera pauses to observe a funeral party of Cadillacs driving by. All of the working-class children filmed on their way to school are well scrubbed, neat and cheerful. Older girls flirt with boys on bicycles. A Smokey Valley playground is seen—a swing slung from a tenement porch. There are white teens and black teens on the street. The black teens are heard speaking English. The camera peers shamelessly through windows. The music varies but is mostly jazz. Children dive from a railway bridge into the river; others play street baseball. A group of young girls play with an alley cat. Night comes. Some teens are filmed in the pin-ball arcade; more teens are sitting on apartment steps. The night is charged with teenagers. The film concludes at a "Coca-Cola Café," where hit parade tunes are being played on a juke box as teenaged boys joke and roughhouse, and where a single, teenaged girl wears a scarf and sips cola.[83] As a literal and symbolic representation of a distinct, urban French working-class culture in North America, *September 5 at Saint-Henri* is an inspired work of cinematic self-making—as Evans expressed it, "probably the most profound expression of cinéma direct."[84]

The Technological Invasion of Canadian Schools

In the early 1960s, further adjustments to the cinematic mirror as it reflected Canadian public schools were being made in the wake of the six educational royal commissions and equivalent inquiries that took place from sea to sea.[85] In addition to paving the way for curricular reform across Canada, the commission reports almost universally recommended public funding for school-based kindergarten programs.[86] Helping to generate popular support for the latter was the "Candid Eye" film *Kindergarten* (1962), a made-for-television look at a kindergarten class at Van Horne Public School at Montreal. The film enjoyed outstanding success in creating popular sentiment for school-based kindergarten classes and was included on a 1962 list of "films most in the national interest" prepared for the federal government.[87]

Much of the charm of *Kindergarten*, of course, is derived from its cute portrayals of young children, but of greater persuasive impact is the depiction of the program itself, and especially the confident manner of instruction by the kindergarten teacher. For example, having considered the effect upon the children of having a burly film crew with several cameras and pieces of sound equipment in her classroom, the teacher (about fifty years old) adroitly sits the children in a circle as they arrive and introduces them en masse to each member of the crew: "Good morning, Mr. _____." She then allows the children to wander and look into the lens of the cameras, which are operating, until they have satisfied their curiosity.[88]

The children return to the circle upon hearing their teacher strike a chord repeatedly on the classroom piano. Back in the circle, they discuss their fears, especially about fires and being stuck in elevators. At the end of the discussion, a black girl (about five years old) leads them all in a "thank you prayer." The children sing "Taxi Song" and play "block scramble." They play with "asbestos clay," and then they settle down to peruse special children newspapers. One happy boy wears a bow tie; a girl who has newly emigrated from France is in tears because she cannot understand what is being said. During free time the children play house. Girls are observed playing with dolls and toy irons; boys are filmed playing in rocking chairs and talking on toy telephones. One girl is filmed pulling boys into a playhouse. "Little Myrtle has been known to have six husbands at any one time," the narrator remarks.

Kindergarten (1962): A made-for-television film about a kindergarten class in Montreal. NFB, 97375.

Not all classrooms depicted by the NFB in the early 1960s functioned as smoothly as the one in *Kindergarten*, nor were all teachers portrayed as being so effective in their methods of classroom management. A made-for-television drama, *The Test* (1961), explored the uproar caused in a community by a teacher who hastily disciplines her grade six class for their casual attitude about cheating on a test. "She's the meanest teacher in the whole school," says one student to another after Miss Fisher fails the entire class. "She's the meanest thing there ever was."[89]

Controversy about the teacher spreads throughout the community and, led by a father, a school meeting is convened to force her resignation. Speaking to her principal, Miss Fisher defends her action: "They [the children] don't care about honesty anymore. They only care about what the others think." At the meeting, attended by at least two hundred parents, Miss Fisher reminds the adults about "the real purpose of school":

The real purpose of school is to make their lives and the world they live in better, happier, and more decent in every way....If success is what counts and it doesn't much matter how it is achieved, then what does it matter that they cheat....Many children don't understand, nowadays, that there is something wrong with cheating.[90]

Her argument strikes a favourable chord among the parents in the audience. The father who organized the public assembly weakly retorts, "It's supposed to be the teacher's job to look after the children," to which Miss Fisher responds, "You're all teachers in this school." At the end of the film, the children write a new test, and Miss Fisher does not resign.

Cute portrayals of young children were part of the charm of the 1962 film *Kindergarten*. NFB.

Although Miss Fisher did not resign in *The Test*, there is an impression produced by the films that follow (including *Kindergarten*) that pedagogical practices of traditional teachers like herself were now being relegated to a formalist past—that a new partnership of discovery was being forged between pupils and teachers which would be mediated by technology. To help explain the neo-progressive curriculum and "discipline-based" learning to educators, and to explore the future of

education, particularly in regard to media technology, the NFB produced *Child of the Future: How He Might Learn* (1964).

The Test (1961). NFB, 95219.

Both Marshall McLuhan, author of *The Gutenberg Galaxy* (1962),
Understanding Media (1964), and *The Medium is the Massage* (1967),
and Jerome Bruner, author of *The Process of Education* (1960), appear
in this film. After watching two nine-year-old boys, playing on a carpet
with a road-race set, McLuhan observes, "the worm's eye view is the
most involving." He suggests that education is "heading into a period of
total involvement," an assessment shared by Bruner who demonstrates a
"playground philosophy of physics" with a class of grade five students.
As the children send weighted cars down a ramp and measure how far
they travel, Bruner comments, "The kind of learning they're getting is a
kind they can use." A parade of educational gadgetry is displayed, all of
it operated by eager children, some of whom appear to be no more than
four years old. The audio-visual aids include 8mm film loops and projectors (heavily invested in by the NFB), "automated" typewriters, projector readers, and a language lab. In one classroom, educational filmstrips
are synchronized with radio broadcasts; in another, children produce

their own animated films; in yet another, high school students record their screenplay of the War of 1812 with 8mm cameras.[91]

The film surveys the contemporary use of television in school classrooms all over the world. In one school, a television character, "Mrs. Rhoda Loganbeel," teaches "algebra over the airwaves"; in another, a Spanish telecast is beamed into a school classroom from an airplane overhead. In a Japanese classroom, students are filmed welcoming television into their school: "The kids made a television room for their new teachers, TV images." McLuhan is critical of this use of television, but he is not especially clear about other possible uses: "It's like treating the motor car like the horseless carriage," he remarks. "You shouldn't use new technology to replicate the old. A huge wastage of opportunity."[92] The media guru delivers a final, enigmatic missive in the film: "The child of the future will program consciousness just as we program curriculum."

The Merry-Go-Round (1966): The Sexual Revolution and Youth Rebellion

In 1966, the commissionership of the NFB turned one full generational circle when Grant McLean, the nephew of Ross McLean, assumed the post in an interim capacity following the resignation of Guy Roberge, who became the agent general for Québec in the United Kingdom.[93] This chance reproduction of a family pattern at the NFB was ruptured in 1967, however, when McLean was passed over by then secretary of state, Judy LaMarsh, as the official appointee. Instead, the position went to Hugo McPherson, a professor of English from the University of Western Ontario, who was, according to Evans, "a recent convert to the glib gospel of Marshall McLuhan" and "whose nomination was accompanied with the words 'highly photogenic.'"[94]

During the McLean interregnum, Canadian children appeared in several films, which in retrospect reflect the simmering social tensions of the mid-1960s—regional and cultural tensions in the films, *Centennial Travellers* (1965) and *Tuktu and His Eskimo Dogs* (1966); class issues exacerbated by poverty in the groundbreaking documentary, *The Things I Cannot Change* (1966); and family issues and gender tensions in films such as *The Summer We Moved to Elm Street* (1966), *This Is No Time For Romance* (1966), and *Once Upon a Prime Time* (1966). But whereas these tensions appeared merely to rumble within the fields of vision of NFB filmmakers, some other issues more directly relevant to Canadian youth suddenly erupted in film productions such as *The Merry-Go-Round* (1966), *The Game* (1966), and *The Shattered Silence* (1966).

The Things I Cannot Change (1966). NFB, S-6037.

The "cultural revolution" of the late 1960s, at first described as a "generational gap," manifests itself in the archival collection as a rupture in the social history of Canadian childhood as it was being scripted by the Film Board—abruptly jarring and re-directing the course of cinematic narratives concerning Canadian youth.

Cinematic teenagers of only a decade earlier, such as Joe and Roxy, who were said to want "all to be orderly and precise...simple problems, simple solutions, simple actions,"[95] were supplanted, by 1967, with filmic images of adolescents protesting on city streets—non-conforming, defying authority, and demanding social change. Plaid, long-sleeved shirts abruptly vanish as the apparel of cinematic boys.

At first the issues of youth were treated as individual phenomena by NFB filmmakers. The initial "gap" between generations, explored rather than explained by filmmakers, concerned respective sexual mores. In *The Merry-Go-Round* (1966), the "sexual revolution" is discussed by a panel of commentators, including the syndicated, newspaper advice columnist, Ann Landers, and a psychotherapist, Albert Ellis.

The Summer We Moved to Elm Street (1966). NFB, S-6064.

"There's been a profound sexual revolution in both the activity and attitudes of young people," comments the narrator of this Tanya Ballan- tyne film. A blues soundtrack plays over the images of beer-drinking teenagers at a party. "Teens are using sex," remarks one member of the panel. "We have a vested socio-economic interest in not changing the inevitable," comments another. Ann Landers complains about a decline in the moral standards of society. In a dramatic sequence, a couple is shown holding hands in a movie theatre, and then, accompanied by a jazz piano soundtrack, the two go outside to "park." The psychothera- pist, Ellis, recommends that teenagers "be encouraged to pet to climax."

"This is your decision," says the boy to the girl in the dramatic narrative. "It has nothing to do with your parents." A discrete, cut-away shot
shows a black female "exotic dancer" stripping in a bar.[96]

"The double sex morality is fortunately disappearing," comments a
panelist, as the girl in the film invites her boyfriend to visit her while she is
babysitting. Unfortunately for the girl, the baby's parents arrive home just
as the teenagers are "necking" on a couch. The outraged parents evict the
two young people, and a telephone call is made to the teenaged girl's
mother to complain about her daughter's behaviour. From the babysitting
fiasco, the two youths next go to a café where a folksinger is performing,
then to the boy's house, where his parents are away, and finally upstairs to
his bedroom. Warns Ann Landers, "Don't get yourself into a spot from
which there is no retreat." Advises psychotherapist Albert Ellis: "It is their
[the teenagers] choice to make, not their parents."

Although described as a sexual revolution, little that was revolutionary had changed about gender roles in the films.[97] In general, community-based portrayals of the late 1960s were still being scripted from the
perspective of boys. Such was the case with a second film of the era
about the sexual revolution, *The Game* (1966), which was produced to
illustrate the emotional consequences of adolescent sexual activity. At
the beginning of the film, a gang of sixteen-year-old boys loiter on the
roof of an urban apartment building. Their leader, who wears sunglasses, a wide leather belt, and a black and white polka-dotted shirt, is
armed with a "BB gun" and a macho attitude. A group of teenaged girls
dressed in bikinis pass by the gang of boys. "We do need some girls,"
says the gang leader. He approaches the girls and obtains a telephone
number from one of them, a slim fifteen-year-old with long, dark,
straight hair, named Nicki. "How do I know what kind of boy you are?"
Nicki asks him later on the phone as he arranges a date.[98]

The two meet at a mall where go-go dancers dance in public. He
says, "Work the minimum; get the maximum; that's what I say." He
wears his sunglasses wherever he goes—inside or out. The two teens go
to her parents' house, where they "neck," and then he goes home. The
boy exaggerates to his friends about his relationship with Nicki. His
friends, who play in a garage band, tell him to bring her to a beach party
where they will be playing the next day. At the beach party, twenty
teenagers are dancing on the sand. Most of the boys are dressed in cut-
off pants; most of the girls are wearing very skimpy bathing suits, and
one girl is wearing a white brassiere and jean skirt. Egged on by his
friends, the boy persuades Nicki to leave the party and go "parking"
with him. Night comes.

The Game (1966). NFB, S-5414.

The next day, at school, he avoids Nicki. Back at home, feeling unhappy, he smokes a cigarette in bed. "Op-Art" posters and a poster for a Beatles album, *A Hard Day's Night*, adorn his bedroom wall. He begins to skip school altogether. When Nicki finally phones him at home, he confesses that he used her merely to impress his friends. "I feel rotten," he says, then he meets with her to break up. Later, he rejoins his gang, but no longer finds their company as enjoyable as he once did. He phones Nicki from a pay telephone, presumably to make amends but, as is often the case with films of this era, the ending is left unresolved.

A second aspect of the "generation gap" explored by the NFB was the rambunctious, occasionally outrageous behaviour of some adolescents. *The Shattered Silence* (1966) looked at two different ways that an older Canadian might deal with unruly teenagers and projected some hypothetical consequences of either approach. Inclined toward a hostile plan of action is "Uncle Moe," who returns home with his wife from the movie *Mary Poppins* (1964) to find his teenaged nephew (an invited guest) embroiled in a gang fight in their living room. Moe evicts all the teenagers from his house, including his nephew, who was an innocent victim of the brawl. Moe's wife, a woman of reason, suggests that Uncle Moe should have taken a few more minutes to find out what the fight was about but, since it is over, she remarks, "Now, just forget it." But Moe cannot forget it, especially when some of the teenagers "rev up" their motorbikes early Sunday morning on the street outside his bedroom window. "They have no right to make our lives miserable," he complains to his wife. His wife replies: "Moe, you're ridiculous." When a neighbour, George, likewise complains about feeling threatened by the antics of the motorbike teens, he and Moe organize a community meeting.[99]

To the two men's surprise, they are out-voted at the meeting by other adults sympathetic to the teenagers. "It's only kids having fun," remarks an articulate bachelor, who resides across the street from George. Those who side with George and Moe appear to have property values, rather than human values, uppermost in their mind—and George's suggestion that the police be alerted to the problem is voted down. "The kids are members of this community, too," observes one opponent to his plan. The group charts an alternate course of action: "Sort the sheep from the goats and discuss our grievances with the sheep." It is a plan that Moe can live with, but not George. The following day, he takes his revenge against the teenagers by secretly pushing one of their parked motorbikes closer to his driveway then backing his car over it. The teenagers are outraged by the "accident." They argue with George about what actually happened and retaliate against his car. The articulate bachelor from across the street exposes George's culpability in the matter and, ultimately, George is ostracized by all his neighbours—teenager and adult alike. Moe recognizes that George's predicament could have easily been his own, and that he chose wisely to tolerate the youth of the community.

By 1967, a new generation of young English-Canadian filmmakers, such as Mort Ransen, Robin Spry, and Patricia Watson, were handed control of the NFB cinematic mirror to explain contemporary events involving their generation to a puzzled older generation—in particular, to explain the Yorkville and Vancouver riots involving "hippies."[100] Content aside, their films are a landmark in the cinematic mirror of Canadian childhood, marking the moment when the postwar generation, to use McLuhan's phrase, began "programming consciousness" about itself.

In the *Invention of the Adolescent* (1967), Watson devised a clever argument based, in part, upon Philippe Ariès' popular history of the family, *Centuries of Childhood* (1962) and also upon her personal fascination with the chain-link fence surrounding schoolgrounds as both a physical and metaphorical barrier—a barrier that segregated children, adolescents in particular, from their historically "normal" participation in adult social affairs. "Yorkville, Toronto, a world of dropouts, love-ins, hippies," begins the narration for the film, over a rapid compilation of the now familiar images of young people of the late 1960s—dancing in circles, hugging in groups, adorned with buttons and carrying guitars, wearing T-shirts, ponchos and jeans, wire-rimmed "granny" glasses, smoking cigarettes and protesting en masse on city streets.

> Young people have more money and more opportunities than ever before. Adults are baffled and angered by their behaviour. Adolescents have been rebellious before, but this rebellion is different...more ominous. Will it happen to my kids?[101]

"Once upon a time," explains the narrator over several images of medieval paintings, "teenagers were virtually indistinguishable from their elders." The selected paintings strongly support this argument. "Often size [of figure] is a clue to age." A second series of paintings similar to the seventeenth century Caravagesque works described by Ariès in *Centuries of Childhood* are screened; they show children gambling and mingling with debauched adults.[102] "The artist was reflecting life as it was then," remarks the narrator, "Nobody worried about the innocence of children, least of all the children."

The narrating voice adds: "Today, children have many years of segregation from all adults but their teachers. We want our children to be children, not little adults." An elementary school teacher is shown leading grade one children in a hand-action song: "Here is our bunny, with ears so funny." Again drawing on Ariès, the narrator describes a change in eighteenth-century portraiture that "exalted all that was childlike about the child...how sweet the paintless smiles of infancy." A credible account of British working-class childhood through the industrial revolution explains how less affluent children were, at last, equally segregated from adult society by means of compulsory mass public schooling: "Now everyone is required to stay at school to acquire the knowledge and skills necessary to take their place in a complex society. Now teenagers are a segregated group. But youth is intellectually and sexually mature."[103]

In a cinematic conclusion strikingly reminiscent of the "shot and shell" endings of wartime NFB productions, a rapid and rhythmic compilation of stock shots is accompanied by a male narrative voice rising to a crescendo. Scenes of high school students being drilled in calisthenics in a gymnasium are followed by scenes of anti-war protestors on the street. "So much in school seems pointless and discontent wells up," explains the narrator. Scenes of young people smoking marijuana ("Sometimes it's a passive withdrawal into a world youth makes for itself") are followed by newsreel clips of the riots in Yorkville and at Vancouver in 1967. The clips in turn are followed by scenes of young children in school, and are finally juxtaposed with a single still photograph of young teenagers seemingly imprisoned behind the chain link fence of their schoolyard. The narrator concludes, "The young have not withdrawn but have been excluded."

The explanation offered by the filmmakers for the "cultural revolution" of the late 1960s is inventive, and it captures the essential intergenerational power struggle that is evident in the images, but it seems inadequate as a historical explanation for such a major adjustment to the cinematic mirror—both in regard to the history of NFB portrayals of Canadian childhood and the social history of Canada as depicted by the NFB. While it is true that by the early 1960s more fourteen to seventeen year olds were in school than ever before, and while there is no denying the generally repressive role attributed to schooling by Watson, the explanation, as it stands, is too unidimensional to be entirely satisfactory.[104]

A superior explanation for the upheavals of the late 1960s in Canadian social history is offered by Owram in his examination of Canadian baby boomers, *Born at the Right Time*. In Owram's view, it was a confluence of four historical forces upon the postwar generation that ushered in "the age of aquarius" and its concomitant rebellion against traditional social values: i.e., numbers, affluence, the link to a turbulent decade, and the child-rearing philosophy of Dr. Benjamin Spock who, during the boom years, "became as essential for child rearing as diapers."[105]

Herein lies the final "other thing" of significance made visible by a survey of the portraits of this era—Spock's invisibility in the film collection, and thus in NFB society. There is no mistaking that Spock's *Com-*

mon Sense Book of Baby and Child Care (1946) was a cultural landmark in both Canada and the United States in the postwar era, and it is a given that the adoption of his child-rearing philosophy by Canadian parents after the war contributed indirectly to the abrupt adjustment of the portrayals of youth produced by the NFB in films such as *The Invention of the Adolescent* (1967), *Flowers on a One-way Street* (1967), or *Christopher's Movie Matinee* (1968). But it is just as certain that parents in the cinematic society created by the NFB archival collection never consult Dr. Benjamin Spock's *Baby and Child Care*—not once.

Far from diminishing Owram's "fourth force," however, this oversight brings to prominence the fact that the National Film Board—like Spock himself—drew heavily upon Drs. Arnold Gesell and Frances Ilg's work, *Infant and Child in the Culture of Today* (1943) to guide parents.[106] Spock's absence from the child-rearing process in postwar NFB society thus presents us with a more fundamental conception of Owram's controversial force—of which the renowned Dr. Spock was but one significant agent.[107] Entered through Gesell and Ilg, a discussion—which all too frequently progresses from the "cult of Spock" through fields of psychology and psychiatry, past Freud, and into a centuries-old debate among philosophers, theologians, and social reformers about the relative desirability of a harsh or permissive approach to child rearing—may now proceed along an alternate pathway. It is a route which, while headed as before toward Freud through the same fields of psychology and psychiatry, may now be seen passing as well through the progressive domain of the American mental hygiene movement.

"The New Generation": Mental Hygiene and the Portrayals of Children by the National Film Board of Canada, 1946-67

That is the achievement of the psychologists. In our own society they are very kind, and do everything for our own good. The tales of what they do elsewhere are rather terrifying.

— Hilda Neatby, *So Little for the Mind*

"How," as the American historian, Sol Cohen, has asked, "shall we gauge the impact of the [mental] hygienist educational campaign, then? How can we document hygienist influence?"[1] Gauging the postwar impact of the child psychiatrists and psychologists has been problematical for historians. The mental hygienists operated in the realm of mass psychology and social relations, within the "mentalities" of generations of boys and girls—who as men and women have left little evidence of changing social attitudes and relationships attributable to changes in mass child-rearing and schooling practices. Evidence exists of the impact of the mental hygiene movement upon postwar parenting literature and curricular documents; hygienist influence is perceptible in baby books, magazines, newspapers, radio

_____

Notes to chapter 5 are on p. 252.

scripts, and films, as well as in the changing language of educational theorists and practitioners. But as Cohen has observed, as to its actual impact upon any society, "there is more evidence than might be supposed, but so far we have not been able to see it."[2]

I argue that the impact of the mental hygiene movement may be seen in the postwar portrayals of Canadian children produced by the NFB, reflected in the changing patterns of adult-child power relations within the families and schools of NFB society. In this chapter, I document the efforts of psychologists and psychiatrists in the postwar collection of films to forge a new generation of young people—a generation whose childhood would be guided by mental hygiene principles and whose adulthood would therefore be happier, more productive, and more self-reliant than any generation before them. The chapter describes a subtle transformation in adult-child social relations that arises shortly after the introduction of the "modern" child-rearing and schooling principles of the hygienists into filmic homes in 1946 and schools in 1953 and traces its progress over two decades as the gulf of power between generations progressively narrows, advancing the control of NFB children over the events of their social mise en scènes. The narrative begins with the children in their homes and schools prior to the start of the NFB mental hygiene campaign and ends with the new generation of young people on Yorkville Street in the documentary *Flowers on a One-way Street* (1967), blocking traffic and flexing their mass, social muscle against traditional authority. But first, a brief historical account of the mental hygiene movement may be helpful to a reader's understanding of its ascendancy in NFB society.

The Mental Hygienists

As Theresa Richardson has observed in her *The Century of the Child: The Mental Hygiene Movement and Social Policy in the United States and Canada* (1989), "the mental hygiene movement originated [in the United States in 1909] with the premise that society could be perfected through the socialization of children."[3] In Canada, where the Canadian National Committee for Mental Hygiene (CNCMH) was founded a decade later in 1918, the movement was broadened in scope to include proponents of the eugenics and mental testing movements, however, according to Cohen, the American mental hygienists "rejected eugenics and all hereditarian assumptions."[4] The path to mental health in the United States, according to Cohen, "was not through breeding a better race, but through molding the personality."[5]

The logic behind the American mental hygiene movement followed from Freudian psychoanalytic theory, and it rapidly gathered momentum in the United States after World War I, especially among leaders in medicine and science. While many of these were skeptical about various aspects of Freud's work, his central idea that childhood experience had a profound impact upon adult life soon became the consensus among them—a consensus of particular benefit to the nascent fields of child psychiatry and psychology. From the outset, the "hygienists" were substantially funded by two related philanthropies: the Rockefeller Foundation (RF) in regard to parent education, and the Commonwealth Fund (CF) in relation to pedagogical practices in American schools.[6]

The American hygienists combined nineteenth-century child saving with the idea that the scientific promotion of well-being in childhood could prevent adult dysfunctions. Happy, healthy children, it was argued, were society's best assurance of a rational and productive adult population. Reinforced by clinical studies of "maladjusted" children in the American juvenile courts, the belief that delinquency could be prevented through mental hygiene practices "spiralled outward and away," to use Richardson's metaphor, first to American schools and then increasingly to the North American family.

According to Cohen, who has written extensively on the hygienists' influence upon American schools, the movement was "the social arm of psychiatry."[7] Early on, hygienists saw a direct causal connection between parental treatment of children and later personality maladjustment but, at first, they tended to dismiss parents as "hidebound and inaccessible." As Jessie Taft, a psychiatric social worker in the mid-1920s declared, "Why spend one's life trying to make over a bad job when children are at hand [in the schools] to be guided into the kingdom of good adjustment."[8] Succinctly put, the hygienist intent in American public schools was to make teachers less rigid, moralistic, punitive, and authoritarian, and to make students happier in school, more successful, and, above all else, more sociable. As hygienist William Healy wrote in a 1933 article in the *Journal of Educational Sociology*, the primary question was not "What does the child learn in school?" but rather, "How does the child feel because of school?"[9]

Amply funded by the CF in the 1920s through the 1930s, the National Committee for Mental Hygiene (NCMH) mounted its campaign for school reform on a variety of fronts simultaneously. Direct intervention included initial funding for a proliferation of "child guidance clinics" and a "visiting teacher" program (social workers trained in the new psychiatry), whose agents would act, overall, as models for

change in the schools. Less directly, according to Cohen, the CF dissemi-
nated "a vast amount of literature on the implications of mental hygiene
that reached community leaders and opinion makers" and utilized fel-
lowships and subventions "to co-opt the helping professions" to a
hygienist point of view.[10] Meanwhile, the NCMH reached college and
university students (most effectively at Yale University) through subject
courses in mental hygiene, while urging teacher training institutions,
such as Teachers College at Columbia University, to lead teachers to a
scientific understanding of children's personality.[11] Ultimately, in the
1930s, according to Cohen, "the NCMH cemented ties with the Progressive Education Association (PEA), then at the height of its influence,
to co-opt the PEA, to make it a 'movement organization.'"[12]

The ascent of mental hygiene concepts to hegemony among educational leaders was swift. By the late 1920s, the idea of the schools'
responsibility for personality development had begun to filter into books
for teachers or teachers-in-training. By the 1930s, the mental hygiene
point of view was firmly entrenched in progressive educational thinking.
Beginning in the late 1930s, hygienist concepts and nomenclature began
to figure prominently in the publications of the National Educational
Association (NEA).[13] Soon thereafter, according to Cohen, "the sensitive
antennae of publishing firms saw which way the trend was moving."[14] A
flood of textbooks on mental hygiene appeared in the late 1930s and
the 1940s. The pinnacle of the NCMH's influence was achieved in 1950
at the historic mid-century White House Conference on Children and
Youth. The conference took as its slogan, "A Healthy Personality for
Every Child."[15]

On the home front, beginning in the mid-1920s, the goals of the
RF's parent education campaign were not dissimilar to the therapeutic
aims of the CF campaign in the schools: to decrease the domineering
and autocratic practices of parents and thus advance the development of
each child's personality.[16] Steven Schlossman traces the origins of the
"modern" parent education movement to the Laura Spelman Rockefeller Memorial (LSRM) and to its senior officer, Lawrence K. Frank,
who was "a champion of...'progressive' educational ideas generally" and
an advocate for the hygienist perspective on child rearing in particular.[17]
In his chapter on childhood and youth in the massive *Recent Social
Trends in the United States* (1933) Frank observed, "The interests of the
parent education and the mental hygiene movements are similar [in
respect to the focus on personality development] and mutually reinforce
each other."[18] Commencing in 1923, according to Schlossman, Frank
administered one million dollars annually for the LSRM, a fund by

which he, "subtly but aggressively nurtured and coordinated the long-since-forgotten parent education movement."[19]

In a similar manner to the CF, which provided funding to the NCMH on several fronts at once in its campaign to transform schooling practices, the LSRM also financed a body of contemporary programs for disseminating child study information to mothers based on "scientific" research in child development. Parent education groups were the initial LSRM venue, in Frank's words, for "giving the parents...a sympathetic awareness of their child's personality needs."[20] The LSRM parent education groups were touted by Frank as "a direct contribution to the mental hygiene movement," but a covert contribution of more significant proportions was *Parents' Magazine*, which was discreetly funded by the LSRM through Teachers College, as well as through Yale, Minnesota, and Iowa Universities, and which "soon became the largest selling educational periodical in the world."[21] As Schlossman records, from the outset of its publication in 1926, *Parents' Magazine* "was certain of LSRM's financial participation, whatever form it actually took": "The eventual arrangement was extraordinarily complex and roundabout; it reflected LSRM's decision not to be publicly identified or officially connected to the periodical, and to rely on its beneficiaries in the parent education movement to exercise quality control."[22]

On the research side as well, according to Schlossman, "Frank successfully used large financial inducements to direct social scientific research in directions he considered 'progressive.' "[23] By the end of the 1920s, LSRM and RF grants were funding child study clinics at Iowa, Columbia, Berkeley, Toronto, and Minnesota Universities—but it was at Yale University, "a bastion of the mental hygiene movement since 1909" that the monographic equivalent to *Parents' Magazine* was ultimately produced.[24] There, at the "Yale School of Medicine, Clinic of Child Development" under the direction of Arnold Gesell, after a "frame-by-frame" analysis of "miles of film" of child development by clinic researchers, emerged the landmark child-rearing text by Drs. Gesell and Frances Ilg, *Infant and Child in the Culture of Today* (1943). Their work gave the stamp of "scientific certitude" to the long held hygienist assumption that social development, like physical development, passed through "normal and natural stages," which, "too often parents lacking in knowledge of child development will punish their children for":

> The long and patient study of child behavior made by Dr. Gesell and other workers in the field has made it clear that childhood's greatest need from birth throughout the formative years is for a parental attitude of enlightened understanding. For this understanding with love

and care will bring to healthy fruition the budding individuality of the citizen of tomorrow's world.[25]

Present at Yale and later at Columbia University during the RF and CF campaigns from the mid-1920s through the early 1930s was the young Benjamin Spock, who took his undergraduate and early medical training at Yale and his pediatric training at Columbia.[26] Here is why, despite being "an overtrained, repressed child of a strong-willed family," as described by Owram, he would choose to advise parents in the *Common Sense Book of Baby and Child Care* (1946) that "what makes your child behave well is not threats or punishment but loving you for your agreeableness," and similarly, in the "Schools" subsection of his book, that a "good teacher" "knows that she can't teach democracy out of a book if she's acting like a dictator in person."[27] Dr. Spock's behavioural advice for postwar parents had little to do with the "common sense" of the time and much more to do with the triumph of the mental hygiene project.[28]

The Postwar Shift in NFB Social Relations

Prior to the introduction of mental hygiene into NFB homes, whatever unfolds for children in a scenario is primarily under adult control, most notably the control of NFB mothers. There is no intergenerational struggle concerning outcomes of scenes in NFB films of this era. The two children who appear in the film *Vitamin D* (1943) may grimace upon taking a tablespoon of cod liver oil, but there is no argument from either of them about having to take it and, afterwards, they smile and wave at their mother on their way out the door. That adults should control the family mise en scène appears to be the expectation of nearly everyone in early NFB society: mothers, fathers, the children and, evidently, the writers, producers, and directors of the film scripts themselves. Typical of the portrayal of family power relations of this era is the following dinner scene from *Supper's Ready* (1944), a film in the "Knife and Fork" series.

Outside a white bungalow in *Supper's Ready,* a twelve-year-old boy wearing a dark sweater over a white shirt and tie, and his younger sister, dressed in a striped dress, brown socks, and brown leather shoes, mow the lawn and tend the garden. Inside the bungalow, their mother, garbed in a plain housedress and aproned, and her teen daughter, similarly attired, are preparing the family dinner. The film's narrator describes the mother's activities: "By looking after her family, she is doing her part in laying the foundation for better feeding of the whole nation. She is keeping them fit and ensuring their health for tomorrow's world." Soon afterward, all three of the children are out on the lawn, playing an informal game of catch. The ball is tossed to their father, an aging labourer who has just dressed for dinner. Although startled, he catches it in time. The mother, austere but friendly, steps outside, wiping her apron. She holds out an arm to gather in her family. "Come on folks; supper's ready...Okay, we're coming...What're we having for supper, mother?"[29] Efficient, disciplined, and content, the typical NFB family of this early era, both urban and rural, functions under the beneficent rule of adults with the willing complicity of dependent children. Gathering her family under her arm like a wing, the traditional mother asserts her natural authority to which her children yield without question. In early NFB schools as well, adults impose structure and discipline and invariably receive orderly, if occasionally somewhat fearful, compliance by NFB children. Typical of teacher-student relationships in NFB society is this exchange from the film A Friend for Supper (1944) in which Tommy, a grade five student who has been daydreaming, is called upon by his teacher, a tall woman in a tweed jacket, to stand up.

> Teacher: Tommy. Are you listening? [Tommy stands uneasily to attention at the side of his desk, squeezing his thumbs in his fists.]
> Tommy: Yes.
> Teacher: I think you were daydreaming.
> Tommy: Yes.
> Teacher: What *were* you thinking about?
> Tommy: Well, I was thinking I'd like to have all the hungry children to my house for supper. [Tommy's classmates burst into loud laughter. Tommy bows his head shyly. The laughter of his classmates ends abruptly when the teacher calls the children to attention.]
> Teacher: All right now class. [The students turn in unison to face the teacher, their hands folded on their desktops.] That's a good idea, Tommy. Who would you invite?[30]

Progressive pedagogies, as well as formal ones, are evident in early NFB classrooms. In progressive schools, pupils engage in more practical and community oriented activities than their formally educated peers, often learning citizenship skills along with their academics. But no matter how much the structure varies, the children's compliance with adult expectations does not. In the film Lessons in Living, for example, the students renovate their classroom when inspired to do so by a school inspector. In Tomorrow's Citizens (1947), the students of an urban elementary school race about city streets, clipboards in hand, acting as junior social scientists, "enquiring about the nature of commerce, discovering the teamwork underneath that makes it tick," a purposeful activity, the narrative voice of Lorne Greene assures the spectator.[31]

More often, however, NFB pupils are found in desks in rows. In a school sequence from *The Children from Overseas* (1940), a film concerning the lives of British evacuee children placed in Canadian homes for the duration of World War II, thirty elementary students sit in fixed desks, each quietly working from a geography textbook. Their teacher, a young man in his late twenties, uses a pointer to indicate Canadian cities marked on a chalk map drawn on the blackboard. One boy, his Toronto Maple Leaf hockey sweater worn over a white shirt, furtively prods the leg of the boy beside him with a ruler, whispers something quickly, and returns to work. The soundtrack voiceover of an English girl says of Canadian boys, "The boys seem to be just like English schoolboys: same tricks and same excuses." The soundtrack voiceover of an English boy complains, "In my opinion five hours a day is rather hard on the brain. Don't you think so too?" At dismissal, all the students stand in unison to the right of their desks, turn together, and walk down the aisles. The same formal dismissal procedure is likewise part of a rural school day in *Out Beyond Town* (1948). In a mirror shot, the teacher stands behind her desk, which is at the front of the class, directing the students with the commands, "Stand, turn, dismissed," to which the students uniformly respond.[32] At home and at school, childhood in the early years of NFB society is firmly governed by cinematic adults.[33] So pervasive is this control that, even in films produced for Canadian children, the mise en scènes are invariably dictated by an adult narrator; so that, quite literally, children may be seen but not heard. Conversely, so respectful are children in these early years of their governance by adults, that the shift in adult-child social relations that occurs during the next decade, the 1950s, is a highly conspicuous one. Indeed, so conspicuous that the anthropologist, Margaret Mead, who makes an appearance in NFB society in 1959, is both able to discern the primary characteristic of the change and astutely identify its underlying cause.

In *Four Families* (1959), Margaret Mead sits in an overstuffed armchair and watches NFB films, which are being screened for her analysis. The films are a series of sound productions without narration—depictions of child-rearing activities (feeding, bathing, dressing, etc.) in four countries: India, France, Japan, and Canada. The Canadian film segment features a farm family of five from Saskatchewan. Without intending humour, the host, Ian MacNeil, introduces the Canadian segment with a comparative comment about women of the world: "In North America, women are believed to have a more dominant position. Some critics even say 'too dominant.' Our next family is North American, a farm family in Saskatchewan."[34]

Mead watches as the Saskatchewan family goes about its business, the family members clearly comfortable with the presence of NFB cinematographers. She structures her comments around the concept of building a culture of independence in North America. Hence, she takes note that the mother helps the eight-year-old boy to take the lead in saying Grace at the table and expects the infant girl to feed herself after the first few spoonfuls of dinner. Mead also notices that during the dinner, although the father sets limits, the boy is allowed to talk back and assert himself, and that during the infant's bath, the mother struggles with the girl over the control of a washcloth. "Another part of independence training," explains Mead, commenting upon what she assumes to be a common cultural practice of Saskatchewan parents; i.e., permitting limited challenges to parental authority in order to promote their children's independence. Moreover, Mead notes, in her experience this is a practice unique to North American families, since she cannot find an equivalent to independence training in any of the other three cultures she analyzes in the series: East Indian, French, or Japanese.

Nor, unbeknownst to Mead, was there any equivalent to independence training in the cultural practices of film families of the early 1940s. While observable instances of what Mead defines as "independence training" become a common feature of Film Board families of the mid-1950s and beyond, independence training is non-existent as a child-rearing principle in the portrayals of these families in the early years of NFB society.

Limited challenges to parental authority, for example, occur with regularity in the 1955 production *The Pony*, a film with a narrative plot that would be familiar to anyone who ever watched an episode of the *Leave It to Beaver* or *Father Knows Best* television series. In the film, two farm children, a boy of eleven and his nine-year-old sister, are forbidden by their father to buy a horse. The children buy the pony anyway (on the girl's insistence) and hide it in an outbuilding until Christmas. When the pony whinnies, prematurely leading the parents to its stall, the parents speak sharply to each other but they are not upset with the children. Instead, the father admires their insubordination: "They've certainly shown a lot of initiative." And when the surprise is revealed on Christmas morning, the mother remarks with pride, "To think the children did this all on their own." A more subtle illustration of what Mead dubbed "independence training" is likewise found in the film when, at the dinner table, the mother speaks brusquely to the boy, who is about to butter his bread before his father sits down: "Just a moment, John!" The boy pauses long enough to absorb the intent of his mother's remark, then ignores her and butters his bread anyway. Instead of reining him in, mother turns away, accepting this limited exercise of his independence.[35]

The Pony (1955). NFB, 74845.

This is a radical departure from films made a decade earlier and, as Mead observed, the difference lies in a novel parenting principle which she calls "independence training." More than a convenient anthropological label, however, it is an actual principle that one may observe being introduced into NFB society immediately after World War II by the mental hygienists, psychologists, and psychiatrists who challenge the merits of adult (particularly maternal) dominion over children and make practices of child rearing a public issue—both in NFB, and Canadian, society.

Mental Hygiene Enters into NFB Homes and Schools

The first of these child psychologists is Dr. William Blatz, who in real life vaulted to worldwide fame in the early 1930s as the nursery director for the Dionne quintuplets.[36] His psychological study of the five sisters was a bestseller. Thus, it was inevitable that one day he would become incarnate in NFB society, playing himself in *What's On Your Mind?* (1946), lecturing a young couple about rearing their toddler:

Dr. Blatz:	I understand, Mrs. Madge, that this is your first child and that the both of you are worried about him.
Mother:	Yes, Dr. Blatz. We're afraid we have a problem child.
Dr. Blatz:	There's no such thing as a problem child, Mrs. Madge. There are problems of child-raising. Children are not born delinquents nor geniuses. They're made that way. We train them. We can train them in any direction in which we want them to go.
Mother:	And he seems to be so highly strung that we're afraid he's on the verge of a nervous breakdown.
Dr. Blatz:	Nervous breadowns come pretty late, but they always come after a very poor young childhood. Now, we know there are certain things in childhood that will make for a nervous breakdown later on. One of them is if parents disagree. Children are very sensitive to the relations between their parents. Another thing is nagging, and I'm afraid mothers nag more than fathers, Mrs. Madge. Nagging, I think, is the worse crime in the parental calendar.[37]

What's On Your Mind? (1946) was among the last of the *Canada Carries On* series to be widely exhibited in the Canadian chain of Odeon Theatres. Since 1940, the short reels had been regularly shown in the theatres prior to screening an American feature movie but, with the end of the war, Canadian public interest in the *Canada Carries On* series waned and the Odeon cinemas ceased playing them. Among the last of the one-reelers of the series to receive wide exposure, *What's On Your Mind?* introduced Canadian cinema audiences to the latest revelations of the psychiatrists working at the famous Allen Memorial Institute in Montreal. In particular, the psychiatrists had discovered that the psychological problems of adults often originated from their early childhood experiences. Through their fingerpaintings and through "the startling new treatment of psycho-drama," psychiatric patients in the film revealed to the doctors how their parents were often at the root of their emotional problems. Fortunately, *What's On Your Mind?* revealed, the psychiatrists had a plan to minimize the damage that future parents could do "Working hand in hand with enlightened parents, psychiatrists hope for a new generation free from hidden fears and resentments, a generation able to face life realistically and handle it unafraid."[38]

The details of the plan for parental enlightenment are not fully revealed in the film *What's On Your Mind?* However, in the admonition given by Dr. Blatz to Mrs. Madge (and the millions of Canadian women who attended the cinemas each month) to cease "nagging" her child, one finds the most critical component of the mental hygiene project as it pertained to families. The hopes of NFB psychiatrists for the "new generation" lay in extinguishing the domineering child-rearing practices of parents, particularly mothers.

The damage caused children by their well-meaning but over-controlling parents was the subject of the *Mental Mechanisms* series of films, which were intended as training films for psychiatrists in the late 1940s. In the series, mothers were frequently portrayed as the agents behind the mental health problems of their children. Calumnies were cast upon them in films such as *The Feeling of Rejection* (1947), in which a young woman, Margaret, becomes withdrawn and overly shy because her mother prevented her from becoming independent as a small child.

Because Margaret cannot disagree or say no, everyone in the film takes advantage of her: her co-workers, salesclerks, but especially her mother, with whom she still lives. Now, suffering from severe headaches, Margaret is referred by her doctor to a psychiatrist, who helps her to see how her migraines are related to her inability to stand up for herself. On the psychiatrist's couch, the psychological wellspring of her physical pain becomes clear in a series of cinematic flashbacks:

Narrator: Gradually Margaret, with the doctor's help, discovers what in her childhood has made her act and feel as she does now. Margaret was sheltered too much as a child. Her well-meaning but over-anxious mother often discouraged her by exaggerating the dangers of everday life.

Mother: [Upon seeing her daughter splash water on the top of a woodstove.] Margaret, stop that! You'll burn yourself, child. Mommy doesn't want her darling baby to be hurt.

Narrator: As she hears the all too familiar "don'ts" her normal need to learn by doing is curbed. She clings to her mother for safety.

Mother: [accompanying various flashback scenes with scissors, hammers, stairs, etc.] No, Margaret! It's sharp. You'll cut your hand. You mustn't do that. You'll smash your thumb. Margaret! How many times must I tell you not to climb. You could fall and break a leg. Darling! Those are sharp scissors! You'll cut off your fingers. Margaret! Little girls don't climb on gates. You'll hurt yourself and get all dirty. Mother wants you to be her good little girl and keep neat and tidy. Love mommy?

Narrator: She depends now too much on her mother's approval. It is safest to avoid all activities which seem dangerous or which her mother wouldn't like.[39]

The Feeling of Rejection (1947). NFB, XSF-2990.

If this much damage could be caused an adult woman by her well-meaning mother, one may well imagine the impact of an intentionally cruel one. The potential consequences of cruelty, in the form of emotional neglect, are explored in the film *The Feeling of Hostility* (1948). In this film, a four-year-old girl named Clare feels insecure when her father is separated from the family because of his career as an engineer. Clare's mother feels resentful that she has been left alone with the child, and when a letter from the father arrives from his worksite (somewhere in South America) mentioning Clare's name more often and with greater affection than her own, Clare's mother deliberately deletes the tender lines written about her daughter when reading the letter aloud, thereby rendering the girl heartbroken. When her father dies in an accident, Clare turns to her mother for affection, but her mother is rapidly out and about, seeking a replacement for her husband. Clare's mother weds a clerk, a bitter individual from a commercial firm, and the manifestations of Clare's hostility begin in earnest, ending with Clare in her early thirties as a single, successful, publishing executive who, in the final analysis as delivered by a psychiatrist from the Allen Memorial Institute, "is neither happy nor terribly unhappy...but she is too much alone."[40]

Not only women suffered at the hands of their parents, according to the films. In the 1949 production *Over-Dependency*, a young man, Jimmy, needs continuous appreciation from others to make his life tolerable. He hates to get up for work and he cannot face his boss. He is psychologically less mature than his wife and far more emotionally needy. As a child, he had learned that being ill would gain him love and affection. Now, he needs constant tokens of affection, or yet another cigarette, to get him through the day. "So much illness that a doctor sees is caused by emotional conflict," the film narrator intones. As a child, Jimmy ("born late and probably unwanted") was looked after by his mother and sister. Even in adulthood, he continues to turn to his mother as a convenient source of comfort—"at the price of never being strong." Ultimately, Jimmy suffers a panic attack at a job interview and, in shame, turns to his doctor, who soon gets to the root of the problem. It turns out that, as a young boy, Jimmy was afraid of his father, who kept him from participating in competitive games. As the film ends, his outlook for recovery is good, although he can only gain his independence with the assistance of his more mature wife.[41]

While each of the early mental hygiene films graphically illustrated how NFB parents could frustrate their children's future happiness through their domineering, overprotective, and dependence-producing parenting practices, it was not until *Know Your Baby* (1947) that a formula for creating a mentally healthy childhood (and neurosis-free adulthood) first appeared on film. *Know Your Baby*, a film with decidedly blue ribbon endorsements, was the first NFB production to illustrate modern parenting practices that were approved by child psychiatrists. Sponsored by the Canadian Committee on Children and approved by both the Child and Maternal Health Division and the Mental Health Division of the Department of National Health and Welfare, *Know Your Baby* begins by conveying an ambiguous warning to mothers of young children ("Damage the emotions and damage the body") before delivering up a modern maxim for the proper rearing of an NFB child: "Respect his demands...if we are sensitive to our baby's needs and make him secure, we are helping him to a happy childhood and a balanced manhood."[42]

The Gesell Clinic at Yale University originated the "respect his demands" principle of child rearing that was so readily adopted into NFB society. Indeed, the title of the award winning *Ages and Stages* series of films, produced from 1949-54, was adapted from a chapter of Gesell and Ilg's renowned *Infant and Child in the Culture of Today* (1943) and in one NFB film, *He Acts His Age* (1949) a child-rearing expert opens their second book, *The Child from Five to Ten* (1946), for reference.[43] Funded by both the Rockefeller and Carnegie Foundations, Gesell was a proponent of child rearing for a "democratic culture," as opposed to child rearing for a "totalitarian 'Kultur.'"

> A totalitarian "Kultur" subordinates the family completely to the state, fosters autocratic parent-child relationships, favors despotic discipline, and relaxes the tradition of monogamy. It is not concerned with the individual as a person. A democratic culture, on the contrary, affirms the dignity of the individual person. It exalts the status of the family as a social group, favors reciprocity in parent-child relationships and encourages humane discipline of the child through guidance and understanding.[44]

Since liberty, according to Gesell, was the life principle of democracy in the state, so too should parents give guided scope to the spirit of liberty which animated the growing child. The child was to be given the opportunity to develop purposes and responsibilities which would strengthen her or his inborn personality, rather than make over and mold the child's character into a preconceived pattern.[45]

"The present century is preeminently concerned with man as an individual," wrote Gesell.[46] Thus, it became the task of parents to interpret each child's "individuality" (personality) and thereafter give it the "best possible chance to grow and find 'itself.'"[47] In raising a child for a "democratic culture," instead of striving for executive efficiency, a mother aimed first of all to be perceptive of and sensitive to the child's developing awareness of its autonomous personality: "Thus she becomes a true complement to him."[48]

Control over the feeding schedule constituted the very heart of the Gesell principle of autonomous development through parent-child reciprocity. Since it entailed the symbolic first struggle of wills between the mother and her child, "the [feeding] schedule thus becomes at once symbol and a vehicle of cultural control."[49] The child, according to Gesell, was "preeminently wise" as to what its feeding needs were, as well as "what he *can* not do and what he *should* not do because of the limitations of immaturity."[50] By deferring to the demands of her child in the matter of feeding, not only was a mother satisfying her child's present nutritional needs, but she was also enabling the healthy development of the child's future personality as well:

> Self demands, if adequately satisfied by the culture, result in optimal growth of personality organization. The cultural pattern must be adapted to the growth pattern, because in the final analysis all individual development depends upon intrinsic self-regulation. There is no adjustment to culture other than self-adjustment.[51]

In the cinematic society of the NFB, modern mothers learn democratic child-rearing principles via their family doctor. In *Why Won't Tommy Eat?* (1948), Mrs. Smith learns that although she may spank her six-year-old son, Tommy, she can't make him eat. She shares her concern about Tommy with her family doctor, from whom she receives a surprising admonition: "Mrs. Smith. You are the problem, not the boy." With her doctor's guidance, Mrs. Smith realizes that she has been tense ever since Tommy was a baby. "Even the tension of a nervous mother's arm can be communicated to the infant," remarks the film narrator at an appropriate moment. "Never go to the table with tense, unhappy feelings. Don't battle over food." Thus, the solution to Mrs. Smith's problem is surprisingly simple: "If he won't eat carrots, don't force him." At the conclusion of the film, the penitent Mrs. Smith is making an extra effort to get to know her son, Tommy, who is responding in kind. "She will have to make an extra effort for a while," intones the film narrator cheerily. "Four months of battling may take six months to cure."[52]

In compensation for surrendering autocratic control over their children in favour of reciprocity in their parent-child relationship, parents were assured by NFB doctors that they were preventing their children's future unhappiness as adults.[53] That there possibly could be accompanying behavioural consequences for families was not initially articulated. Indeed, it was not until the late 1940s and into the early 1950s that the *Ages and Stages* film series addressed the anxiety being expressed by some NFB parents concerning the modern problems of democratic child rearing.

The Problem with "Personality"

He Acts His Age (1949) is the first film of the *Ages and Stages* series. It opens with dozens of small children on a holiday picnic with their parents, running among the wild grasses and flowers of an idyllic summer field. The message conveyed by psychiatric consultant C.G. Stodgill, M.D., throughout the film is that children's emotional development is similar to their physical development; it is not static. To the father who wonders why his four year old has begun to question the authority of the family ("What's happened to him? He was alright last year.") or to the mother who asks of her sulky and resentful nine-year-old daughter, "Is this rebellion just a phase, or have I done something wrong?" the reassuring answer from Dr. Stodgill is the same: "They're just growing, that's all."[54]

By the early 1950s, in films such as *Frustrating Fours and Fascinating Fives* (1953), those parents who employ modern child-rearing practices continue to express self-doubts about the undertaking ("Mother begins to wonder if she is bringing him up the wrong way") and their concerns are paralleled by the doubts of significant others: "Granny is not so sure that mother isn't making a mistake with these modern methods." At the age of four, the narrator of *Frustrating Fours and Fascinating Fives* notes, manners can never be counted on. At this moment, Roddy, a four-year-old boy, says to his mother: "You big dirty bum." "His behaviour seems to have deteriorated," notes the narrator cheerily "It is only a matter of moments before he is in trouble again." The solution, as before, is "humour and more patience" and to "guide them with affection," because "of course he'll soon be five."[55]

At age five, a remarkable change comes over Roddy: "At five, Roddy is an independent little person who can entertain himself....He helps set the table....He loves routine....At breakfast, he is the centre of attention." The implication is clear: as Roddy matures physically, he will mature emotionally as well. The child's developing attitude of independence is stressed positively and repeatedly: "It's fun to be with them as they learn to be independent....Roddy goes to school by himself....He enjoys the independence."[56] Happiness and independence are hammered into the films, again and again, as the desired outcomes of democratic child rearing—a democracy to be obtained by the wide-scale relaxing of parental control over their children.

As Cynthia Comacchio has observed in her *Nations Are Built of Babies* (1993), it is difficult to ascertain how the great array of child-rearing information that became available in the interwar and postwar period was applied by Canadian parents, or whether its use ultimately resulted in any change in child-rearing practices. Any impression of change, she has concluded, "must remain speculative."[57] While this is true for Canadian society as a whole, pockets of Canadian society *were* studied in the early 1950s to determine that very thing.

During the early 1950s, research projects into the reception of modern parenting practices among selected segments of Canadian society were being undertaken by groups with a special interest in the mental hygiene project. The early outcomes of "democratic" child rearing among one such segment of Ontario society is documented in the book *Crestwood Heights* (1956). For *Crestwood Heights*, the authors—John Seeley, R. Alexander Sim, Elizabeth Loosley, et al.—were commissioned by the CNCMH and the University of Toronto to record, in part, their impressions of the impact of modern child-rearing practices on the affluent Toronto suburb of Forest Hills (named Crestwood Heights in the book).[58] Crestwood mothers, according to the authors, had rapidly become "banner bearers" for expert approaches to parenting.[59] Indeed, the authors were struck by how easily Crestwood mothers rejected their own experience in favour of expert advice.[60] Although husbands occasionally resented the experts with their psychological know-how and permissive notions of child rearing, Crestwood mothers "tended to be people for whom the most recent deliveries of science on human nature had an overwhelming appeal."[61]

> The feeling among women is widespread that since human nature and social life are perfectible the answer ought to be readily available and can be learned from the right expert, and having been learned will be put into practice either automatically or with a modicum of effort.[62]

As a result of the "modicum of effort" made by Crestwood mothers, the Crestwood family had undergone noticeable changes since the introduction of mental hygiene in the early postwar period, appearing to the investigators to be "a little like a country which, having operated under an authoritarian form of government, has suddenly switched to a democratic form, without too much preparation for the change."[63] In theory (and in practice in many Crestwood families) parents had followed expert child-rearing advice, endowing their children with considerable liberty for personal growth along with constant assurances of love and emotional security. The objective in doing so was to bring about the early psychological emancipation of a child from her or his family.[64] But in the process of emancipation, the investigators noted, the families had developed some unforeseen problems.

A central problem observed by Seeley and his research team involved confusion over the allocation of power among family members. Indeed, in some family circles, the authors noted, "the distinction between child and adult was by no means clear."[65] Small children in particular, the investigators observed, were bewildered by the multitudinous choices of behaviour presented to them and many of them, consequently, became minor nuisances:[66] "The old edict that a child should be seen and not heard no longer holds in Crestwood Heights. Young children join in the conversation of their elders, frequently interrupting the talk of the grown-ups."[67]

Others wielded enough power to disrupt major family patterns: "If a television program for children changes its schedule without warning, the family meal hour may have to be changed, unless the adult members are prepared to accept enforced silence and semi-darkness."[68] And, in what was potentially a problem of larger proportions, older children generated worries for Crestwood parents by employing their new-found liberty to play "kissing games." Parents in Crestwood Heights frequently complained about this last trend, but felt powerless to reverse it, since they felt that "other children and other parents set the pace."[69] Noted the researchers of the kissing games: "if this trend were fully generalized it would entail the collapse toward youth of the entire life experience."[70] And noting the dynamic of modern families whereby "others" could set the pace for children against the wishes of parents, the authors remarked: "The price which is paid may well be a new kind of acute dependence on the approval of a rather large, ill defined, and possibly threatening 'they', the peer group of the wider society, allegiance to which is replacing deep emotional ties to the family."[71]

Despite the anxiety of the Crestwood Heights community that all was well, and despite blemishes and imperfections most discernible in the behaviour of its children, Seeley and the other investigators remained convinced of the benefits of the child-centred culture of Crestwood Heights although they allowed that "given the nature of culture, any attempt to alter it raises the problem of an unanticipated result in the long term."[72]

The researchers were comforted primarily by the logic of the mental health approach to parenting.[73] Children reared democratically would be less shackled in their progress toward autonomy and, thus, on the whole, must logically live happier, more productive and independent lives than those raised by traditional, "autocratic" methods of parenting. If their logic seemed insufficient, then they offered the concrete example of maturing Crestwood adolescents, sixteen to nineteen year olds, "whose general pattern seemed to be one of acceptance of the adult values and way of life."[74]

Indeed, the majority of the North American medical establishment was optimistic regarding the outcome of the mental health project. Among practitioners of psychiatry during the formative and expansion years of mental hygiene, the prognosis had been overwhelmingly positive. They conceived of mass modern child rearing as a social bridge to a future free of crime, mental disturbance, and industrial inefficiency.[75] They envisioned a future populated by a new generation of productive, sociable, independent, and happy adults. But not all psychiatrists during the postwar expansion of mental hygiene shared the majority opinion concerning the movement's beneficial impact.

Writing in 1952, the American psychiatrist, Hilde Bruch, M.D., in her own child-rearing guide, *Don't Be Afraid of Your Child*, sounded a rare note of warning about psychologized child rearing: "The failure to recognize the essentially valid and sustaining aspects of traditional ways and of differentiating them from harmful measures has resulted in a demoralized confusion of modern parents and thus had a disastrous effect on children."[76] Bruch forewarned of "the great possibility of misinterpretation of popularized advice."[77]

> The fashion of child psychologists and psychiatrists to speak in sweeping, dramatic terms of the crushing effect of authority and tradition, the fear that even the most innocent appearing act or a carelessly spoken word might harm a child or damage her or his future happiness, the philosophy of permissiveness has become so widespread that parents have been made afraid to use authority and discipline."[78]

Far from achieving its proclaimed goal of producing "greater stability, more security and more happiness in later life," Bruch predicted a different result arising from psychologized child care: "Today's young people raised under the slogan of 'permissiveness' often do not seem to develop a superego, or such an inefficient, contradictory one that they are helpless prey to outer influences, insecure and dependent on others, like leaves in the wind."[79]

Bruch claimed that the difficulty for most parents in giving the freedom of decision to their children was "the simple fact that they are supposed to put into practice something they never experienced themselves."[80] Even J.R. Seeley, a major architect of the Canadian "Mental Health Project" had admitted by 1959 to this unanticipated problem:

> One finds parents convinced of their impotence, clinging to doctrine in the face of confronting fact-at-hand, robbed of spontaneity (or,

equivalently, forcing themselves as a routine to "be spontaneous"), guilt-ridden, dubious about their own discriminatory capacity, in double tutelage—to the child himself and to his agent, the "expert"— penetrable, defenseless, credulous, and sure only that, while it doth not yet appear, the day of salvation is at hand.[81]

Still, parents would try, Hilde Bruch postulated, to raise their children in a way they perceived society to demand, since it was the conviction of most parents that "the worst possible fate of a child is to be different."[82] To such children, Bruch prophesied, there would be transferred the haunting fear of not being popular, of being left out, a fear accompanied by a compulsive search for approval, for friendship, and for popularity among their peers—"the group," whose values and standards would be "in turn easily influenced by mass propaganda."[83]

The Problem with Peers

In NFB society, the spectre of "the group" becomes the subject of discourse in several films in the late 1950s. The year 1957 alone saw five films produced, in part, to address the growing problem of peer influence in the wake of declining adult authority. In the film *Being Different* (1957), part of the *What Do You Think?* series, a twelve-year-old boy weighs the consequences of being rejected by his usual group of friends if he pursues an interest in collecting butterflies, which he developed during his summer holidays. "Nobody does that unless they're crazy...or girls," warns his closest buddy. "People will think you're a creep chasing butterflies; you'll have no friends, because no one chases butterflies."[84]

In the film *Who Is Sylvia?* (1957), one of three films produced for the *Perspective* television series, the friends of a fourteen-year-old daughter of an urban, working-class family become the subject of portrayal. Although Sylvia's parents are described as "the main architects of her life," it is clear that Sylvia is being remodelled by her peer group: "The gang is supreme, the kids, the crowd," comments the narrator. "They must constantly prove that they are not the oddball."[85]

In the narrative, Sylvia is coerced by "the kids" into having a party after school at her house while her mother and father are at work. Arriving home early, Sylvia's mother finds two of the young people necking in a hallway. She is upset and evicts them all. Embarrassed, Sylvia runs sobbing to her bedroom. "Is she going to turn out like some of them do?" Sylvia's mother asks her husband that evening.

Asleep in her room, Sylvia dreams about her mother as a more understanding individual. In her dream, Sylvia's mother jokes good-naturedly about finding her young friends necking. "Good sport, wasn't she," remark Sylvia's friends as they leave for home. In Sylvia's dream, her mother bids farewell to her friends by saying, "Come anytime." As the film ends, the narrator, speaking for Sylvia, observes, "You can't be a person when you belong to someone, like a kid." He neglects to add, however, that to be a "kid" in urban NFB society in the late 1950s, one must now belong to "the group."

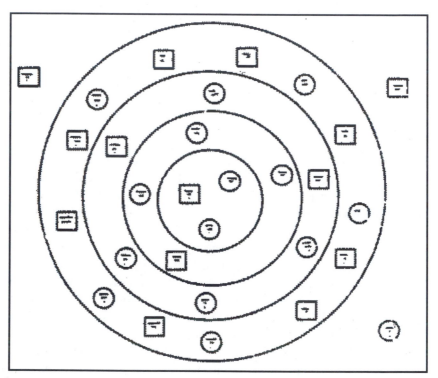

Sociometric Chart.

Ironically, although the ascendancy of "the group" is of concern to NFB parents in the late 1950s, since the early 1950s (influenced by the mental hygienists) the school system in the cinematic society had been elevating the importance of a cohesive, social personality for children. With the production of *Shyness* (1953), a training film for Canadian teachers, the importance of peer sociability among schoolchildren enters the consciousness of teachers for the first time. A kindly male, a grade six teacher with a perpetually supportive smile, narrates the story of what happened in his classroom after a visit from a psychologist, a professional-looking woman in a business dress who administers a socio-metric test to his class:

> It all began one day last September. A psychologist came from the child guidance clinic in our town to give the children what she called a sociometric test, a test to find out how they rated as sociable individuals. They had to answer a lot of questions, like "What three children in this class would you choose to go with you to the school party?" "Whom would you choose to join the stamp club, or the sewing club?"...and so on. It seemed a bit like a popularity contest to me, and I didn't take it too seriously, at least that day.[86]

Later, the results of the sociometric test are returned to the teacher by the psychologist, in the form of a sociometric chart. The teacher is surprised by how accurately the chart depicts the sociability of his pupils, but more surprising to him is its identification of three children completely outside the circles, three children whom nobody picked as a friend: Jimmy, Robert, and Anna.

> They were quiet, well-behaved children. Too quiet perhaps. Certainly not the ones I had thought of as difficult. But they were the friendless ones...[and] unless we do something for them now, when they are still young, they may have ahead of them the lonely frustrated life of the shy adult.[87]

Suddenly alert to his new responsibility, the teacher refers the three children to a clinical psychiatrist, who delivers his judgement upon each child following a brief interview: Jimmy is emotionally sick, the victim of a "jealous" and "overprotective" mother, and in need of specialized help from the child guidance clinic; nothing at all wrong with Robert, who likes to be alone to pursue his scientific curiosity; but Anna, a pretty ten-year-old girl, is "the typical shy child," the victim of a mother who was too demanding ("Of course she meant well"). Anna's emotional health becomes a concern to all her schoolteachers, but especially to her classroom teacher, the film narrator, who does his part by organizing his dayplans to include tasks that enable Anna to join in cooperative ventures with others.

Sol Cohen has labelled the mental hygiene movement as practised in American public schools as "a scheme for assisting and guiding the development of personality."[88] The ideal, "well-adjusted" personality was deemed to be assertive, active, and, most of all, sociable.[89] Hygienists rated aggressive behaviour as the least serious behaviour problem in a classroom.[90] Shyness, daydreaming, passivity, introversion—these traits were tagged as indicating potentially disordered personalities. Personality development also included "a tacit assumption by the schools of a broad parent-surrogate function."[91]

Mental hygienists called upon teachers to sacrifice their sense of authority and to provide the sort of classroom climate that would encourage the child to "show himself for what he is" and not inhibit or repress feelings or behaviour for the sake of good discipline.[92] Suppression of the child was said to be psychologically harmful to the child.[93] One of the key planks of the hygienist consensus was to persuade teachers to view children's misbehaviour scientifically instead of moralistically: to pay less attention to the children's overt behaviour and more attention to understanding the motives behind it.[94] The ultimate goal of the mental hygienists was to alter the teacher's "attitude" (a key hygienist word) toward children to ensure a correct psychological disposition toward their pupils, and thus to make the children happy, efficient, and productive.[95]

Shyness (1953). NFB.

The NFB film *Child Guidance Clinic* (1956) was produced to explain the concept to the Canadian public as part of the *On the Spot* newsreels for the nascent CBC television:

Out of every 100 Canadian school children it is estimated that at some time in their lives 5 will be committed to a mental institution, 2 will go to prison, and at least 5 more will be an emotional problem to themselves, their families or their teachers. In other words, 12 out of every 100 Canadian school children need help. ON THE SPOT is here in Toronto this week to learn more about a plan that is helping to stop this waste in human lives.[96]

The *On the Spot* television reporter who has made these opening remarks watches as a Toronto school principal, a Mr. Montgomery, chats with a puzzled-looking eight-year-old boy dressed in winter togs. After the principal has finished his conversation and pats the departing boy on the shoulder, the reporter engages Mr. Montgomery's attention:

Neil Lloyd:	I was amused to see that little youngster come up to chat with you in the playground. When I was at school the only time we saw the principal was when we were sent up to his office for well-deserved punishment.
Principal:	Well, I remember those things myself all too well. But I think the changing attitude of principals and teachers is made a great deal of difference. [*sic*] The school no longer regards it as its main function to simply teach academic skills. Educators are now interested in the child acquiring habits and attitudes that will make him a happy child, a more successful student, and a better and more useful citizen...training these children to be happy, well-integrated and creative human beings, each in his own way.[97]

The reporter and the principal then climb the concrete steps into the old brick school building and open a door into a classroom, where they observe a socially active body of young children wandering from table to table, working at art projects, and being supervised by a somewhat harried elderly woman who hands out praise and quick tips to the myriad young people who come to her.

As with the film *Shyness*, co-scripted by J.R. Seeley (who would soon be renowned for his work on *Crestwood Heights*), there is an aspect of these NFB schools of the early mental hygiene era which, with historical hindsight, is at least worthy of an aside. That is, how respectful of all teachers *all* the schoolchildren are in the films, especially the disturbed children. In his opinion, Seeley expected this element of classroom interaction to be further improved by the adoption of mental hygiene practices into Canadian public schools: "Far from creating disrespect for the teacher, other teachers, or authorities," wrote Seeley, "since the method is directed to 'understanding,' it can only increase respect where respect is due."[98] Like so much that was promised by the mental hygienists, this too would fail to come to pass.[99]

Of what does come to pass in NFB schools in the decade following the introduction of mental hygiene, the following are most conspicuous: a) expressive play and social interaction become an increasingly important part of elementary education; b) social issues occupy a significant part of intermediate and secondary education; c) formal discipline and structure become less prevalent in all classrooms; and d) facilitation of large-group discussion becomes the mark of a successful teacher. Less conspicuously, the purpose of schooling in NFB society becomes clouded, more often posed as a question in the films than as a statement of philosophy. In one training film, the teachers criticize their professional roles as authorities and automatons; in another, the educational theorist Jerome Bruner criticizes the lack of intellectual activity in their classrooms.[100] In a film made for television, parents challenge the authority of teachers to discipline their children; and indeed, television itself, in a film with Marshall McLuhan, is offered up as a more challenging teacher than teachers and schools.[101]

Advancing Problems in the 1960s

Possibly the most remarkable thing noted by Cohen and Richardson about the mental hygiene project is that its diffusion into society went forward with scarcely any research.[102] As early as 1919, "Dr. E.E. Southard warned that the mental hygiene movement was being launched as a matter of propaganda rather than a matter of research."[103] Similarly, Robert S. Morison of the Rockefeller Foundation observed in 1950 of the epistemology of mental health, "There have been several times recently when I have felt that the leaders of American psychiatry are trying to establish truth on the basis of majority vote."[104]

American school reform activities were founded on tenuous research bases at best. Of the $10,000,000 Commonwealth Fund (CF), Cohen is most disparaging: "The truth is the [Commonwealth] fund really didn't know what it was doing. It was armed with money and solutions looking for a problem....Who could have known how flimsy the foundation on which the Program was erected would, with the benefit of hindsight, turn out to be?"[105]

Despite the inadequacy of their research foundation, mental hygienists refashioned NFB parenting and schooling practices in the postwar period. For their part, parents of this cinematic society of the late 1950s become resigned to following the tenets of modern parenting. Both the commitment to and lack of confidence in the enterprise are best summed up by a father in the film *Making a Decision in the Family* (1957). When his daughter, a fifteen-year-old bobbysoxer, makes plans to go with "the gang" to a barbecue on the very day that the family traditionally attends their Aunt Sarah's birthday party, the father confides to his wife, "I guess we can't force her to do anything, really. Still, she's got to have some discipline. Kids! Sometimes it's hard to know what to do."[106]

By the early 1960s, there are very few dissenters among NFB adults to the mental health practices of democratic child rearing. Symbolic of the hygenic fait accompli are parallel scenes from *He Acts His Age* (1949), an older film in the mental hygiene series, and *The New Baby* (1961) the last of the NFB films with a prescriptive, mental hygiene message. In the earlier film, a jealous four-year-old boy, Roddy, sprinkles baby powder on his aunt's dress and draws her ire; in the corresponding scene from the later production, a jealous four year old similarly attacks his aunt Emily's dress, but this time receives her attention and love. By 1961, modern child rearing is practised universally in NFB society.[107]

Subsequent to this universal acceptance, another, less subtle, transformation in social relations between adults and children becomes observable in the celluloid society. Most illustrative of the transformation is the film *The World of Three* (1966). As mischievious as the NFB filmmakers had portrayed Roddy in the 1949 production *He Acts His Age*, they could not have fathomed the full scope of childhood unleashed that becomes evident in this cinema direct production. In *The World of Three*, the youngster, Lucas, yells at and strikes his mother, breaks a vase, tears down pictures, kicks toys, and screams in rage, as his mother attempts to guide his behaviour with love and understanding and occasional ineffectual discipline: "Lucas! [Vase breaks.] Now, Lucas, look what you've done. You're a very naughty boy. I've told you a hundred times not to play with that vase. [Lucas goes into a rage.] You're a very naughty boy. Stay here. Lucas, Lucas, Lukey! Now listen...Lucas? Stop!"[108]

Although scenes of children hitting parents in mid-1960s NFB films are not yet common, scenes of children yelling at adults become unexceptional. Illustrative of the trend is the best-selling film of the late 1960s and early 1970s, *Phoebe* (1964). Phoebe is an adolescent girl with a problem that hearkens back to the earlier worries of the parents of *Crestwood Heights*: she is pregnant. When her mother (who always walks around the house carrying a lit cigarette) asks Phoebe why she spends so much time in the washroom, the girl shouts at her to leave her alone. Her mother, who is unaware of the pregnancy, retreats, and Phoebe is left to herself, to deal with the questions of who to tell and what to do. Shot in the French new wave style of cinema, with hand-held cameras, shock and jump cuts, *Phoebe* heralds further transformations developing in the NFB culture of childhood, as a group of adolescents at a beach party wear cut-off jeans and Mexican ponchos and dance in circles—the first "hippies" to appear in the cinematic society.[109]

Phoebe (1964). NFB, S-3017.

Ultimately, among the youth of NFB society in the mid-1960s, the usurping of adult authority that has been evolving for a decade within NFB families expands to include institutions outside of the family—schools, in particular. In the film *No Reason to Stay* (1966), attitudes polarize between high-school teachers, who complain that "kids have no respect" and students who explain "we're living in the instant, and they [the teachers] don't understand that." It is noteworthy that the bias of the filmmakers leans heavily toward the students. While the teachers are portrayed as dry and humourless ("Do you find the word 'intercourse' funny?") rebellious students are portrayed as heroic, best illustrated by a daydream scene in which the main character, sixteen-year-old Christopher, puts his history teacher on trial: "You don't interest; you bore. You don't challenge; you put to sleep."[110]

In the course of the film narrative, Christopher decides that what is offered by the school is not education, and he decides to drop out. ("I'd give my right arm for an education, but for a piece of paper...no!") He goes to the school counsellor to make the arrangements but is told that first he will have to speak to the principal, who works in an adjacent office, and that to see the principal first he will have to make an appointment with the school secretary. Here, the film suggests, lies the crucial difference between a tradition-bound, adult society and the new generation. Without hesitation, Christopher exits the counsellor's office, opens the adjacent door into the principal's office, and yells "I quit!" without ever having made an appointment.

No Reason to Stay (1966). NFB, S-5124.

Flowers on a One-way Street

Surveying the faces of the protesters seizing Yorkville Street in the NFB cinéma-direct production *Flowers on a One-way Street* (1967), one is struck by their youth, the average age appearing to be less than twenty-two. Even the oldest were but infants when *What's On Your Mind?* appeared in Odeon Theatres in 1946, with its warning to Canadian mothers to cease nagging their children or assume responsibility for their future neuroses. As helmeted police wade into the mass of young people, attempting to move them from the pavement, one notes their confident defiance of authority, a conviction that their cause will prevail, that their demands will be respected. They are of one mind; they are cohesive, hand clapping, and chanting in unison: "Close our street....Close our street."[111]

They are the peer group that their parents dreaded: "the rather large, ill defined, and possibly threatening 'they'...easily influenced by mass propaganda."[112] At the same time, this study suggests, they are the happy, productive, and self-reliant generation promised by the mental hygienists to the very same parents. I shall return to both aspects of their "personality" in the concluding chapter of this book since, as does Owram for late-1960s Canadian society, I attach considerable importance to the events documented in *Flowers on a One-way Street* in regard to both late- and post-1960s transitions within the cinematic society.

Conclusion

In summary—unlike Canadian society, for which the connections between postwar child-rearing practices and the behaviour of baby boomers must necessarily be labelled a "controversial" factor, and unlike American society, for which there may be "unseen" evidence of the hygienist impact yet to be discovered—in NFB society, the reflected progress of mental hygiene practices impacting on real society is both conspicuous and supportive of Owram's "fourth factor." Moreover, the nature of its impact, usurping power from NFB parents and teachers, suggests that the mental hygiene movement might well be added to the "mechanisms through which electronic media bring about widespread social change," catalogued by Joshua Meyrowitz in his monograph, *No Sense of Place: The Impact of Electronic Media on Social Behaviour* (1985):[113] "Children who have television sets now have outside perspectives from which to judge and evaluate family rituals, beliefs and religious practices...the family is no longer an all-powerful formative influence."[114]

"Given the nature of culture," warned John Seeley in *Crestwood Heights* (1956), "any attempt to alter it raises the problem of an unanticipated result in the long term."[115] Simply stated, the mental hygienists had not anticipated that nature abhors a vacuum. As parental power vis-à-vis their children decreased, the power of children vis-à-vis their parents increased; as adult authority over children decreased, the authority of children over other children increased—a situation of dubious social utility, especially after the early 1950s when television, perpetually fascinating to children, penetrated Canadian and, hence, NFB society, the consequences of which Seeley had only barely anticipated. In the coming years, the new medium would commence to expand the children's vision of what their peer group was about, beyond communities like Crestwood Heights, to include all of North America. Then, in NFB society at least, the first wave of the new generation would seize control of the larger mise en scènes of the late 1960s.

A Progressive State of Disequilibrium: Social Relations in the Cinematic Society, 1968-89

Order is not a pressure which is imposed on society from without, but an equilibrium which is set up from within.
— José Ortega y Gasset, *Mirabeau or Politics*

The young child which lieth in the cradle is both wayward and full of affections, and though his body be but small, yet he hath a (wrongdoing) heart, and is altogether inclined to evil....If this sparkle be suffered to increase, it will rage over and burn down the whole house. For we are changed and become good not by birth but by education.
— Robert Cleaver and John Dod, *A Godly Form of Household Government* (1621)

Endnotes are the road signs of historical research, signalling to us what routes to follow for the best vantage of our primary sources. Recurring notes among the secondary literature I used for this study led me to two separate viewpoints from which to see what happens next within the

---

Notes to chapter 6 are on p. 258.

families, schools, and communities of NFB society. They are Ellen Key's views on child rearing in her treatise, *The Century of the Child* (1909), and those of post-1950s psychologists into both past and (at the time) contemporary research findings concerning family relations. There are other points of view to consider, of course. Indeed, since the 1960s there has been a proliferation of perspectives to be taken into any historical account and I have attempted to incorporate these, wherever appropriate, into the narrative of cinematic social relations that is imposed by the films themselves. But, ultimately, the views of Key and the psychologists are most germane to my understanding of the entire, transient postwar panorama of NFB portrayals of Canadian children and, hence, it is along the intellectual and social paths they traversed that this study now embarks.

Ellen Key: The Century of the Child

Among the child-rearing literature of the early twentieth century, Ellen Key's *The Century of the Child* is unique. Not solely for the egalitarian child-rearing attitudes it espouses, although it easily surpassed the most liberal of other works in this regard: "Homes which send out men and women with the strongest morality," wrote Key "are those where they stand on the same level, where, like a good elder sister or elder brother, parents regard the younger members of the household as their equals."[1] Nor does its uniqueness originate from the fact that Key had no children of her own by which to form her opinion (neither was she married, yet she had also published *Love and Marriage* [1911]). Nor is *The Century of the Child* unique because it had a limited readership among the general public, nor because it did not reflect 1909 child-rearing praxis. Such features are not uncommon to this type of literature.[2]

Rather, the distinctiveness of *The Century of the Child* lies in its vision of motherhood as a means to effect transformations among adult society, particularly in regard to the "Woman Question." Whereas the great body of child-rearing advice of her times was being produced to raise children suited for a social world created by adults, especially men, under continuously changing social conditions, Key postulated that women (as mothers) could change the social conditions of posterity within contemporary childhood itself, particularly in the domain of social relations.

> Women in parliament and in journalism, their representation in the local and general government, in peace congress and in workingmen's meetings, science and literature, all this will produce small results

until women realise that the transformation of society begins with the unborn child, with the conditions for its coming into existence, its physical and psychical training....Nothing will be different in the mass except in so far as human nature itself is transformed, and that this transformation will take place, not when the whole of humanity becomes Christian, but when the whole of humanity awakens to the conciousness of the "holiness of generation."[3]

Every human being who was socially alive, wrote Key, was aware that the "right to control one's life is the emptiest phrase to describe reality in a society built up on a capitalistic basis. It is doubly empty where woman is concerned."[4]

Mankind remains the same though its acts may take different shapes. Thinkers will always find new ideas, scholars new methods and systems, artists new aesthetic creations, but on the whole everything must remain the same. Only when woman heeds the message which life proclaims to her, that, through her, salvation must come—will the face of the earth be renewed.[5]

Not surprisingly, considering the message proclaimed by her own life, the salvation through child rearing that Ellen Key prescribed for society met with the conditions of her own childhood. Daughter of a Swedish parliamentarian of Scottish descent, her mother of Swedish noble descent, Key was both reared and schooled for independence. According to one of her biographers, Havelock Ellis, during her childhood Key was introduced to academic and athletic exercises usually reserved for boys, since "[her] mother overlooked her daughter's indifference to domestic vocations and left her free to follow her own instincts, at the same time exercising a judicious influence over her development....It may easily be believed that a girl of so much individuality of character, so impetuous and so independent, proved a difficult child to manage and was often misunderstood."[6]

As Barbara Ehrenreich and Deirdre English observe in their *For Her Own Good: 150 Years of the Experts' Advice to Women* (1978), it would be easy even today to misunderstand Key and dismiss *The Century of the Child* as "just another advertisement for female domesticity."[7] But Key, in fact, had made a discovery: "a discovery of the *power* of women."[8]

[N]ow it is as if the masculinist imagination takes a glance over its shoulder and discovers it has left something important behind in "woman"'s sphere'—the child. This child—the new child of the twentieth century—is not valued, like the child of patriarchy, simply as an heir. This child is conceived as...a means of control over society's not-so-distant future. This child cannot be left to women.[9]

Ellen Key.

Left to Key, parenting and schooling practices for "this child," which she named "the new generation," would have aimed at the free development of "egoism" in humankind. That "none should tyrannise over, nor suffer tyranny from the other" was the essence of her advice for the development of healthy egos.[10] Hence, she saw corporal punishment as an evil to be forsaken: "I experience physical disgust in touching the hand of a human being that I know has struck a child; and I cannot

close my eyes after I have heard a child in the street threatened with corporal punishment."[11] Only somewhat less objectionable was the child-
rearing maxim that "as the twig is bent, the tree is inclined": "*Bent* is
the appropriate word, bent according to the old ideal which extinguish-
es personality, teaches humility and obedience. But the new ideal is that
man, to stand straight and upright, must not be bent at all, only supported, and so prevented from being deformed by weakness."[12] To Key, "the
strongest constructive factor in the education of a human being" was the
"settled, quiet order of home"—an environment in which parents and
children lived together in "freedom and confidence," each possessing
"full freedom for their own personal interest; where none trenches on
the rights of others."[13] Further, to prevent "soul murder in the schools,"
she prescribed "home schooling" for young children, while schools for
older children "should be nothing more but the mental dining-room in
which parents and teachers prepare intellectual bills-of-fare suitable for
every child."[14]

From the collective "egoism" that would thus develop among boys
and girls (and mature among men and women), Key hypothesized, woman would convince man and society of the following truths: "that woman is not solely a sexual being, not solely dependent on man, the home
and the family, no matter what form these may exist."[15] Then woman,
Key believed, having been emancipated through the home and family,
would return to the home and the family to exert her natural power to
shape posterity since "through our posterity, which we ourselves create,
we can in a certain measure, as free beings, determine the future destiny
of the human race."[16]

As with much of the child-rearing literature of the early twentieth
century, Ellen Key and *The Century of the Child*, as well as a dozen other motherhood advice authors of the first decade of the twentieth century, influenced only a small proportion of middle and upper class
readers.[17] Meanwhile, parenting practices throughout most of Europe
and North America continued to be influenced by family and neighbour,
homespun wisdom, common sense, practical experience, and, to a
slightly increasing degree, by the home visits, well-baby clinics, and
health lectures made by public health inspectors, physicians, and
nurses.[18] However, unlike the majority of advice authors who published
guides in the initial years of the century, included among Key's readership was Lawrence K. Frank who, in *Recent Social Trends in the United
States* (1933), in addition to alluding to the progress being made by the
parent education movement, extolled, in the manner of Key, "the possibility of directing and controlling [future] social life through the care

and nurture of children," since "the social life of tomorrow is already determined by the children now living and being born."[19] Frank quoted directly from *The Century of the Child* to give this point emphasis:

> As Ellen Key expressed it, "...'holiness of generation.' This consciousness will make the central work of society the new race, its origin, management, and its education; about these all morals, all laws, all social arrangements will be grouped. This will form the point of view from which all other questions will be judged, all other regulations made."[20]

"Holiness of generation," the phrase conveys ecumenical overtones—an appropriate concept for Frank and Key to share. For both social theorists, through "holiness of generation" future society might be perfected by the management of childhood present. For both, the family would be the major vehicle of control over "society's not-so-distant future." And for both, the model family structure to be adopted by the masses would exercise more egalitarian internal power relations than was presently the case.[21] Frank and Key had differing visions of what social outcomes could be expected from democratizing family relations en masse. For Frank, the change would lead to the eradication of poverty, delinquency, crime—even war; for Key, it would shepherd society toward the resolution of "the woman question." But regardless of their differing calculations, both shared a common conviction that, in the end, such a positive change could only better the "settled, quiet order of home."

A Change of Mind: Post-1950s Psychological Research into the Family

Herein, perhaps, lies the greatest irony concerning the mental hygiene movement. Credible research into functional family power relationships did not take place before the early 1960s. Reviewing the research up to 1975, psychologist Theodore Jacob characterized family studies prior to the late 1950s as "methodologically weak or inadequate...vulnerable to major interpretive difficulties."[22] Among the unexpected discoveries of post-1950s psychological research into families, Jacob reported Amerigo Ferreira's 1963 finding "that children in disturbed families were more dominant than children in normal families," and Anthony Schuham's 1970 finding that "a completely equalitarian structure...existed in disturbed families and a hierarchical structure in normal families."[23]

In regard to that latter study, the author, Schuham, noted how pre-1960s family studies tended "to view the normal family as equalitarian and the disturbed as authoritarian."[24] On the contrary, Schuham reported, (as with studies by G.H. Vandenberg and James Stachowiak [1966] and Elliot Mishler and Nancy Waxler [1968]) his research revealed "that at least a moderate tendency toward "authoritarianism" typifies normal family functioning."[25] As late as 1967, psychologists such as Stanley Murrell and Stachowiak had begun their research with the hypothesis that "clinic [troubled] families would have more autocratic and more rigid patterns of interaction than non-clinic [normal] families," yet had produced findings "at variance...with the general assumption that "disturbed families" are more rigid than "normal families.'"[26] The power struggle that resulted from equalitarian family practices, reported Schuham, left "the disturbed family system...impaired in its capacity to resolve conflict between its elements [and thus] in *a state of flux or disequilibrium* to a much greater extent than the normal family."[27]

From Family to Community: The Expansion of Disequilibrium in NFB Society

As I have demonstrated in earlier chapters, a developing state of disequilibrium within the cinematic families created by the NFB (an equalizing shift in the allocation of power between adults and children) becomes a widening phenomenon from the mid-1950s onwards.[28] A similar state of flux in power relationships may be observed progressing within NFB schools by the mid-1960s, and, by 1967, the phenomenon can be seen pervading NFB society as a whole. From families to schools and communities, spilling from one to the other to the other, a seemingly axiomatic principle of equalizing power arrangements now suddenly pervades the power structures of the cinematic state itself.[29]

In 1967, reflecting the egalitarian attitudes of the new society the Film Board commenced its "Challenge for Change" programme (designated "*Société nouvelle*" by the ONF), an innovative philosophy of documentary film production that reallocated representational voice to the previously voiceless—a sociological parallel to the practice of "democratic" child rearing promoted in NFB society twenty years earlier and with parallel consequences.[30] By the early 1970s, traditional hierarchical authority was diminished at the Film Board as shifts in power over filmic voice and vision led to formerly powerless "units" of film production being replaced by more autonomous "studios."[31] By the mid-1970s, these would include Studio D, the women's studio at the NFB which, by the late 1970s, would gain hegemony over the cinematic portrayals of Canadian children.

Reared for independence and schooled for sociability, the new generation does, in fact, reform society after 1967, just as the hygienists had hoped—but not by creating a crime-free society distinguished by social harmony and industrial efficiency as promised by the child psychiatrists and psychologists. Rather, the postwar generation fashions a profound transformation in social structures and relations—a society distinguished by the ascendancy of feminism and cultural plurality, a decline in patriarchy (social leadership by men and boys), the diminution of the public school as an authoritative educational force and the "monolithic" family as the dominant family structure.[32]

As the new generation becomes increasingly adult after 1967, reflections of Canadian society undergo dramatic transitions in the cinematic mirror as NFB women and girls increasingly provide social leadership—first within families, then schools and communities—while men and boys flounder, at times in open rebellion against their adult selves. This chapter follows the evolution of the new generation of postwar NFB children and the development of a "new society" up to the mid- to late 1980s through a filmic gaze upon portrayals of children—both new generation and "next generation"—beginning with their families in the late 1960s.

Parental/Paternal Retreat from the NFB Family

One of the most striking features of late 1960s and early 1970s NFB portrayals of children is the demise of their parents as a subject of focus. In a turnabout from the films of the 1940s, in which children were most often cast in supporting roles in an adult world, in the films of the late 1960s and early 1970s, the roles are more often reversed—with adults cast in the supporting roles. Children often appear in the films of the era without any reference to their parents at all; at most, they include only brief shots of their parents—even in films about child rearing. The mothers in *Child Part II: Jamie, Ethan, and Keir: 2-14 months* (1973), for example, are "extras," picking up their infants when they topple out of chairs; their fathers are the NFB cameramen filming them. In *The Burden They Carry* (1970), a Swedish/NFB sex education advocacy production, a photographic slide of a father changing a baby (the first such portrait) and another of a mother breast-feeding are the only family references shown to a class of elementary school students being filmed during a sex education lesson. In *Summer Centre* (1973), working-class parents are briefly observed watching television in the evening as their children wreak havoc at a suburban, recreation centre. Parents become peripheral in family settings; children become the central focus.

Inuit mother and son from *Stalking Seal on the Spring Ice* (1968). NFB.

Among the rare exceptions to the rule of child centricity in family portraits are the anthropological depictions of Inuit families in the *Netsilik Eskimo* series. These are purportedly authentic portrayals of the Pelly Bay Inuit prior to 1920, when few Netsilik would have met Euro-Canadians. A typical film of the series is *Stalking Seal on the Spring Ice* (1968). In the film, three members of an Inuit family—a father, a mother, and a son—pitch their cariboo-hide tent at the edge of the Arctic ocean. The mother organizes the camp and tends the dogs as the father goes off with a harpoon onto the spring ice. The four-year-old boy stays back at the campsite and plays alone. The father spots a seal sunbathing by a hole in the ice and he lies down, making seal noises and seal movements. The seal regards him with only minor misgivings. When the father has slid very close, he leaps up and harpoons the seal before it can dive into the water. Back at the camp, the mother and father skin the seal, cutting the skin into narrow strips. The boy takes the strips, washes them in a pool of water, and sets them out on the rocks to dry. The parents cut off chunks of meat from the seal and eat them raw—he using his snow knife, she an ooloo. That night in the tent, as the mother tends the seal-oil lamp, the parents talk and the child plays between the two. The pre-contact Inuit family as portrayed by the NFB in the late 1960s functions much like the cinematic families of the late 1940s and early 1950s, with adults at the centre of the depiction and operating with a high degree of equilibrium.[33]

But, as film historian Wolfgang Ernst has noted, every film—even a "film aiming to deal with some past period or event"—shows the present, not the past.[34] In the very structure of this depiction of traditional Inuit life of the 1920s, a late-1960s shift in power relations is discernible. The patriarchal voiceover (i.e., the male narration commonplace in earlier NFB documentaries about the Inuit) is absent from *Stalking Seal on the Spring Ice*, replaced solely with dialogue in Inuktitut among the family members. That is not to say that an Inuit voice has replaced the dominant voice of past NFB narratives about the Inuit, since the film narrative itself is constructed by the latter. But the absence of a "voice of God" soundtrack is a retreat in the degree of authority over narrative evident in the past, i.e., a step away from traditional paternal NFB documentaries—especially about indigenous peoples. It is the structural equivalent of cinematic children appearing without their parents.

Although their parents disappear, NFB children do appear with their grandparents during this period. The first-ever Film Board portrayal of grandparents with their grandchildren is found in *The Wish* (1970). Twin girls, robust, precocious, flaxen-haired children of twelve years of age arrive (without their parents) by train to spend their summer vacation at their grandparents' idyllic home in rural Ontario. The clean environment by the lake, the soft-spoken vibrant elderly couple—pillars of middle-class Ontario—and a soft-focus lens filter render the film an emotional paradise. Grandfather takes the girls fishing while grandmother bakes fruit pies. The girls dress up in their mother's old clothes. There is a constant reference to the past through photographs. Grace is sung at dinner. The girls do their chores with little resistance. At the conclusion of the film, the grandparents and grandchildren dwell for a prolonged time in a cemetery, locating departed family members.[35] A similarly nostalgic theme is found in *Gore Road* (1972), a family flashback film of an even more abstract nature to a mythical simpler time. A man stands behind his grandfather's portrait in a rural farmhouse; the resemblance between himself and the painting is startling, and it starts a flow of still photographs of infants going back through the decades and into the nineteenth century.[36]

It is perhaps not surprising to find children in films without their parents but with their grandparents at the very time when divorce rates in Canadian society (led by baby boomers) were soaring, nearly tripling in number from 11,000 in 1968 to 30,000 by 1970.[37] Perhaps it is, as Margrit Eichler has speculated in her *Families in Canada Today* (1988), that "the importance of grandparents as a source of enjoyment increases when parents are separated or divorced."[38]

As the new generation grew numerically within the population of parents and voters (and filmmakers) in Canadian society, there was a growing perception as well—as recorded by Gallup pollsters—that power relations within "the family" were in transition. In a Gallup survey released 17 March 1973, 49 percent of Canadians thought that the dominant role of the husband in the family was declining, as compared to 39 percent who did not think so.[39] Corresponding to these perceived shifts in family power relations, fundamental debates were occurring within the NFB itself in regard to power over documentary voice. Whereas, in the past, representations of voice had belonged almost exclusively to a hierarchical production structure consisting of director, producer, sponsor, and executive administrators up to and including the Government Film Commissioner, in 1967 the Film Board commenced the Challenge for Change program, an experiment allowing filmic voice to originate from the subjects of the film itself. Beginning with the Fogo Island Communication Experiment in 1967, Challenge for Change had, by 1980, produced 83 films (not including the *Netsilik Eskimo* series), which advanced alternative voices into Canadian society through the NFB.

Labelled by its first executive producer, George Stoney, as "government-sponsored subversion," Challenge for Change was a heterogeneous approach to facilitating communication between disadvantaged communities and those with power.[40] The Fogo Island project provided a cinematic opportunity, for example, for the residents of the Newfoundland island to argue (successfully) for funding to rehabilitate their fishing industry. A later film, *Up Against the System* (1969), allowed welfare recipients to articulate complaints directly to government officials about their victimization by the welfare system.[41] Another film, *You Are on Indian Land* (1969), became the voice of the Mohawk Indians of the St. Regis, Ontario, reserve following their blockade of an international bridge over a dispute with customs officials. This latter film, *You Are on Indian Land*, was edited by Kathleen Shannon, an enthusiastic supporter of Challenge for Change, who shortly thereafter began the lengthy process of lobbying for and organizing (successfully in 1974) Studio D, the women's studio at the NFB. Shannon credited the experience of watching reactions to the film by the Indians ("of helping the voiceless to gain their voices") as being the catalyst in her transformation to feminism.[42]

The course of development of Studio D is of interest from a variety of perspectives but, for the purposes of this study, perhaps none quite so interesting as the strategy employed within Studio D to overcome institutional disequilibrium internally. A passage from Gary Evans' *In the National Interest* explains:

> The manifesto of Studio D was a practical "in-house" agenda, calling for ways to bring women's influence to bear on programming, in particular through the presence of professionally qualified women in numbers equal to men. "There are decades, centuries, millennia of repressed or forgotten history and meanings to be explored," Studio D proclaimed, and underscored the fact that it was men's as well as women's history because current themes, now perceived as women's themes, were "virtually universal." No eyebrows were raised over the intended virtual segregation of this group into what critics soon called a women's ghetto. At this point, the women showed little interest in a possible contribution by progressive men who might share their outlook.[43]

Within their own studio, Shannon and her women colleagues (film equipment handlers to producers) were able to establish their own equilibrium, governed (according to Evans) by "the wholeness of women articulating their own needs."[44] The resulting body of films was undoubtedly the most ambitious effort since Grierson to cast a unified reflection in the NFB mirror; i.e., to project a feminist vision of Canadian society into Canadian society. But whereas Grierson's audiences had been born prior to the war, Shannon's audiences had been raised after. In matters of education, therein lay a significant difference.

Sir! Sir! (1968): An Educational Admonition

In the films of the late 1960s, the disequilibrium manifested in Film Board families since the mid-1950s becomes even more pronounced at their schools—perhaps profoundly so in the Candid Eye production, *Sir! Sir!* (1968), in which the roles of teacher and student are reversed for a cinematic experiment. In this odd about-face set in an urban, elementary school, two eleven-year-old boys take on the task of teaching a dozen teachers who, almost unanimously and without prompting, adopt the attitudes and behaviours of unruly students. Virtually the only time the actual teachers may be said to be under the control of the youngsters is during a drama activity, for which the class is asked to "pretend you're something under the water." Only then do the adults do as they are told rather than arguing or causing problems. At the end of the film, one of the boys remarks to a filmmaker, "If I had a class like that I wouldn't teach for a million dollars. There should have been at least some people who were good."[45]

Paradoxically, it is the loose structure of educational drama that offers behavioural challenges for an actual teacher in the film *Mrs. Ryan's Drama Class* (1969). Again set at an urban, elementary school, the teacher in this Candid Eye production has a difficult time channeling the energies of a raucous group of boys and girls (caucasian and Asian) ranging in age from ten to twelve years old, who take part in her after-school drama course. "She's got to have discipline," one child suggests, as some boys commandeer gym equipment unrelated to their acting assignment and Mrs. Ryan appears powerless to stop them. While at the end of the first afternoon she seems deflated by the experience, by the end of the film Mrs. Ryan succeeds in gaining the useful participation of even the most troublesome child—most effectively in a play about a museum where statues come alive and kill the patrons.[46]

If NFB students of this era are filmed being attentive to the lessons being taught them, it is usually due to something extraordinary about the lesson or about the students themselves. In *Loops to Learn By* (1970) for example, groups of students cheerfully operate clattering 8mm film loop projectors, viewing simple operations over and over to "help to find meaning and pattern in apparent disorder." Language arts, mathematics, and physical education are three subject areas for which the continuous loops are said to be especially helpful. "The repetition breaks down the mystery of the subject to be learned," explains the narrator in praise of the machine, oblivious to the parallels to be drawn to formalist teaching practices in disfavour in NFB society since the mid-1940s.[47]

The schoolchildren filmed in a sex education film, *The Burden They Carry* (1970), are also highly attentive to the instruction they are given, at both the elementary and secondary level, but it appears to be the subject of the lesson which attracts their earnest interest: human sexuality. Even given this topic, however, some flippant interjections are heard from the adolescent group. ("What's the big deal? You do your own thing.") Yet their spontaneity also generates creative thought at a level unachieved since *The Gifted Ones* (1959), as when one boy earnestly suggests the development of "a type of gum chewed by girls that would turn red if no sex was allowed and turn green if it was."[48]

Aside from these circumstances, however, in these late years of the 1960s and the early years of the 1970s, it is only at an institutional school for the mentally handicapped, in the film *Danny and Nicky* (1969), that NFB children appear genuinely appreciative of their time in a school classroom. Only at this annex school are these institutionalized, mentally disabled children recognized as individuals. In contrast, individuality for most other NFB youngsters of this period appears to be a group phenomenon—a group "otherness" related to the intergenerational disequilibrium that is pervading NFB communities.

Danny and Nicky (1969). NFB, S-7974.

Rural-Urban Community Differences

Of late-1960s to early-1970s communities depicted by the NFB, conflicts between cultures of youth and adults are most evident in large urban areas and least evident in remote, rural areas. Of the latter, the smallest amount of generational change (and coincidentally the least intergenerational tension) occurs between the remote Newfoundland youth of Fogo Island and their elders. A part of the Challenge for Change program, the cinema-ethnographic *Children of Fogo Island* (1968) documents the young of this north coast island as they engage in pastimes that were clearly a part of the lives of Fogo Island children of generations before them, including labouring alongside adults—the youngest children shown haying with adults of the island and the older children shown helping in the processing (drying) of fish.

Clubhouse in *Children of Fogo Island* (1968). NFB, S-8005.

The film begins with an aerial view of the island community, followed by a shot of six boys (aged ten to twelve) heaving together to haul a heavy, wooden platform over the rocks of a cove. Throughout the film, the children's spoken English is so heavily accented that much of their dialogue is incomprehensible to west coast ears (although most Newfoundlanders would follow it easily). One eight-year-old boy strides among the rocks on extremely tall stilts. Two girls (aged eight and nine) handle a dory in the cove. Elderly women, as well, are filmed out and about in row boats. Numerous handmade toy boats appear in the water, including dugout sailboats, which the children tow behind their dinghies. All of the craft used by the children appear to be handmade— including a sailboat with a sackcloth sail on which several boys sail. Incongruously, a rough-hewn, plywood contraption is hauled across the water by some of the children, a mock float plane with a broad tail upon which is written "Expo 67." In the fields above the cove, eight more children mount their stilts against a barnside, then stride away. Meanwhile, back on the rocks of the cove, the wooden platform initially seen at the beginning of the film has been transformed into a clubhouse. One young boy plays an accordion at its door while first one, then another, begin to stepdance.[49]

In contrast, at a considerable distance culturally as well as geographically from Fogo Island, in the community of Westmount, Montreal, the skateboard becomes the symbol of change and youthful resistance to adult authority in Claude Jutra's *The Devil's Toy* (1969). Dedicated "to all victims of intolerance," the film documents early skateboarding on tapered plywood boards bolted to steel rollerskates. The appearance of the young skateboarders is equated with nuclear weapons: "needing only pavement to proliferate." Several shots follow of adolescents skateboarding down the street directly at the camera, an exhibition of early skateboards and riding techniques. Both boys and girls ride the skateboards, sometimes both on the same board, one piggybacking on the shoulders of the other. Some stunts look extremely dangerous. The police arrive and take the skateboards away under a city bylaw and return them later at a city arena, where they are of little use. "For the moment we are safe," remarks the narrator, "but beware, for the youth of the world are on the move and their aim is to take over."[50]

Wow (1969). NFB, S-7923.

As Doug Owram has observed, a distinguishing characteristic of the youth culture of Canada in the late 1960s and early 1970s was its recreational use of drugs—marijuana in particular. Marijuana use in NFB society is practically non-existent before 1969, even in the film *Flowers on a One-way Street* (1967), although Owram suggests it was used liberally during the actual events depicted by the film.[51] The drug is finally featured in *Wow* (1969), an indulgent film produced in Montreal, in which four adolescents "toke up," following the ritual prescribed by Jon Ruddy in 1966: "Deep drag, pass it on, suck in air, hold it in—hold it in!—then exhale."[52] To this sequence, the young people in the film add the expression "Wow!" prior to acting out adolescent "takeover" fantasies, including smoking "dope" in school, blowing up houses before a game of volleyball, and running naked down a street with a ribbon tied around the neck. "Most of all I want to shock people," says one teenager. "It's the adults' fault. I swear it is."[53]

In another seemingly drug-induced film narrative, childhood in the suburbs surrounding Toronto in the early 1970s becomes abstracted to the point of near incomprehensibility in the Queen's University production *One/Two/Many/World* (1970), a film project adopted and distributed by the National Film Board. The film begins with a thirteen-year-old girl, dressed in colourful flowing garb, flying a kite on a beach while being watched by an eight-year-old boy. Within a brief span of psychedelic time, the eight-year-old is also observed in pyjamas playing with metallic toys, dressed in a tuxedo and being driven to an expensive home in a chauffered limousine, back on the beach watching the girl draw landscapes, dressed in a policeman's uniform directing traffic, dressed in scholastic apparel spelling "improbable" on chart paper, and so on, until at last a battle of little boys takes place on the beach with many dramatic deaths. After the conflict, the boy and girl run along the sand with a colourful caterpillar in tow, leaving the mise en scène to an adult male in a bowler hat who emerges out of the lake and walks deadpan toward the camera.[54] Possibly, the film was meant to symbolize the metamorphosis of children into adults, boys into patriarchs; or perhaps the film was merely intended to be psychedelic. Whatever; *One/Two/Many/World* exalts the freedom and imagination of male childhood, while expressing a loathing for the constraints of inevitable male adulthood.

Produced by film students who themselves were part of the new generation, the film supports Christopher Lasch's contention in his 1978 book, *The Culture of Narcissism: American Life in an Age of Diminishing Expectations* that, for the new generation, "the fear of growing up and aging haunts our society."[55] To Lasch, the traditional child was dependent and repressed at home but became freed by adulthood, whereas the child reared under the mental hygiene regime was freed in childhood but looked forward only to the bondage and repression (and invisibility) of adulthood.[56] The paradigm is useful to the study of two distinct contingents of NFB young people rebelling against the conditions of adulthood in the films of the early 1970s—a rational contingent of boys and girls who engage adult society over topical issues such as ecology, and an irrational contingent who engage in seemingly wanton destructiveness.[57] Typical of the rational contingent are the mix of children aged eight to ten years in *A Time to Consider—Ecology* (1972).

In the film, pastoral scenes of young children and nature are juxtaposed against scenes of industrial pollution, clear-cut logging, and other ecological ravages. Included in a wide-ranging discussion among the children are environmental issues concerning oil tankers, animal slaughter, phosphates in detergents, and recycling depots for telephone books. One young boy with shoulder-length hair suggests that filters be put on smokestacks; an eight-year-old girl suggests that new products be banned; a third child suggests that hunting seasons should be controlled, while others suggest that governments should "make sure things don't get too big," or that they should "shut down everything when pollution levels get too high." Rather than agree with or challenge their suggestions, the narrator poses an adult question: "The question for us is what heritage will we leave our children?"[58]

Within the irrational contingent of NFB youngsters, on the other hand, a second dichotomy develops: those who use drugs to escape a lack of direction in their lives, as in the films *Almost Everyone Does* (1970) and *Brian at 17* (1973), and those who direct their hostility against adult society through violence or vandalism, such as the thirteen-year-old in *Paper Boy* (1971), in whose hands a rolled newspaper is a dangerous projectile. Both types of young people gather for the production *Summer Centre* (1973) which, according to its NFB catalogue synopsis, "re-enacts the anarchy that occurred at a summer recreation centre in Richmond, British Columbia."[59]

In the film, a new boy in a subsidized housing project attends a poorly run summer drop-in centre for teenagers. Intended to keep teenagers out of trouble, the place becomes a hub of activity for those wishing to create trouble, as evidenced by a chalk notice board outside the old church housing the centre, upon which is written "10:00 pm— Gang Bang on Linda Thorpe." After a concert at the centre, during which many of the teens smoke marijuana, the activities of the youngsters become more and more outrageous—from fist fights to pear fights on private property, to a situation that has the potential of becoming the gang rape promised on the church agenda. Too late, the operators of the centre, themselves only in their early-twenties, take action, realizing that the "soft-pedalling" attitude they have taken with the teenagers has hurt the program. At the conclusion of the film, a core of troublemakers threaten to burn down the church after the operators threaten to close the summer centre, but the night passes without incident.[60]

The threat against the church in *Summer Centre* brings to mind J. Donald Wilson's recollection of the concerns of Canadian adults in the early 1970s over, among other things, the kinds of teenage behaviour depicted by the film: "The wisecrack, "Is nothing sacred?" was no longer funny; it had become a serious question."[61] By the mid-1970s, a full 62 percent of Canadians in a Gallup Poll expressed a belief that, in society as a whole, there had been a "general breakdown in respect for authority, law and order,"[62] and yet as late as 1974, strong arguments were still being publicly advanced in favour of creating a culture of childhood still more independent from adult authority. In his *Birthrights* (1974), Richard Farson extolled the idea:

> In the developing consciousness of a civilization which has for four hundred years gradually excluded children from the world of adults there is the dawning recognition that children must have the right to full participation in society....We have replaced ignorant domination of children with sophisticated domination. Even the most permissive approaches [to child rearing] seem embarrassingly authoritarian....There is no way to be a good parent in a society organized against children. There is no way to have a liberated society until we have liberated children.[63]

But the liberation of children from family control had ceased to be a direct theme of Film Board productions since the early 1960s. Instead, in the mid-1970s, particularly after the formation of Studio D, themes of liberation develop for "the family" itself.

I'll Find a Way (1977): Planting a New Equilibrium in NFB Families

Families were the initial sites of disequilibrium (contested power relations) in NFB society during the mid-1950s; likewise, families become the first sites of a new equilibrium introduced into NFB society during the mid-1970s, a result of cinematic leadership by Studio D. But while the women's studio restored the concept of equilibrium within families,

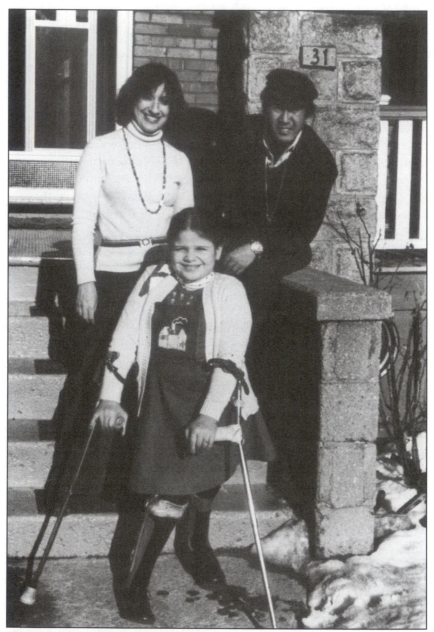

I'll Find a Way (1977). NFB, S-16204.

the families themselves differ distinctly from those depicted in the late 1940s and early 1950s, both structurally and in their functioning.

Studio D productions of this period reinvolve parents in the family picture, while continuing to advance the child's narrative voice (seemingly unscripted) to the fore. Often, these are portraits of children of immigrant families or portraits of children with disabilities to overcome, which they manage to do through family support. The most acclaimed of these is the documentary *I'll Find a Way* (1977), about Nadia de Franco, a nine-year-old girl with spina bifida.[64] De Franco's Italian Canadian family is depicted throughout the film as having harmonious, happy, and mutually supportive family relations—their "supporting" role elevated by their love of their disabled daughter.[65]

I'll Find a Way is one of a series of documentaries produced by Studio D under the multicultural program of the NFB. The origins of the 1971 federal government policy of multiculturalism (and reactions to it) were diverse and are better discussed elsewhere,[66] but, suffice it to say, the National Film Board, seeking a raison d'être for the seventies, was delighted to find itself with a newly assigned role as one of the policy's major purveyors, as was Studio D similarly pleased to have an amply funded venue for a production series portraying contemporary, Canadian social relations.[67] The Studio D series includes *Gurdeep Singh Bains* (1976), a film in which the strength of Sikh family life is attributed to its embrace of the Sikh religion, and the character of Sikh children attributed to Sikh traditions of child rearing. The film downplays the patriarchal structure of Sikh society by cleverly weaving a feminist perspective throughout the narrative, especially through Gurdeep's grandmother, who is depicted as the chief protector of Sikh religious values in the family.[68]

A third, Studio D production in the series is *Beautiful Lennard Island* (1977), a film that portrays the eleven-year-old son of lighthouse keepers of English Canadian ancestry. The boy, Stephen Thomas-Holland, his older brother, and their parents, live on a small island off the west coast of Vancouver Island and embody feminist ideals of a functioning "democratic" family unit. The family members appear to share equally in both the work of the lighthouse and the work of the household with little observable functional differentiation. A clue to the arrangement of power relations within the family comes from Stephen's comment: "Here, the byword is teamwork when there's work to be done, otherwise people are free."[69]

Among alternate visions of power relations within the NFB family, a Challenge for Change film, *Cree Hunters of the Mistassini* (1974), documents three Cree families of northern Québec who leave their settlement in the fall and fly by float plane into the wilds to live on whatever they can catch. For the Cree families, harmony among family members appears to develop from their universal acceptance of traditional differentiation of roles. In the process, the families become advocates for a traditional lifestyle with such overwhelming success that, according to Evans in *In the National Interest*, "the day after [the film's] local exhibition, the men of the town left en masse for the bush to regain contact with a way of life they felt was fast slipping away."[70]

Beautiful Lennard Island (1977). NFB, S-16077.

In the film, the three families live together in a lodge constructed by the men from logs cut by the women (who also buck firewood with their chainsaws). Teenaged daughters haul moss to fill in the chinks and insulate the lodge. The smaller children learn to work by watching their parents and then by helping them. The three families coexist happily together, even in the confined space of the lodge. In the evening, they dine on a bear that one of the men has shot. Afterwards, a father amuses his youngest children while other children play "cat's cradle" in the dark. One teenaged daughter plucks feathers from fowl shot by a father. "What does a mother teach her daughter?" asks someone from behind the camera. "Everything," is the reply from a mother. During the day, a father teaches his son how to hunt beaver. His wife skins the beaver, while the teenaged daughters apprentice at the craft by skinning rabbits. Very young children play in the snow and watch fish pulled out of the fishing nets. The men drum in the evening in the lodge, and everyone—fathers, mothers, and children—seems very happy operating within a traditional organization of social relations.[71]

Cree Hunters of the Mistassini (1974). NFB, S-13097.

How very different is the family felicity in another Challenge for Change film, *Would I Ever Like to Work* (1974), one of a series of six NFB films about working mothers. The film advocates the end to what Eichler in *Families in Canada Today* has described as "a structural disadvantage for women," i.e., a lack of publicly funded daycare. The single mother in the film is on welfare, unable to work because she is unable to afford daycare. She swats a kid as she talks on the film. Her children eat beans and french-fried potatoes. She needs daycare to "get away from these monsters....It's always mommy this and mommy that." She was sixteen when she married and fifteen when she first became pregnant. One of her children has very blotchy face sores. Children are a real burden to her life, she claims. She appears extremely bitter.[72]

Approved daycare centres (nursery centres), absent in NFB society since *What's on Your Mind?* (1946), become an alternative to modern, family child-rearing practices for NFB families of the mid- to late 1970s.[73] *Day Care—The Newest Tradition* (1978) begins with a sepia-tone photograph of a mother and child that fades to the motion of an urban street. "The city is no place for kids," remarks an anonymous male passing by. "The family is no longer as strong as it was," contends the female narrator. "Let us start working toward a new vision of the family....Society has abdicated its traditional role toward children....The role of the day-care is to do all the work normally done by the family....It's up to you and parents like you to tell your politicians that you need more day-care."[74] The woman from the sepia photograph is the narrator. She and her son, and others who have "split families," are seen to be in need of daycare but are shown to be blocked by waiting lists or financial want.

The advantages offered by daycares for families are persuasively detailed but few, if any, disadvantages are.[75] In place of any social counterarguments to daycare, family resistance to child care outside of the home is presented as the obstacle to be overcome. The narrator's "Grampa" wants to keep her son at home when she goes to work, "to watch the plumber." The mother feels terrible, "not like a good parent." But "daycare prepares the child for what the world really is..." (shots of happy children on a field trip to a bakery) and, in the film's happy resolution, Grampa becomes a volunteer at the day-care centre—thereby joining the cause and fulfilling a purposeful, useful, and traditional role in a contemporary, "nursery school" setting.

NFB Schools Midway through the Baby Boom Generation

Given the rise in public discontent concerning Canadian schools during the mid- to late 1970s, it is interesting to observe the actual graduates of a rural high school filmed in 1974 at Penticton, British Columbia.[76] In the opening reel of *Pen-Hi Grad* (1975), forty teenagers are standing or sitting on a hillside, drinking beer, hooting and hollering. Most wear jeans and T-shirts; some wear jeans and hockey sweaters. One long-haired adolescent leaps over another, gyrating his hips wildy at the camera. Others spray bottled beer at each other. A teenaged girl wearing a cap with Mickey Mouse ears and carrying a bottle of beer calls out to the filmmaker, "It feels really good to be graduating because I hate school." A resounding cheer from the others follows her remark. From behind her, a long-haired boy wearing a jean jacket says, "It feels like I'm mating." Another, sporting an afro hairstyle and likewise carrying a stubby bottle of beer shouts out in a slurred voice, "Graduating is like a piece of cake. You always want more. I'm coming back next year, man." Beside him, another graduate finally gains the attention of the crowd and the camera: "Twelve years of nothing. If you didn't put anything into it you won't get nothing out of it." "Yeah, man," agrees the student with the afro, after pausing to consider the remark.[77]

In other NFB public high schools of the same era, the state of disequilibrium heightens between students and their teachers. Schooled for sociability at the elementary level, high school students appear less amenable to academic instruction than ever in the past, and more capable of exerting cohesive group pressure to thwart it. Illustrative of their social power is the depiction of grade nine students with a "teacher-on-call" in the film *Happiness Is Loving Your Teacher* (1977), a film which illustrates the hidden warmth of personality beneath the exterior of even the most obnoxious adolescent once separated from "the gang." In the film, a young male teacher wearing a green, knitted-wool sweater and who is also wheelchair-bound arrives in a suburban classroom. There, the students are milling about or sitting on desktops talking loudly. As he wheels into the room, the teacher says, "Sit down, please," and he coughs to clear his throat.

"Who are you?" a student's voice is heard from the din.

"Sit down...I'm your substitute teacher...Can I have quiet please?...Could you close the door for me?"

The students move slowly into their desks. One bangs the lid of his desktop. Another throws a paper dart.

"I'm Mr. Todrick. I'm replacing Mr. Coglin for a couple of days."

"Oooohhh...yay!!" There is a lot of chatter and laughter.

"We're going to study grammar today."

This announcement is followed by loud groans, laughter, and catcalls: "Why don't *you* study it?....Good point....Good shot...We're here to learn not to make fools of ourselves...etc."

"Now...now do you think this is a joke?" asks Mr. Todrick.

"Yep!" a student's voice can be heard from the din.[78]

Not all public schooling in late-1970s NFB society is depicted as being so ineffective and unappreciated by students as in the above examples. But where NFB public school programs are depicted positively, they often portray alternative educational programs, especially innovative programs being offered to students formerly institutionalized in NFB society: i.e., native Indian students and mentally handicapped students.[79]

The film *Wandering Spirit Survival School* (1978), for example, extols the benefits of "a new school for Indian children," where "self-determination for Indian education" is the goal. At the urban Toronto school, the day begins with an elder burning sweetgrass and leading prayers for those in prison and having alcohol problems. In addition to providing the basic skills required under the education act of Ontario, the school offers a native Indian curriculum, which the children are said to appreciate. One leader wears an American Indian Movement (AIM) button on his cowboy hat. He tells the story of Nanabush and the birch tree to a group of highly attentive children aged nine to eleven. The children report having had social problems in regular schools: "They were yukky." An eleven-year-old girl says, "I like learning the Indian stuff. I like the powwows."[80]

Wandering Spirit Survival School (1978). NFB, S-16819.

Likewise finding their curriculum valuable are the mentally handicapped children of a special class at Kane Public School in Toronto. In *Let's Get a Move On* (1978), these children, aged twelve to sixteen, are filmed training to ride on the Toronto public transit system (TTC). At the outset of the film, they are recalling "phrases-of-use" on the TTC, using the "Language Master" (audio-tape cards) for phrase identification. Arriving at a subway station by bus, they receive their "destination cards." Their objective is to take a train to a designated station with a buddy, acquire a transfer, and return to the original station. They carry a quarter with them in case they become lost. Back at school, they share their experiences and solve problems they encountered as a group. "This school is worthwhile," says one boy. The stated goal of their teacher, a young woman who wears a jean jacket and jean pants, is to get the children to blend into the community and be able to travel on their own: "Teaching the kids to cope in this tough, competitive world."[81]

For "regular" NFB schoolchildren of the late 1970s, a practical training for the tough competitive world outside of the public schools is available outside of the public school system through cadet training, or so it is advertised in the film *Challenging the Future* (1977), co-sponsored by the Department of National Defence and Cadets Canada. Especially innovative over past NFB films about cadets is the emphasis placed on recruiting girls to the organization. Girl cadets are filmed in charge of platoons and shown building "bailey bridges," parading with all-girl units, and working together with boys—literally, head to head. "It [Cadets] is increasingly popular among teen girls," remarks the narrator. A visiting British cadet points out that there are no girl cadets in Britain whereas, "Here they furnish them." As with prior recruitment films, weapons training and driving lessons are featured, but so are trips to museums "to broaden cultural horizons," as well as exchange visits between francophone and anglophone camps. Citizenship and leadership are said to be the twin goals of cadet training, but the predominant sales pitch is, "worthwhile things are to be learned here."[82]

Teach Me to Dance (1978): Patriarchy in Trouble

Meanwhile, in the portrayals of NFB communities, previously unheard voices surface to challenge prior visions of the past and future. Not surprisingly, where children are concerned, these voices emerge from the most historically silenced of NFB children: NFB girls. Representative of the revisionist histories suddenly evident in the NFB archival collection is Anne Wheeler's, Studio D film, *Teach Me to Dance* (1978). This narrative takes place in rural Alberta in 1919 and involves two girls, one British and the other Ukrainian, both eleven years old. After school (a two-room building with a Union Jack flying over it), the British girl visits at the home of the Ukrainian family, where she is given a bowl of borscht and a gift. Later, to a tune played on a balalaika, her friend dances a mazourka as the British girl bounces joyfully on the knee of her friend's Ukrainian father. Together, the girls decide that this dance would be perfect for the two to perform at the Christmas concert at the school.

For the concert program, however, both the girls are compelled to learn the poem "Children of the Empire" ("From little isles they came, to spread..."), and one is reprimanded by the woman teacher for speaking Ukrainian at school to other Ukrainian children. Equally unsettling for the two, when the father of the British girl discovers that she is being taught to dance the mazourka by the Ukrainian family, she is barred from visiting the Ukrainian homestead. Neither girl can comprehend the logic of one culture dominating another, particularly when the repressed culture seems much more fun than the other. Hence, the British girl decides to override her father's orders and learn the mazourka, which she and her Ukrainian friend agree to present as a surprise at the concert.

Teach Me to Dance (1978). NFB, S-16718.

In *Teach Me to Dance*, white, Anglo-Saxon boys play the parts of racist bullies who enforce the "English-only" rule at school. The female teacher is portrayed as being uncertain of the justness of the rule, but she is also depicted as a lackey of the British fathers, whose racism seems bent upon making the Ukrainians servile. The crisis, of course, comes at the Christmas concert when the girls attempt to dance the mazourka after the choral reading of the poem. The outcome is a brawl among the men and boys of both cultures but, for the two girls, the result is cathartic. Despite being forcibly separated, they appear filled with resolve to continue to work together to right the injustice of cultural inequity.[83]

Achieving cultural and political equity within Canadian society is likewise the theme of *Nunatsiaq—The Good Land* (1977), produced by the Inuit Tapirisat organization. In matters of voice, the film is the reciprocal of films of the 1940s and 1950s. A female Inuit child narrates over a compilation of images that include landscapes, archival photographs, and a modern Inuit settlement, but primarily speaks over images of Inuit adults. "This is our land," she begins. "We the Inuit were here before Columbus, before Cartier, before Martin Frobisher, before the Vikings....The land is my heart and soul. It will be the land of my children and their children." She protests that the penetration of Euro-Canadian society came too quickly for the Inuit to comprehend what was happening. "No one ever consulted us...maybe if we knew then what we know now, we wouldn't have given such a friendly welcome to the explorers, the sailors from the whaling ships, the traders, the mounties, and the schoolteachers."[84]

Her narrative expresses bewilderment as to how the Inuit became acculturated but, on behalf of her people, she resolves never to "lose ourselves in your culture, to become second class citizens in your society and never find our own identity again." She takes charge of that identity by switching back and forth in her usage of singular and collective, first-person pronouns. "I want to make my contribution to Canadian society, but I want to be an equal partner, not a colonial subject. I must perserve my way of life or I'm nothing."

> The white man has brought clocks and calendars to our land and perhaps we should be thankful because we can see now that time is running out. We must find ways to govern ourselves, so that we can be allowed to determine our own social, economic, and political destinies...or we will be lost for all time as a very special group of people within the country.[85]

Once unable to speak even for themselves, the voices of children (most notably girls) by the late 1970s speak on behalf of entire cultural communities. Children's voices are clearly considered to carry substantial weight with audiences, since immigrant and indigenous cultures use them during this era to advance their own voice and to create favourable shifts in their own power relations with the dominant "other" in Canadian society. At their point of liberation, however, in NFB families of the early 1980s, morbid symptoms are now beginning to appear within the culture of fatherhood.

Feeling Yes, Feeling No (1980): Men in Trouble

Neil Postman, in his *The Disappearance of Childhood* (1982), argued that ever since the advent of television in the 1950s, the differences between adults and children had been steadily disappearing.[86] According to Postman, "in the television era, there are but three stages of life: infancy, the adult-child, and senility."[87] Based upon his observations of the medium, Postman concluded that children on contemporary television shows did not differ significantly in their interests, language, dress, or sexuality from adults on the same shows.[88] He considered this to be a significant change from images of the pre-television era: "Is it imagineable except as parody that Shirley Temple would sing 'On the Good Ship Lollipop?' Her language would consist of a string of knowing wisecracks, including a display of sexual innuendo."[89]

Postman theorized (using a mirror analogy) that television was both creating, and was affected by, "the disappearance of childhood"; i.e., it both determined and reflected the social realities of post-1950's childhood. In regard to childhood sexuality, the steady "disappearance of childhood" from 1950 to 1979 (as Postman saw it) coincided with a trend to give children a sexual image on television and, likewise, with a significant rise in reported cases of sexual abuse of children.[90] While Postman's hypothesis is speculative, it is interesting that in NFB families, where power relations between children and adults had been similarly in flux over the very same period, the sexual abuse of children by family members now surfaces as a major social issue as well.

The first film distributed by the NFB to deal with the sexual abuse of children, *Sexual Abuse of Children: A Time for Caring* (1979), was independently produced in California and established concepts which later became conventional in NFB productions on the subject. In its soundtrack, the film establishes that "most of the victims are female; most of the perpetrators are male," and, through its images, it also establishes that most of the perpetrators are fathers. The American film also identified the chief psychological consequence to a victim of abuse: "If someone else wasn't responsible, then it must have been me."[91] As with the Californian film, which begins with a father warning his daughter about strangers when he, in fact, is the danger, the first Canadian production, *Child Sexual Abuse: The Untold Secret* (1982), opens with a father compelling his daughter to stay home with him while the mother goes shopping.

The dramatic scenario which unfolds in the University of Calgary production affords five Alberta girls (aged thirteen to sixteen) the opportunity to tell their personal stories (dramatized on film) about sexual abuse by their fathers in their homes.[92] One of the girls recalls having told the family's priest about the problem, "but he didn't believe it could happen." Another reports not realizing that her relationship with her father was unusual until she saw a television commercial about the abuse of children. The five girls advise other children to "tell somebody; it'll help a lot." "Children rarely lie about sexual abuse," remarks an expert at the conclusion of the film.[93]

In the same year, the NFB produced *No More Secrets* (1982), a film in which the list of family perpetrators of sexual abuse grew to include brothers and uncles. In the production, two girls and two boys (all aged ten years) meet in a clubhouse, where one girl sneaks a diary from the other and learns that the diarist's brother watches her when she showers. The other children advise the girl to tell her brother to stop—a strategy that successfully brings about a resolution to the problem in an animated segment that follows. One secret now out, two of the other members of the club likewise reveal abusive situations in their families. A boy complains about his uncle, who wrestles with the boy in order to touch "his privates" (the first reference to molestation of boys by family members); again the advice is "tell him to stop." The other girl discloses that her father puts his hands under her covers at night; for her, the advice is to tell another adult. In every case, the children assure each other that "It's not your fault."[94]

Feeling Yes, Feeling No (1984). NFB, S-18469.

Among NFB productions of this period dealing with family sexual abuse, the *Feeling Yes, Feeling No* (1984) series was most widely distributed. The films helped children define sexual abuse (unwanted looking at or touching of parts covered by bathing suits), advocated full trust of their point of view, identified men as potential offenders (expanded now to include both male family members and family friends, as well as strangers), and offered children a means of preventing abusive situations by shouting "No!" and by reporting offenders.[95]

A significant consequence of the sexual abuse series of films was that NFB fathers now bore a stigma once reserved for NFB mothers, as the chief potential danger to the mental health of their children—another of several social turnabouts since the 1940s. Fathers were prime offenders as well in NFB films that, for the first time, dealt with alcohol and drug abuse within families. (According to CIPO-Gallup, alcohol consumption had been rising steadily in Canada since the war.[96]) "My dad can't figure out why I don't hang out around him anymore," remarks a ten-year-old girl in *Children of Alcohol* (1984). The reasons become painfully clear as the children disclose the horrors of living in homes where there are alcohol problems. "It makes me want to stop and not go on any farther," says a twelve-year-old boy. "At Christmas, fight, fight, fight—booze wrecks everything." But, from the same child, a thread of hope for the future: "I believe my dad when he says he'd like to quit."[97]

In the same vein, countering beliefs of negative psychological effects of separation and divorce upon children, especially from an alcoholic situation, is the Studio D production *It's Just Better* (1982). The film supports Eichler's contention that "there is now increasing evidence that divorce may not be half as significant for children as had been thought."[98] It portrays a family of eleven, a mother and her ten children, who cooperatively maintain a Cape Breton farm without the support of the father, an alcoholic who abandoned the family. A team effort, a non-gendered collaboration ranging from woodcutting to haircutting, keeps the family functioning. In one scene, the mother and a daughter are observed successfully repairing a truck engine. "The children's pockets are usually empty," remarks the mother, "but their lives are exceptionally well filled." "We make things instead of buying them," explains her twelve-year-old son, who expresses hope that his father will return someday, rid of his alcohol dependence.[99]

Overwhelmingly, early 1980s NFB families are distinguished by their plight (most often with fathers at fault), but films of this period are equally remarkable for their expanding definition of what constitutes a family. A variety of family forms begin to appear in the cinematic society, ever widening in scope as the decade progresses. Few, however, ever achieve the singularity of structure portrayed in the NFB documentary *The Followers* (1981), a film about the Hare Krishna organization in Canada.[100]

At the start of the film, robed Hare Krishnas are filmed out on the streets of Montreal, followed about by laughing, unsupervised, city children. Later, some Krishna girls (aged four to seven), wearing long, western-style, print dresses are seen inside a temple with their mothers. Krishna parents, for the most part, appear to be white men and women in their early twenties—the last wave of the new generation. One father in the documentary, a young Krishna devotee, daily dons a wig and a suit and tie to sell Krishna products door-to-door. His child, a boy of three, is shown at his apartment in Montreal in Krishna garb—a pony-tail haircut, white painted nose bridge, and a new Krishna shirt. The boy's mother is filmed cooking and sewing for the family group and playing with the child. Children in Krishna society appear to be cared for primarily by the women. The family structure as portrayed in the film is highly patriarchal. Renunciation allows a husband to escape his family responsibilities to seek higher spiritual enlightenment if he wishes—but no such escape from her husband and children is available for a wife. During their dance ceremonies, men dance separately from the women and children.[101] Despite outward appearances and claims of harmony, an epilogue to the production discloses that some of the young women initiates seen in the documentary quit the temple shortly after the film was completed.[102]

At the other end of the familial structural continuum, only one NFB family from this period bears a strong resemblance to families from the distant past in NFB society—the family in the Studio D slice-of-life of rural Newfoundlanders, *Julie O'Brien* (1981). "In her province the past is not forgotten," reads the catalogue account of this film by Beverley Schaffer. More accurately, the past appears to be incorporated into daily life, material and otherwise, in the rural community of Tors Cove where the film was produced. Julie O'Brien, a twelve-year-old girl, wears an assortment of fashions during the course of the documentary, ranging from nearly contemporary bell-bottom jeans to a blue, wool bonnet more typical of NFB children from the late 1950s. As with her wardrobe, Julie's attitudes and opinions on family and community life recall popular sentiments of earlier periods.

"Being the oldest, you have to have lots of responsibility," she says in a lyrical accent much more comprehensible to west coast ears than previous portrayals of rural Newfoundland children. Among her responsibilities as documented on film, she stokes a wood-fueled, Moffat kitchen stove in the morning to cook breakfast for her two sisters, helps her mother with the family washing by pulling the clothes through a wringer-washer and hanging them up to dry, helps to bring wood home on a horse-drawn sled with her father, and cleans the toilet with Comet cleanser. On the weekend, she attends a community dance for young teens, where two girls are filmed doing "the bump," and where boys and girls do "close waltzing." The "usual age to get interested in boys is around twelve or thirteen," she reports.[103]

During a sermon at a Sunday church service, with the family in attendance and Julie dressed in a plain blue jumper, a Catholic priest warns his congregation to prepare for change. He offers the metaphor of a pebble cast into a wide puddle to allude to changes coming from afar. But Sunday evening at the O'Brien house, instead of gathering to prepare for apocalyptic waves, Julie's extended family gathers for a spirited game of cards, followed by step-dancing by her "pappy" (grandfather), and a family singsong led by her "nanny" (grandmother) and her "nana" (great-grandmother), who is ninety years old. Where "the past is not forgotten," the film, *Julie O'Brien*, seems to suggest, the changing present is of minor concern. It is an odd sentiment in NFB society of the late 1970s, where the past is rarely remembered—even at NFB schools in which, at a considerable distance from Tors Cove, an extraordinary change is now beginning to take place.

Julie O'Brien (1981). NFB, S-18021.

This Is Me (1979): Rising Relativism in NFB Schools

One of the most striking features of NFB portrayals of children at school during this period is the absence of classroom teachers. When children appear within school contexts, they often appear by themselves, becoming de facto teachers to the viewing audience. An example of the innovation is in the NFB production *This Is Me* (1979), a film intended to promote creative expression in art and social discourse at the upper-intermediate elementary school level. In the film (which is introduced by an animated panoptic eye), several Montreal schoolchildren (aged eleven to thirteen) are occupied in an art room without a teacher, where they produce a variety of work in mixed-media—primarily oil paintings on glass and large, cut-paper collages. Dubbed over and intercut with filmed segments of the children pottering about with art materials are sequences where they interpose, apparently spontaneously, stream-of-consciousness thoughts for the cameras on ethereal subjects as diverse as clouds, God, life, dreams, and the soul.

Student 1:	Our life is the same as electricity. It's like a great big spirit that comes right into us. My body becomes its slave.
Student 2:	My soul is like my twin brother or sister inside of me. It's something inside me that tells me what to do. It's a person in my skull looking about for ideas.
Student 3:	Dreams come from the inside and go out. When you feel tired, it's your soul that is tired of being locked in. Your soul takes off and comes back in the morning.[104]

Social relations among adolescents frequently become a subject for examination under similar conditions in NFB schools during this period. In recording six teenaged boys at a school cafeteria, for example, the Vancouver region produced *Being Male* (1980), a film that focuses on the formation of concepts of adolescent masculinity.[105] The group's first revelation: big boys do cry. One student discloses how he cries when leaving friends; the others are empathetic. Concerning what it means to become "a man," they accept a definition advanced by a member of their group that it has to do with the development of stamina. On learning to be "male," they are in near agreement: "You soak it up from all over." The discussion reveals that, as a group, they believe in the power of peer pressure to shape the outcomes of masculinity. A boy is drawn into "male stupidity" because of friends: "fighting even when you know you don't want to fight," getting into a car with a reckless driver, "smoking pot and being stoned in school," "there's no way to get out of

it if you don't want to lose all your friends and be a loner....You overcome what you have to do because you don't want to be bugged all the
time." One member concludes, "there should be no [male] image at all,
but things aren't like that."[106]

Girls Fitting In (1980). NFB.

A parallel discussion ensues among adolescent females in *Girls Fitting
In* (1980). Unlike the boys in *Being Male*, the girls smoke cigarettes as
they talk. Says one of her habit, "smoking shows that you're not goody
two-shoes." Projecting a self-image is a common theme in their discussion ("You're always worried when you leave home about your appearance....I was trying to make an impression..."), but "you don't show that
you're good at something," especially since "people get down on smart
girls." One girl generalizes that to advance her image, a girl must
"knock down someone else to build up yourself." Relationships with
boys are central to their discussion about images, especially the social
inequities they perceive in these. Says one, "It's extremely acceptable to

have a boyfriend...it shows you are capable of loving, but not acceptable to have a few—unlike boys—or you have a reputation." Another provides insight into the source of reputations; ie., "a bad reputation exists more among girls than the guys," although a third girl refutes this, saying, "I think that women's liberation has come too far to let that happen." Gradually their talk turns to problems of achieving "women's liberation" ("I feel pressure not to be equal or better than boys...they get turned off when you're better than them,") and at last to graduation: "We'll say we'll keep in touch with each other, but we never will."[107]

When they do appear on film, teachers are often depicted as material handlers and facilitators of group discussions who validate statements made or opinions held by students on a subject, rather than acting as authorities on the subject itself. Hence, relativism, especially in NFB elementary classrooms of the period, is elevated to a new level of appreciation.[108] In *Gifted Kids* (1984), the pedagogical practice is demonstrated by a teacher who generates an open-ended topic for discussion among a group of ten- to twelve-year-old "gifted children." The discussion that ensues is interesting to compare with the conversation that takes place in an earlier film about intellectually gifted children, *The Gifted Ones* (1959). In the 1984 production, the teacher is distinctly younger and less confident than the teacher in the earlier film. More telling of the program itself, while the gifted children in the 1959 film have their own classroom, the students in the 1984 production are taken from their regular classrooms to participate in a pull-out program. Hence, the setting is much more informal in the latter production. The 1984 "gifted kids" sit in a circle on a carpeted floor in a sparsely decorated classroom, as does their teacher. There are four boys and two girls in the group.

Teacher:	I thought we'd spend some time right now and talk about the future. I know that several of you have really unique ideas, and they're different from what I've heard expressed perhaps in the past. So, Kevin, you're sort of our most unique thinker about the future. Can you give us an overall view?
Kevin:	Well...I think the future is going to be in quite a chaos because at the rate we're going now the population of the world will be terrible and people will be practically living on top of each other...
Teacher:	[Dubbed over image of Kevin talking] These students are our future problem solvers, and I think it's really important that they get a chance in their school career to work

> on solving problems and making decisions and planning real things.

Corrine: [Picking up from what Kevin has been saying] I don't think cloning is very necessary. Well, you'd sort of said something about genetic research and they're already doing the first clones and that, and I think it's stupid because there are lots of children that their parents abandoned them, and they're left without parents and other people are trying to clone themselves and make million little me's.

Kevin: If you clone someone like Albert Einstein, then when the original died the clone could go on, and he would be an exact duplicate of the first guy, well pretty well the same, so he would go on, and he would make his contributions and we'd clone him, and when that clone died, then they'd go on, and you would have your continual resource of scientists and maybe they could help solve some of the problems.[109]

It is surprising, given the advancements made in NFB society in the education of "regular" and mentally handicapped NFB children, how very little improvement can be discerned in the education of gifted children since the late 1950s. And yet this, according to the narrator of the film, was one of the few districts in North America at the time (Coquitlam, British Columbia) to provide a specialized program for gifted children. In NFB schools since the early 1960s, just as the mental hygienists had advocated for American public schools from the 1920s onward, socialization appears to have surpassed intellectual development as an educational goal. And as the socialization of NFB children is primarily shaped by their peers (as suggested by the films *Being Male* and *Girls Fitting In*), the authority of adults as educators is supplanted by children. Thus, teachers virtually disappear, and, as Postman observed of North American education in his *The Disappearance of Childhood*, "we are left with children who rely not on authoritative adults but on news from nowhere."[110]

Starbreaker (1984): Revitalizing the Wizard's Planet

Technology and community become the entwined leitmotif of film productions of the early 1980s involving children. In *Ida Makes a Movie* (1979), the eight-year-old daughter of a single mother wins first prize at a film festival when her roughly constructed 8mm home movie about

Starbreaker (1984). NFB, S-18408.

littering is misinterpreted by a panel of judges as a brilliant anti-war statement. In *This Is Only a Test* (1984) a shy sixteen-year-old Edmontonian girl wearing a bandana that reads "work tirelessly for peace" leads a three hundred kilometre march from Cold Lake, Alberta, to Edmonton to protest cruise missile testing. And in *Starbreaker* (1984), produced by veteran NFB filmmaker Colin Low, a thirteen-year-old girl and her twin brother crash land their bubble-shaped spaceships onto a desolate world, where the heroine rescues her brother and teaches an ancient, male wizard how to bring his sterile planet back to life through the power of music. Common to each of these, in addition to their technological references, are the strong social and intellectual leadership roles now taken on by girls and (where they are included) the weak supporting roles assigned to boys—a complete reversal of films from the 1940s through 1960s. This is particularly true of *Starbreaker*, which is narrated by the girl and in which the highlights of the part played by the boy are 1) his rescue from a trance by his sister and 2) his operation of a cassette tape player when instructed by the girl to switch it on. The successful outcome of the girl's plan to save her brother and revitalize the wizard's planet depends on an acceptance of her leadership by the others (i.e., an equilibrium established under her direction) which they follow without resistance. In the wake of the children's departure from the wizard's world, great crystals break through the desolate surface of the planet and a city grows—born of feminist hegemony and rock and roll.[111]

Despite the optimism expressed by *Starbreaker* for the future of gender relations in society, equilibrium remains a scarce commodity in most NFB families of the mid- to late 1980s. The common occurrence of parental separation and divorce in Canadian society by the middle of the decade finds reflection in films such as *The Umpire* (1985), which portrays the agony of a suburban mother attempting to explain to her sons that their father has deserted her.[112] In the film, two young boys wait for their dad to arrive home to umpire their baseball game. "Maybe dad got hit by a sniper," says the older boy. His mother replies, "Philip, sometimes people who love each other don't get along too well." The mother, her sons, and a multicultural mix of children set up to play baseball on an old baseball diamond, with the elder boy taking on his father's usual role of umpire. The mother smiles benignly at the end of the game, as Philip finally realizes that his dad won't be coming home. As the three return to the car, her bravado breaks down, and she cries and tells the boys a separation is imminent. The film suggests that the two boys will now be taking on more mature responsibilities within their shattered family—a suggestion that reflects the belief of some social scientists that "children growing up in one-parent households grow up a little faster."[113] In NFB families of this period, children who "grow up a little faster" may either create or alleviate disequilibrium within their family. Both are true of the heroine in *Hayley's Home Movie* (1987). In the film, twelve-year-old Hayley is the only child in an affluent family in which separated parents are dating others. Hayley is nearly equal to both parents in the allocation of power relations within the family. The following scene, in which Hayley stands frowning outside the kitchen while her mother removes burnt cookies from the toaster oven, produces a dialogue typical of their relationship.

Mother: You be absolutely sure to clean up in here.
Hayley: Why? It's not messy....When is your date coming?
Mother: I'm meeting him at a restaurant.
Hayley: How come? Why doesn't he come here?
Mother: It's just easier that way. He's an old friend of mine from my ballet days.

Hayley and her mother in *Hayley's Home Movie* (1987). NFB, S-19363.

Hayley: Does he know about me?
Mother: Sort of.
Hayley: Does he have kids?
Mother: I don't know.

> Hayley: Who else is going?
> Mother: No one.
> Hayley: Are you going to kiss him?
> Mother: Oh, come on. That's enough Hayley. I've got to go. I want this mess cleaned up.[114]

Hayley's father calls on the telephone. After the call, Hayley packages the cookies to take to his house for a surprise visit. "Aren't you going to leave us some?" asks her mother. "I thought you were on a diet," replies Hayley, "and I thought you were going out." Hayley's visit turns out to be a surprise for her as well, as she discovers her father relaxing with his girlfriend. Again the dialogue is revealing of the power relations in the family:

> Hayley: Who is she? And what's she doing in your bathrobe? The one I gave you.
> Father: Look, Hayley. Please. I'll explain this to you some time later. Okay?
> Hayley: Why can't you tell me now?
> Father: Because I just can't...don't argue with me.
> Hayley: I think this is gross.
> Father: Hayley, I want you to leave. Okay? You shouldn't have come without calling.
> Hayley: You always said to come here anytime.
> Father: Well, I don't care what I said. I've changed my mind. Now out.
> Hayley: I'm never coming back here then.
> Father: Well, okay, good. That way I won't have to keep repairing my VCR.[115]

Outraged by his flippant remark, Hayley smashes the box of cookies onto the floor of her father's exercise room. That night she runs away from home. The outcome, a reconciliation of sorts, leads Hayley to remark of her family life: "And they all lived happily for as long as possible."

Disequilibrium in the relationships between parents and children in NFB society during the late 1980s is not solely a problem of "split-families" but it almost always signifies a dysfunctional family. The severity of the dysfunction seems to correspond with the severity of the disequilibrium. Take, for example, the NFB production *Wednesday's Children: Vicky* (1987) and, in particular, this exchange between a mother and her sixteen-year-old daughter:

Mother: Where have you been?

Vicky:　Out.

Mother: I want to know where.

Vicky:　I said out.

Mother: Fine. You keep that up. But I'll find out. Go and wash that junk off your face and get ready for school.

Vicky:　I'm tired and I'm going to bed. It's been a long night.

Mother: You little tramp.

Vicky:　(Slaps mother hard.) Me! At least I like the guy I screw.[116]

Wednesday's Children: Vicky (1987). NFB, S-19419.

As the story unfolds, it is revealed that Vicky has been spending her evenings breaking into homes and committing petty theft with her boyfriend. Moreover, it becomes apparent that it is Vicky's father who is the root of this NFB family's problem. During Vicky's birthday party, her father arrives home late and drunkenly welcomes Vicky's aunt with an unwelcome kiss on her lips. Just prior to her husband's arrival, Vicky's mother had been telling the guests at the party about her sister: "She was the first hippie on the block. (Turning toward her sister.) But at least you were happy. Vicky looks so angry."

As much as depictions of unhappy families, it is again the explosion of diverse family portraits that mark the film productions of the mid- to late 1980s. Manifold in their structures, their organization, and functioning, NFB families of unique composition or novel characteristics replace modern families at the mainstream of the cinematic society. However, as Judith Stacey notes in her *Brave New Families: Upheaval in Late Twentieth Century America* (1990), such families are rarely sites of blissful relations: "the postmodern family is a site of disorder instead, a contested domain."[117] At root of much of postmodern family disorder, Stacey contends, are not feminist reforms, but rather postindustrial economic transformations, which have the effect of drastically revising the organization, experience, and distribution of paid work, with accompanying drastic disruptions in family economies.

This is certainly the case with the first "two-earner" family to appear in NFB society—a family in which the father undergoes a struggle for his self-esteem and for the respect of his eleven-year-old daughter after he loses his job and cannot find another. In *Left Out* (1987), the daughter, Amy, is overjoyed to learn that her class at school has won a trip to Québec, but later is horrified to discover that her family cannot afford the three hundred dollars required for the excursion because her father is laid-off and the family must live on her mother's income alone. At first Amy neglects to tell her friends she won't be travelling with them. She is embarrassed by her father and when he appears as a volunteer at her school while she is rehearsing a song on stage, she pretends not to know him. Her callousness causes him extreme pain, but he applauds enthusiastically anyway, pretending to be an appreciative onlooker rather than a proud father. Remorse brings Amy around to telling her peer group that she will not be accompanying them to Québec and she feels instantly better for having told them the truth. As the lyrics of her song persuade a viewer, "If I've got someone who really cares, then I'm not left out."[118]

Other diverse family groupings portrayed in this period include the extended family living together in *The Silence Upstairs* (1985), a film which deals with abuse of the elderly; the racially blended family portrayed in *Differences* (1986), a film concerning the pressures exerted on a twelve-year-old white boy and a seven-year-old Indian girl living under the same roof by externally generated prejudice; the film *Blueline* (1985), about a young man who discovers that he was adopted as a child and who takes his anger out against his adopted family; and (in a truly disequilibrating experience), *The Movie Movie* (1986), an eight-minute film detailing the construction of a filmic family, illustrating how "you're being told how to feel by the pictures that you see" by the editing, music, camera work, make-up, and acting—a production that aims to liberate viewers from the authority of films themselves.[119]

Differences (1986). NFB, S-19255.

Internal conflict is common to all but the last of the above-mentioned film families but, likewise, there is an abiding orthodoxy in each film about a more stable family life to come through greater understanding and tolerance of individual differences. In the cinematic society, it is a message that hearkens back through the decades to its introduction in films of the postwar era and, ultimately, to its origins at the Gesell Institute at Yale where its positive outcome ("It exalts the family as a social group...") was judged to be inevitable.[120]

Head Full of Questions (1989): The Social Invasion of the School

Of the eight films screened for this period (1985-89) in which a school was a context, only one portrays a classroom teacher as a significant player. In two others, teachers are present, but only in "bit parts"—in one as a supervisor in a detention room, and in the other operating a 16mm film projector and posing a discussion question at the conclusion of a film. In the majority of NFB schools in the late 1980s, outside experts use the forum to present information to students, or students use informal opportunities while at school in order to discuss contemporary social issues. In either case, teachers are usually absent.

War is foremost among the subjects pursued at NFB schools in the late-1980s, both regional and global. In *The Children of War* (1986), a Studio D production, a panel of children from nations torn by civil strife—Ireland, East Timor, Namibia, Guatemala, and El Salvador—address an assembly of junior secondary schoolchildren at a school in Montreal. Horror stories are told by members of the panel ("If they tell you to 'lick my shoe,' you would lick it"), some of which are revealing of the panelists' own rigid cultural and political beliefs. An Irish Catholic boy, for example, expresses a desire for his entire country to be united, "but the Protestants force the north to stay a part of the U.K." For their part, the Canadian children in the audience seem unable to comprehend both the level of hate that leads to torture of civilians, and the cycle of regional violence itself. As one boy asks from the audience, "Would you ever fight back against the...uhhh...opposing team?"[121]

In *Bombs Away* (1988), although the issue is global war and what an individual can do to prevent it, the conflict is more localized. A competition develops between two fourteen year olds, a boy and girl with differing tastes in popular music, both vying to be the disc jockey at a school dance. Having shown the class the NFB film *If You Love This Planet* (1985), their teacher asks the students, "What can we as a class do together to stop nuclear war?"[122] Despite her recurring nightmares of nuclear holocaust, the girl (Leanne) declines an invitation from her friend to join her on a peace march. "Only weird people go on marches," she tells her friend. Meanwhile, the competition with the boy, Peter, for the disc jockey position deteriorates into name-calling and leads to the sabotage of her personal journal. Ultimately, it is their mutual desire for global peace and a joint effort to make the peace march a success that leads to a truce between the two. Following Peter's apology for the vandalism of her journal and his compensatory offer to cede to her the disc jockey position, the two teenagers become friends. Similarly, through cooperation rather than confrontation, the film suggests, lies a parallel path to global peace.

Other subjects brought into NFB schools by outside agents during this period include sex and legal rights. For the former, two actors from Vancouver's "Green Thumb Players" replace classroom teachers as instructors in *Head Full of Questions* (1989), a film providing answers to a list of questions about sexual matters submitted to them by a diverse group of schoolchildren aged nine to thirteen:

Children:	Why do men and women make love? How does a baby come out? How does the baby get inside the mother? Why don't babies have teeth when they're born? What are condoms? Why isn't there just one sex? Why do only women have periods? How does the sperm move around? Why does a man have to stick his penis into the lady to have a baby?
Woman:	(Looking at slips of paper) These are great questions...[123]

The actors, a white woman and a black man, do not answer the questions of the students directly. Rather, they introduce the children to an animated cartoon couple, "Fred and Anna," who are of early college age. The animated characters provide answers as to "why and how" people have sexual relations through a series of explicit cartoon sequences illustrating "a good loving relationship," from attraction to conception. Gay and lesbian relationships are included in the film, and sexually transmitted diseases (including HIV infection) and the use of a condom are explained.[124]

Among the adults featured as instructors in NFB schools during this period, the sole teacher with a significant role is the 1988 winner of a Canadian Teachers Federation national teaching award, Richard Edwardson, an elementary schoolteacher from British Columbia. In the film *The Dig* (1989), Edwardson engages his grade seven students with an exceptionally large-scale discovery learning project in archaeology. Over the course of the project, he employs a wide variety of teaching strategies—including tableaux and simulation games as well as formalist strategies. For his unique effort, he commands the respect of his pupils to a degree unseen since the early 1950s.[125] In NFB high schools, on the other hand, not even a cameo appearance is made by a high school teacher. Instead, as in the early years of the decade, NFB adolescents (teenaged girls for the most part) are the real instructors of their peers.

Such a group are the teenagers in the film *Thin Dreams* (1986), in which six NFB girls (age fifteen to sixteen) set out to discuss "chubbiness" and diets, but wind up speculating instead about the origins of their desire to be thin. The girls hypothesize that a thin-conscious culture has been created through television and movies by a cinematic process that links body shape images with personalities, so that "books [women] *are* judged by their covers"—a stereotyping process of useful application to advertisers. The girls are surprised by the outcome of their discussion, since they expected at the outset to discuss ways of getting thin. "It feels good to talk about our bodies, to have brought it out," says one.[126]

And again, it is an adolescent girl who instructs others in the final educational context of this period, *Canadian Portraits* (1989). Answering an exam question for a high school history course, the teenager introduces viewers to the peoples of Canada who are often left out of Canadian historical textbooks—blacks, Inuit, Jews, Vietnamese, Poles, Sikhs, and Chileans—of whom she remarks rhetorically, "If it weren't for them, we wouldn't have a country, right?"[127]

The Magic Quilt (1985): A Cinematic Patchwork Society

In addition to signifying the ascendancy of girls in NFB schools of this era, the cinematic essay, *Canadian Portraits*, reveals a semantic change occuring in "the new society" during the period as well—a change in the use of the term "community" itself. Formerly a reference to a group of people occupying a limited geographical space, the term "community," by the late 1980s, is as often used in films to describe like racial or cultural attributes (i.e., "cultural communities") within NFB society. As with the young woman in *Canadian Portraits*, who leads adolescents into the discovery of a new cultural history, so too do NFB girls created by Studio D offer imaginative leadership for younger children in regard to preserving the mosaic created by Canada's cultural communities—their work best illustrated by the film *The Magic Quilt* (1985).

The theme of a new social equilibrium established and ordered through feminism lies beneath *The Magic Quilt*. In this semi-animated, Studio D film by Bettina Mayline, a culturally diverse group of children (aged 8-12) run down a grassy hill and find a fabric quilt on a picnic table. It quickly becomes clear that the animated quilt is magically reflective of the cultures of the children who hold it. The children take the quilt into a cabin to avoid a tapestry rainstorm and find a magic map of Canada on it. Ironically, at first one child incorrectly identifies the map as being that of Yugoslavia. Several children fight over and rip the quilt. Although a few of the children are indifferent to the torn fabric ("Who cares? There wasn't any magic."), some of the girls begin to repair it, saying, "Sewing's a girl's job." A boy asks, "What's a boy's job then?" A girl replies, "Ripping it up." As the narrative proceeds, the boys learn to sew just as well as the girls ("This isn't so hard!") and when the quilt is repaired, its magic again functions. At the end of the film, the children have a party outside the cabin and, supported by a group of multicultural adults, use the quilt to toss each other high up into the air.[128]

Rather than express concerns about tears in the seams between patches in the cultural quilt, however, actual cultural communities more frequently voice concerns about the torn fabric within the patches themselves—i.e., family concerns. In articulating these, the film narratives reverberate with the effects of past and present social invasions of families. The documentary, *Richard Cardinal: Cry from a Diary of a Métis Child* (1986), for example, expresses the plight of "15,000 native children [who] are wards of their provinces." Cardinal, a Métis foster child, commits suicide, leaving behind a tragic diary recording the events at twenty-seven "alternate home placements"—a litany of physical and emotional abuse beginning at age six, including memories from his first placement, in which he and his brother were whipped with their pants down in front of the three daughters of the foster family. "What Richard needed most," comments his brother, "was to go home. His funeral was the best social service that was provided for Richard, because his family was finally brought together."[129]

Equally family-conscious is *Sitting in Limbo* (1986), which explores the relationship between low self-esteem among black male adolescents in Montreal and the high incidence of single mothers within the black community—a condition which, in the United States, prominent social observers from the 1930s onwards have traced to the violation of black families during the slave trade.[130] Blacks have never fared well in NFB society.[131] The docu-drama *Sitting in Limbo* suggests that growing up fatherless may cause some young black males to develop personalities incompatible with holding down long-term jobs and maintaining family relationships—a dynamic which results in a self-perpetuating family cycle within the black community. "Sooner or later you're going to have to stand up strong," is the message to black males in the reggae soundtrack to the film. But exactly how the cycle is to be resolved and black strength achieved is not revealed.[132]

Even within one of the most closed NFB cultural communities since *The Hutterites* (1963), family concerns originating from a social invasion (of a more contemporary sort) are evident. *The Old Believers* (1988) takes us to "northern Alberta at the edge of Holy Russia," where an archaic sect of the Russian Orthodox Church resides. The members of the sect, who migrated from Russia to China to California and then to Alberta in the years following the Russian revolution of 1917, call themselves "the Christians," and they believe they are the last on earth. For more than seventy years, they have co-existed alongside, but have resisted intrusion from, "the polluted outside world." But their children have recently added leather jackets and fast cars to their usually ornate

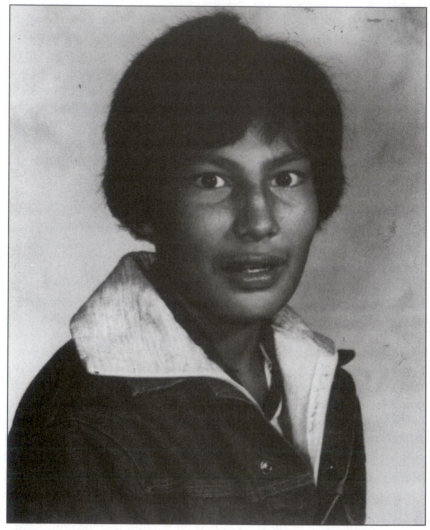

Richard Cardinal: Cry from a Diary of a Métis Child (1986). NFB, S-18729.

apparel, threatening the traditional community with the distinct possibility of assimilation into mainstream culture. At the close of the film, a group of families of "Old Believers" visit the West Edmonton Mall, where the mothers laugh at the children recklessly driving bumpercars. "When the end of the world comes," one mother jokes with insightful irony, "it will probably begin here in the West Edmonton Mall...the world is disappearing into the market place."[133]

Conclusion: The New Generation and the Next Generation in NFB Society, 1968-89

Veronica Strong-Boag, in her "Home Dreams: Women and the Suburban Experiment, 1945-60," suggests a pandemic explanation for post-World War II gender events: "the daughters of the suburbs, examining their parents' lives [began] to ask for more."[134] Almost certainly, that is the case—but why did so many daughters ask for more when those of prior generations had not? Unmistakably, they were responding to ideas advanced by "second wave" feminists, such as Simone de Beauvoir and, later, Betty Friedan, via myriad media unimaginable to earlier "daughters" but how was their consciousness awakened on such a scale to the possibility of asking for more? I suspect that a significant factor in their awakening was the adoption of modern child-rearing practices by the "mothers of the suburbs" and elsewhere, which was in part the very praxis proposed by Ellen Key as the solution to the "Woman Question." With a quote from Nietzche, Key set forth her goal for mothers of the next (twentieth) century: "I will that thy victory and thy emancipation shall yearn for a child. Living memorials shalt thou build for thy victory, and for thy emancipation."[135]

Modern child rearing was to a large degree, of course, aimed at emancipating children of both sexes from domination by their mothers. But, in NFB society at least, a complex side effect appears. As mothers loosen control over their children, fathers lose dominion over their families. The phenomenon is in evidence in NFB films as early as *The Pony* (1955). The son and daughter in *The Pony*, having learned to exercise their independence from their mother over minor rules, further exercise their initiative and override the orders of their father concerning larger rules about animals on a mechanized farm. "I'm going to find out what's going on around here," says the father to his wife after he hears the pony whinny. "And I suppose you're in it right up to your ears."[136] The man's supposition is correct, but the connection is not as direct as he presumes. His wife has not given the children permission to purchase a pony. The children have done so on their own—but only as a consequence of the independence training provided by her. Developments within the NFB family of this decade are analogous to what later occurs within the cinematic society as a whole.

In NFB society in the late 1960s and early 1970s, young adults of both sexes of the new generation are eager participants in the creation of a "new society," free from traditional social hierarchies: i.e., patriarchal social structures. But whereas for NFB "daughters" this is an "asking for more," for NFB sons it amounts to asking for less, since it is a rebellion against assuming their traditional power and authority as patri-archs—a disdain for male adulthood as signified in the film *A One/Two/Many/World* (1970). Little wonder that J.R. Seeley observed in *Crestwood Heights* that Crestwood fathers were considerably more uneasy with the new notions of child rearing than mothers: "rarely will he come wholeheartedly to endorse the democratic and permissive norms now seeping into the family."[137] In NFB society at large (and within the NFB itself), after 1967, patriarchal structures are continually challenged and weakened as the new generation of NFB men and women together raise the banner for general liberation from men.

In the cinematic state of disequilibrium that results a new society emerges, in which males may be said neither to rule nor exactly to be ruled; but one in which (through Studio D at first, then swiftly through all the studios and regions) NFB females emerge to ideological domi-nance, especially girls, whose cinematic ascendancy is projected to audi-ences composed mainly of their Canadian counterparts—both boys and girls. This rise to prominence for girls in the cinematic society is a direct consequence of the hegemony over childhood images gained by the film-makers at Studio D after 1974—a hegemony so complete that, as with *Starbreaker* (1984), even veteran male filmmakers unassociated with Stu-dio D adopt the principle of featuring girls in strong leading roles. Coin-cidentally, these images function in concert with the paradigm of socia-bility adopted at NFB (and Canadian) schools since the early 1950s—a coincidence of particular significance given the psychological observa-tions of J.R. Seeley et al.:

> It is they [women] who, instead of taking direct individual-to-individ-ual action, organize, work in concert, know and use the techniques of group pressure, and so secure alteration in the circumstances of the group. Men tend to use a psychology of individual differences...women tend to use a social psychology...quite frequently to secure collective and cooperative alteration in the ways of groups.[138]

Within the schools of the "new" NFB society, the impact of psycho-logical engineering is widely perceptible. "The group" challenges the teacher over educational power relations. By the late 1960s, assertive pupils in elementary classrooms exist in numbers capable of provoking complex discipline problems. By the late 1970s, their high school coun-terparts mock their teachers and their schooling to an extent unthink-able to a prior generation. By the early 1980s, classroom teachers have all but disappeared from view within NFB schools, succeeded at the elementary level by outside agents and at the secondary level by adolescent NFB girls.

Meanwhile, in depictions of NFB families, despite the hegemony held by Studio D over childhood images and the early appearance of a new equilibrium, the manifestation of "lone parent" families, abusive scenarios, diverse groupings, and emotionally disturbed children all mark the reign of a state of disequilibrium, which is of concern to NFB families and communities alike, and, moreover, recall the concerns expressed by an unnamed member of J.R. Seeley's *Crestwood Heights* research team:

> At least one of the authors strongly felt both systems—the social and the personal—to be exceedingly labile, not to say fragile, dependent on a concatenation of circumstances difficult to guarantee in the modern world. But this is impression, and what could be added to it would be more impression.[139]

An overall impression of the change that occurs to families, schools, and communities in the NFB "new society" is that each loses a once well-defined boundary and becomes susceptible to social invasion. In the personal sphere, gendered characterizations are especially unstable. NFB men, once the gentle after-dinner playmates of NFB boys and girls, guardians of the "sacred newspaper reading time," and organizers of the family vacation, are just as likely to be depicted as sexual predators, drunks, racist troublemakers, or family deserters. On the other hand, NFB girls of the next generation fare best of all in the imagery. Their voices, once silent, are now capable of speaking—of asking for more— for entire cultural communities. Boys of the next NFB generation become the silent gender, uncertain partners in the new equilibrium.

At the root of these transformations in NFB society lies a shift in the power relations between children and adults, boys and girls, and men and women, brought about as a consequence of the mental hygiene movement and functioning in conjunction with postwar feminism.[140] Simply stated, the NFB "daughters of the suburbs" who ask for more, ask sons with diminishing expectations.[141] In the resulting struggle for a new equilibrium (advanced by the NFB into Canadian society) a state of disequilibrium arises (reflected by the NFB from Canadian society)—a consequence effected, in part, by the mass application of a seemingly axiomatic paradigm about family power relations, the origins of which may be traced to *The Century of the Child* itself.

Conclusion: The Century of the Cinematic Child

How often does the hand that rocks the cradle unwittingly
plant the seeds of permanent ill-health!
— Charles Martin, *The Mental Hygiene Movement in
Canada* (1930)

"The Motion Picture: a Mirror of Time" was the title of Marjory
McKay's article in 1959 concerning the historical value of the NFB
archival film collection.[1] In this study, I have argued that there is a
mirror-like quality to the motion picture narratives within this unique
body of films, that the NFB collection is, in effect, a cinematic looking
glass in which transient images of Canadian society are preserved as
"NFB society." It is a society in cinema, for which a coherent social history may be re-created by the simple juxtaposition of filmic narrative
images.

This study has been a re-creation of a half-century of childhood in
this cinematic mirror. But more, it has been a study of changes within
the primary socializing structures of NFB childhood—the changing
social life of families, schools, and communities. Each of these structures
has been transformed over the fifty-year course of the portrayals, each
appearing to have been affected by the progressive engineering of the

---

Notes to chapter 7 are on p. 267.

conditions of childhood in early and postwar NFB society. Each structure loses some clarity of definition it once held; the boundary of each becomes less well defined; but most importantly, each body loses some of its former authority over the social lives of children—a role that is increasingly taken up by cinematographers.

It may be argued, of course, that NFB children—the events and outcomes of their portraits—have always been governed by Film Board cinematographers. And in fact, that is true. What changes, however, is the relationship of NFB filmmakers to the children they portray. The relationship evolves from one that is nearly always mediated by adults in family, school, and community scenarios to one, by the 1980s, that rarely is. That is, parents, teachers, and community leaders in the cinematic society lose their influence over children at the same time as NFB cinematographers gain more and more direct control over them.

Of all the narratives that impose themselves over large series of films in the NFB archival collection, this one—that the progressive engineering of society created children more susceptible to cinematic socialization—is the least pronounced but possibly the most significant. It is the sole social narrative to run through the entire five decades of portrayals, and it is the connecting thread through each of the others. Its significance lies both in its rootedness in progressive projects of the 1920s through 1930s and in its contribution to the search for an intellectual model of how electronic media produced widespread social change after the 1950s. It is a metareflection in a mirror that Grierson built for "our moods of resolution." And, as Grierson saw it, "It is in our moods of resolution that we may be expected to build the future."[2]

Before the Beginning

Ted Magder, in his *Canada's Hollywood: The Canadian State and Feature Films* (1993), remarks of the National Film Board, "Only in Canada could an autochthonous culture begin to impose itself on itself."[3] For much of the archival content of the NFB, that is true. The collection contains a vast amount of the "what was"—the physical, social, and intellectual realities—of Canadian life reflected to Canadians in their cinematic mirror from 1939 onward. However, concerning one important aspect of that filmic image, Magder is mistaken. Alterations to the primary socializing structures—families and schools—that were made in the mirror during the 1940s and 1950s were not autochthonous to Canada at all. Rather, they were almost wholly constructed by American progressives in the 1920s and 1930s and transplanted under the auspices of "National Health and Welfare," for the most part, into the cinematic representation of Canadian society.

In her *The Romance of American Psychology: Political Culture in the Age of Experts* (1995), Ellen Herman makes a pertinent point about the importance American progressives attached to these socializing structures.[4] According to Herman, by the mid-1930s, the concept of "national character" was in ascendance among influential progressive thinkers such as Frank. Originating from the work of cultural anthropologists such as Gregory Bateson, Ruth Benedict, Margaret Mead, and Edward Sapir, at the heart of the concept lay a compelling logic: if individuals embodied their society and societies embodied the collective personality of their people then the institutional vehicles of socialization for a nation, from child rearing to teacher training, worked to produce a collective personality structure—i.e., a national character.

> In a pivotal 1936 article, Lawrence K. Frank, an advocate of clinical approaches whose influential foundation posts had included the Rockefeller Foundation and the Josiah Macy Jr. Foundation, pointed out that if nations had characters, then it made sense to think of "society as the patient."[5]

"Society as the patient" could be remedied, or so it seemed, by reforming national socializing structures.[6] Frank's prescription for national character reform, of course, included implanting the "democratic" schooling and child-rearing structures of the mental hygienists into the socializing matrix. A generation schooled from birth in the experience of democracy should, logically, become the unfailing safeguard of democratic culture. Gesell made this very point in his preface to the LSRM-funded *Infant and Child in the Culture of Today*: "Were it not that the democratic countries are bent on strengthening the very cultures which are being assailed [by totalitarianism] one might well wonder why this book should be written."[7] Through Gesellian child-rearing praxis, democracies could be inoculated against the disease of autocracy—and have their social problems doctored simultaneously—by what was literally a clinically prescribed treatment of their national character.

The model was fraught with both known risks and incalculable perils. Reformers knew that treating social problems by altering the structures upon which social order rested was not without risk. Theresa Richardson in *The Century of the Child* (1989) observes that Frank, who has been described as "the procreative Johnny Appleseed of the social sciences,"[8] once commented that trying to solve a social problem was like "trying to cultivate a flower without the fruit."[9]

The dilemma for reformers who wanted to solve crime, disease, poverty, delinquency, and war by way of mental hygiene was that they did not want to change any of the structures that had caused the problems. The effort was to make social institutions "work better" without altering their basic character.[10]

In fact, the flower could not be cultivated without permanently changing the character of the fruit. To cultivate the flower of the new generation, progressives consciously altered the character of social institutions without calculating what would result beyond one generation. That is, they appear not to have contemplated that the flower produced the fruit and that the fruit produced the flower, not in one cycle, but continuously, and that by altering the ability of one to produce the other, each might unwittingly change the character of the other, generation after generation.

Nor had they wholly considered the importance of another socializing structure in the cultural experience of children, the cinema. In *Recent Social Trends in the United States* (1933), Frank made only fleeting references to motion pictures:

> The patronage of commercial amusements by children and young people is one of those subjects about which there is general knowledge but not much actual record. The attendance of children at moving pictures has been under scrutiny by various groups. For our present purposes it is sufficient to point out that children are attending moving pictures in large numbers and are apparently receiving a considerable amount of their education thereby, particularly in human relations and more specifically in courtship and marriage.[11]

Frank observed that "those in control of commercial moving pictures and radio broadcasting [were] influencing the rearing of children" and cited a Commonwealth Fund (CF) study concerning the limited value of films in the public school classroom but on the whole, he concluded, "the possibilities of using moving pictures in the guidance of youth awaits further exploration."[12]

In fact, a series of studies concerning the physiological, emotional, and social effects of moving pictures upon youth, the Payne Fund Studies (PFS), were being completed just as Frank was writing his chapter for *Recent Social Trends in the United States*. But unfortunately for the PFS, a brouhaha erupted upon their release that almost immediately damaged their academic credibility.[13] Indeed, their initial scholarly reception was so tarnished by the vocal "anti-movie" bias of the instigator of the studies, the Rev. William Short, that only recently, as Garth Jowett, Ian

Jarvie, and Kathryn Fuller observe in their *Children and the Movies: Media Influence and the Payne Fund Controversy* (1996), "have these volumes of research stemming from a major school of social science begun to be accorded the recognition they deserve as excellent mass communications research."[14]

Among the credible findings of the educators, psychologists, and sociologists who published their research in the twelve volume MacMillan series entitled *Motion Pictures and Youth* (1933) were those dealing with retention of information from various movies. At the end of six weeks, even very young children remembered 90 per cent of what they knew on the day following the show. Furthermore, three months after seeing a motion picture they remembered as much as they did six weeks after seeing it: "In some cases, as with "Tom Sawyer," they remember more at the end of six weeks and still more at the end of three months."[15]

Another revelation from the studies was that children of all ages tended to accept as authentic what they saw in the movies. They readily accepted falsehoods as facts. In general, the researchers found, "children accept the information in the movies as correct unless it is flagrantly incorrect."[16] As to the effect of motion pictures upon the social attitudes of children, the researchers found it was "substantial" and "cumulative."[17] According to W.W. Charters, chairman of the PFS and Director of the Bureau of Educational Research, Ohio State University, "they demonstrated the fact that two pictures are more powerful than one and three are more potent than two...that continued exposure to pictures of similar character will in the end produce a measurable change of attitude."[18] While the authors of the research concluded that "shifts created by exposure to a film have substantial permanence," they also found that the movies could conflict with one another in the direction of their influence: "a good film may be followed by a bad, an anti-Chinese film may be neutralized by a pro-Chinese movie."[19]

In the main, the studies provided a scientific foundation to some lay perceptions concerning the educational efficacy of motion pictures. Children remembered what they saw in the movies, believed what they saw in the movies; the movies could shape the social attitudes of children, then reshape them if necessary—but more. According to Jowett, et al., some PFS researchers "succeeded in moving well beyond a position that is still taken for granted in public thinking about the role of electronic mass media in society."[20] Typical of their insights into the social force of the movies is the following passage taken from Paul Cressey's unpublished study for the PFS, "Boys, Movies, and City Streets":

The ultimate factor to be noted in all the controversy regarding the movie is that the cinema is really an agency in "speeding up" communication....Thus the cinema is bringing to remote centers with more facility "foreign" (i.e., locally unapproved) patterns of life which before were not presented. Significantly, its contribution is not merely to facilitate the contacts of local citizens with those elsewhere (as with the telephone) but whole patterns of life as unities are presented. "Psychological mobility" rather than spatial mobility is here involved but it is nevertheless very real mobility.[21]

And this conclusion was given by two University of Chicago sociologists, Herbert Blumer and Philip M. Hauser: "motion pictures play an especially important part in the lives of children reared in socially disorganized areas."[22]

The influence of motion pictures seems to be proportionate to the weakness of the family, school, church, and neighbourhood. Where the institutions which traditionally have transmitted social attitudes and forms of conduct have broken down...motion pictures assume a greater importance as a source of ideas and schemes of life.[23]

Hence, moving pictures had enormous potential as a medium for socializing children at a distance but, as it stood, their influence over children was effectively counterbalanced by existing family, school, and community structures—the same structures that had become the focus for progressive reforms in the century of the child.

NFB Society in the Beginning: The Grierson Years

Social order, social stability, social control—those were the watchwords of the academic and social world to which Grierson gained admittance as a student at the University of Chicago in 1924.[24] When the LSRM placed him under the tutelage of some of the foremost progressive intellectuals in the United States in the mid-1920s—including Charles Merriam of the University of Chicago, Beardsley Ruml of the United States Social Science Research Council, and Walter Lippmann—it impressed upon the young Scotsman the ideals that would be synthesized into the very tenets of early-NFB society, a "progressive democracy" in which citizens inevitably welcomed the reform of their institutional practices by outside experts.

From the outset, NFB documentaries were a psychological bridge between the Canadian public and the reform of their social systems. To successfully bring Canadian public opinion over the bridge and into public action, early NFB documentaries projected a close likeness of the Canadian audience—the "what was" of the audience—resolving a narrative about "what ought to be." Consequently, holistically over the larger body of films, a metanarrative emerges of Canadians as a healthy, productive, thoughtful, and, above all else, cooperative people. The paradox in this metanarrative, of course, was that from the outset NFB society was a progressive society without progressive socializing structures.

Only one change in the socialization of children was incorporated into the Canadian imagination during the Griersonian era. *Lessons in Living* (1944) is a progressive vision of education which, along with a philosophical bent readily attributable to John Dewey, bears some notable similarities to the 1920s and 1930s New York City progressive experiment in education: the "Little Red School House," as described by Sol Cohen in his *Progressives and Urban School Reform: the Public Education Association of New York City* (1964).

> Children in the Little Red School House...were given many opportunities to learn "from direct experience." Trips into the neighbourhood were much employed. Activities, of course, were all important: "Here some two hundred small workers don overalls and go about their occupations," building, hammering, painting...[25]

The traditional practices that progressive education was meant to replace may be seen in a number of early NFB productions, especially those in which pedagogy was not the particular focus of the film.[26] The pedagogical differences are striking, particularly in the area of socialization. In general, in traditional classrooms in both rural and urban settings, pupils learn textbook-based material independent of their peers in an adult-directed, highly structured and disciplined setting, while in the progressive classrooms, children work in cooperative teams on large scale projects of novel design under adult supervision. Neither of these educational models survives wholly intact past the 1940s in the cinematic society. Instead, with the introduction of the mental hygiene paradigm in the early 1950s, a synthesis of the two occurs, which evolves by shedding the traditional and advancing towards the attainment of a derivative of the original progressive structure—i.e., a neoprogressive structure.

Postwar NFB Society: Re-rocking the Cradle

Because mental hygiene principles of child rearing were not introduced into NFB society before 1946, there are numerous examples of family structures which typify traditional socializing patterns within this institution, and some variants as well. As a body of work, with the exception of single-parent families, these paint what is probably too rosy a picture to be considered a credible representation of typical Canadian families of the era, yet they present a remarkably consistent reading of "the family," and, since NFB society is a society of perceptions, they may be said to accurately reflect the perceptions of Film Board cinematographers concerning what constituted normal Canadian family life.

Most striking is the ease of relationships within the families—between mothers and fathers and between parents and their children. These relationships appear to be guided by mutually established patterns of expectations based upon domestic roles. They are not maintained by punitive measures, but they are authoritarian.[27] The patterns of dominance vary. Mothers dominate home life in films such as *Supper's Ready* (1944), *Rural Health* (1946), *Something to Chew On* (1947), and *Out Beyond Town* (1948). Fathers dominate the home in films such as *Lessons in Living* (1944), *Early Start* (1945), *Mother and Her Child* (1947), and *Fitness Is a Family Affair* (1948).[28] In several productions, no clear picture of the hierarchic social arrangements between the parents emerges—often due to a paucity of shared footage in a film—but it is fair to say that children of this era never dictate the events in the portrayal of a family.

Whether or not a mother dominates her husband in the NFB family of this period, she virtually always controls the children. Food plays an important part in this control. Mothers in early NFB films are frequently seen purchasing, preparing, and serving food. They also can be seen instructing their daughters in food craft. Fathers, although they may attempt to influence their children's choices (more often by grumpy or stubborn behaviours than by reason), seldom exercise direct control over their offspring. At home, for the most part, fathers undertake leisure activities with both their sons and their daughters; they bring them gifts and provide them with pocket change. They allow their sons access to their tools. They motor children about; they take them on vacation. They put money aside for their education and worry about them when they are ill. But it is the NFB mother—efficient, supportive, and frequently aproned—who controls them.

As rosy as NFB family social relations may seem during the early 1940s, they actually improve from the late 1940s to the mid-1950s. Mothers learn to relax and enjoy the personalities of their four-year-olds; fathers discover that they may reason with their adolescents; children respond in kind; the family structure remains stable. Capturing the spirit of family life during the early postwar years of modern parenting are the opening scenes from *He Acts His Age* (1949), the introductory film in the *Ages and Stages* series. As the film begins, dozens of happy children clad in light summer clothing, some hand-in-hand with their parents, others racing ahead, sing their way through Technicolour fields of daisies on their way to a picnic: "What shall we do when we all go out, all go out, all go out; what shall we do when we all go out on our holiday?"[29] As if to answer, a flaxen-haired, four-year-old girl dashes from her parents' side, picks a spray of daisies, runs back, and presents them to her mother with a hug—an apt metaphor, perhaps, for the brief golden era in family life that had now begun.

It was a *sine qua non* that children reared to be mentally healthy during the first five or six years of their life at home should enter a school environment where mental health was of equal concern. It is not a happenstance, then, that psychological concerns finally make their appearance in a cinematic classroom in 1952, six years after the baby boom had begun in Canada and almost thirty years after American progressives first introduced hygienist practices into educational structures in the United States. Whereas there had been attempts to implant the cooperative practices of progressive education within NFB schools in the early and mid-1940s, the mental hygiene aspects of the educational paradigm are neglected until the first cohort of the new generation are on their way to school.

Hygienist principles are introduced into schools in the cinematic society through the teacher training film *Shyness* (1952). In a later film, *Child Guidance Clinic* (1956), an urban, Canadian school principal, while articulating the goals of his elementary school, echoes the aims of the American Progressive Education Association (APEA), following its adoption of the agenda of the National Committee for Mental Hygiene (NCMH) in the 1920s:

> The school no longer regards it as its main function to simply teach academic skills. Educators are now interested in the child acquiring habits and attitudes that will make him a happy child, a more successful student, and a better and more useful citizen.[30]

Resistance is not the problem in the implementation of hygienist practices into NFB schools of the mid- to late 1950s. Just as in *Crestwood Heights*, where researchers reported variation from school to school in adopting "the common ideology" of mental hygiene, there is an uneven transience in NFB schools of this period as well—but little doubt, as in Crestwood Heights, that mental hygiene is the dominant ideology. On the contrary, overzealousness for the psychologized classroom poses a greater potential problem for the progressive paradigm. In *Crestwood Heights*, for example,

> One earnest, well-informed, and competent teacher, on two different occasions, inquired with a genuine air of worry and distress whether the researcher thought the short prayers she used at the conclusion of her kindergarten classes would harm the children in the sense of making them over-dependent, or of risking authoritarian elements in their characters and thinking.[31]

Demonstrating a similar zeal for psychological concepts, a teacher in the NFB production, *Popular Psychology* (1957), transforms a once secure parent into a neurotic one. In the film, a primary grade teacher bandies about terms like "group adjustment" as she informs a mother that her son is not an outgoing child in the classroom. The mother quickly becomes distraught about her son's ability to socialize in a group. "Perhaps the child is wise to consider what the group is about before participating," remarks the boy's father. "If reading these things about psychology disturb you, stop reading them." The mother wails in reply, "But we can't avoid psychology. It's like air!"[32]

Like air, consideration for the development of the personality of children is quickly diffused throughout the schools of NFB society. So subtle is this change in teachers' attitudes that it seems insignificant at first. But with the implementation of mental hygiene into NFB schools, a complete package of American progressive practices had been set in place over traditional Canadian structures for the socialization of children.

In the Middle: The NFB Family, School, and Community as the New Generation Matures

The flowering personality of the new generation in NFB society from the mid-1950s to the late 1960s is accompanied by little change in the physical structure of the family—just as Frank had hoped with American society.[33] On the other hand, a growing number of portraits reveal a web of complex social tensions novel to the cinematic society developing within family relationships—a dynamic exacerbated by pressures exerted on family boundaries by sibling peer groups. Despite the presence of internal tensions and external pressures, however, most NFB families remain stable structures up to the mid-1960s.

During this period, technological and production advances in film-making—lighter motion picture cameras and sound equipment and "candid eye" techniques—enable a more "authentic" representation of Canadian practices of child rearing to emerge than in the past. Cinema-direct films such as *2 1/2* (1964) and *The World of Three* (1966) offer evidence of the popular acceptance of democratic child-rearing practices in middle-class Canadian homes by the mid-1960s and a candid view of the effects of these practices upon infant children—both boys and girls—who freely explore their environments and just as freely express their personalities.

In contrast to their pre-teen children, role-bound parents in films such as *The Summer We Moved to Elm Street* (1966), *This Is No Time for Romance* (1966), and *Once Upon a Prime Time* (1966) exhibit some early symptoms of a growing malaise within the family system. Escape without abandonment is the predominant theme in the portraits of the parents in each of these films. Alcohol is the means of withdrawal for a father in the first production. For the mothers in the other two films, romantic fantasies are a safe means of desertion. In *This Is No Time For Romance*, the mother of four daydreams that she is being attacked simultaneously by a half-dozen, handsome young men in unbuttoned, plaid shirts; in *Once Upon a Prime Time*, a neglected mother fantasizes riding off into the sunset upon a white stallion with an American motion picture cowboy.

Families with adolescent children are represented in mid-1960s films such as *Phoebe* (1964) and *The Shattered Silence* (1966). The adults in both these productions are bewildered and perplexed by contemporary adolescent behaviour. In the first film, a frazzled mother, a cigarette chain-smoker in a housecoat, makes ineffectual attempts to communicate with her daughter, Phoebe, who is pregnant. In the second film, *The Shattered Silence*, a benevolent but short-tempered uncle learns to cope with what, from his perspective, is an insolent attitude on the part of his nephew's adolescent acquaintances. Both narratives are expressions of an intergenerational gulf that had been widening in the cinematic society since the late 1950s, becoming a pronounced divide by the mid-1960s—a rift soon to be characterized as "the generational gap."[34] Even before it was identified by name, the generation gap was finding expression in the schools of NFB society. In the film *No Reason to Stay* (1966), an adolescent student defines the gulf between high-school teachers and students as a difference in consciousness: "We're living in the instant, and they don't understand that."[35] His comment brings to mind Hilda Neatby's critique of progressive education in her *So Little for the Mind*

(1953): "[Progressivism is] almost exclusively preoccupied with the present; the child comes to live in a two dimensional world without depth or background."[36] What progressive education in NFB society lacks in depth throughout the 1960s, however, it makes up in breadth, especially at the elementary level.

The 1960s are remarkable for the educational innovations introduced into NFB elementary schools. Kindergarten, Cuisenaire Rods, new subject methodologies, television and other audio-visual technologies, computers, "discovery learning," and "educational drama" all make their initial appearance in elementary classrooms over the decade. Innovation is, in fact, the predominant theme of the more than twenty NFB films concerning education produced during the 1960s and, as a consequence, the predominant impression created by the bulk of the films is one of a public school system embarking upon rapid, sweeping, and irresistible change.[37] The images of grade six children who sit transfixed in their desks as their regular classroom teacher parses a sentence on the blackboard in the film *The Gifted Ones* (1959) are in sharp contrast to the images of grade six children in the film *A Search for Learning* (1966), clustered around tables actively engaged in a discovery learning project while their "advisor" (their teacher) encourages them to "say whatever you think." Elements of an older order in elementary schooling remain visible even late into the decade, as in the film *We're Gonna Have Recess* (1967), in which urban school children line up after recess to walk single file into their brownstone school.[38] But adherence to convention is the exception to the rule by the mid-1960s and is far more suggestive of the recency and unevenness of the transformation taking place than of any counter-movement to it. In the main, it is the organizational conditions of the innovations themselves—i.e., they frequently require cooperative group work or "stations work"—that oblige teachers to restructure the classroom physically and socially in the mid- to late 1960s. But there is another dynamic in play as well. Films such as *Sir! Sir!* (1968) and *Mrs. Ryan's Drama Class* (1969) suggest that elementary students of this era are far more capable of exerting pressure on teachers to reshape their instructional practices. Such films suggest that the dynamics of the student body include more pupils less willing than those portrayed in earlier films to remain transfixed in their desks for any length of time to attend to direct instruction, or to work quietly from a textbook, or to suffer authoritarian teachers in silence—as demonstrated as early as 1961 by the rebellious grade six pupils depicted in *The Test*. There is a perceptible difference in group character that distinguishes grade six students in mid-1960s NFB society from those of the late 1950s—an attitudinal divide that becomes conspicuous over that narrow band of time, but which is masked, to a large degree, by the neoprogressive restructuring of the intermediate classroom to accommodate "the child of the future."[39]

Nowhere is this divide—this "generation gap"—more conspicuous in the cinematic society by the late 1960s than in the NFB community. In fact, so wide is the chasm by 1967, that two distinct communities can now be perceived existing side by side: a community of young people emerging into adulthood from the postwar socializing structures of Canadian society and an older community—two very different bodies with characters understandably at odds with each other.

Moral conventions and civic laws are flaunted by the younger group, especially in urban settings. In 1967, masses of youth of both sexes may be seen rioting in Vancouver or blocking Yorkville Street in Toronto. A cinematic "riot act" concerning the occupation of Yorkville is read by the chairman of the municipality of Toronto, William Allen, Q.C., in the documentary film, *Flowers on a One-way Street* (1967):[40]

> It has to be established and known for once and for all that in metropolitan Toronto, when there is mobs [sic] and gangs who seek out as a group to defy law and order then they are going to be treated exactly as the circumstances call for.[41]

Much to the surprise of the Toronto City Council, no sooner have the young people been cleared from the street by city police than a large number of them occupy the council chambers while the councillors are out to lunch. The young people demand to be heard. One young "hippie" describes what happened as the city councillors (controllers) returned to the chamber:

> I sat down in the mayor's seat, while the other kids took over the seats of the other controllers, and the rest of the kids just sat down. The Mayor, Dennison, came in and tried to push me out of his seat; nudged me and started yelling at me, and I quietly told him we weren't going to leave until Dave [David DePoe, the group's leader] had been heard, and if Dave wasn't heard we were going to stay there until he was heard.[42]

It is a landmark event in the cinematic society. The peaceful coup d'état staged by the young people at city hall is an apt signifier of the coming of age of the new generation of NFB kids. They are confident that their demands will be respected, that "a rule's only a good rule if the circumstances demand it,"[43] and their confidence is not misplaced.

After a few moments of wrangling, the seats are returned to the elected officials, who agree to allow DePoe to speak to council without following protocol. The mayor and the majority of the councillors are hesitant about compromising but uncomfortably conscious that the motion picture cameras are rolling.[44] One controller remarks, "I submit that we are encouraging the revolutionary viewpoint that they have in their mind."[45] When this revelation comes, it is twenty years too late to stop the social revolution that is augured by DePoe's address to council: "It appears to a lot of people that there has been a breakdown in democracy," Depoe reads from his notes, "hang-ups on rules and that sort of thing."[46]

The NFB cameras follow the young people as they leave the council chambers and return to the street. By 1968, the revolutionary viewpoint they represented would begin to radically alter not only the socializing structures of NFB society, but also the structural characteristics of the NFB itself. In a remarkable parallel to changes brought about in the previous generation to family power structures, the Film Board initiated its "Challenge for Change" program, by which filmic voice was given to groups and cultures that had been seen but rarely heard in NFB society—especially indigenous cultures, the poor, and women. An eventual outcome of this change of philosopy was a restructuring of film production at the National Film Board in the early 1970s from its centrally controlled "unit" system to a more autonomous "studio" system. The most renowned of the studios thus created was Studio D, the women's studio, which was staffed by mainly new generation female filmmakers who set out in 1974 to cinematically explore "the woman question" independent of their male colleagues—and who, ironically, took the cinematic child along with them.[47]

At the End: New Fruit, Next Flower

Perhaps Christopher Lasch in his *The Culture of Narcissism: American Life in an Age of Diminishing Expectations* (1978) indirectly comes closest to describing the national character of NFB society after the new generation comes of age and begins to rear and school "the next generation." Lasch argued that the mental health movement in postwar American society had produced a narcissistic culture, causing the collapse of a prior "cult of intimacy."[48] As a result, Lasch contended, "our society has made deep and lasting friendships, love affairs, and marriages more increasingly difficult to achieve."[49] With the collapse of abiding intimate relationships, Lasch argued, "reality has come to seem more and more like what we are shown by cameras."[50]

In NFB society, the inability of the new generation to maintain traditional family, school, and community relationships is almost everywhere evident.[51] From the late 1960s onwards, the pace of change is dramatic. The assertion made by a single mother in *Day Care—The Newest Tradition* (1978) that "the family is no longer strong as it was," is a truism by the late 1970s in the society in celluloid.[52] Physical and sexual abuse emerge as problems within cinematic families, as do drug and alcohol addictions. Separation and divorce become commonplace, and ultimately the family as a monolithic unit is replaced by a wide variety of family types: single parent, blended, or innovative groupings. A newly separated mother in the film, *The Umpire* (1985) best pinpoints the dilemma faced by parents who were reared for independence as she explains her separation to her son: "Philip, sometimes people who love each other don't get along too well."[53]

Likewise, the community suffers from internal problems compounded by loss of definition—quite literally so, as the meaning of the term "community" in NFB society comes to include groups of people with like characteristics as well as people of a fixed geographical location. The golden years for community involvement with young people, from the 1940s through the 1950s—years when adult organized activities for children and youth included pursuits such as cadets, agricultural clubs, choirs and art clubs, Boy Scouts and Boys' Clubs, Junior Forest Rangers, horsemanship and swimming clubs, Atom and Pee-Wee hockey leagues, Little League Baseball, modelling classes, hot-rod clubs, and majorettes—are replaced by dark days best represented by *Summer Centre* (1973), in which community property is vandalized by teenagers operating from a recreation centre. Community-based organizations for young people dwindle in number as successive waves of the baby-boom generation advance toward maturity, then virtually vanish from the cinematic society by the late 1960s, only making a brief comeback in the early 1980s when gymnastics squads and ringette clubs for girls appear in the NFB film catalogue synopses.[54]

It is in the public school, however, that the most significant outcome of the rift between generations now becomes evident. The NFB mirror, always sensitive to trends within Canadian society, begins to reflect the usurpation of the socializing role of teachers to a cinematic state. During the mid- to late 1970s, just as parents are being reduced to secondary or even minor roles in the postmodern NFB family (their power to shape posterity thereby cinematically curtailed), the stature of elementary school teachers is likewise diminished, while at the secondary level, teachers, for all intents and purposes, vanish. In a curious effect, as their traditional socializing structures become debilitated, everywhere the result on screen sees NFB children of the next generation more and more fashioning their own destinies with less and less visible guidance from NFB adults. By the 1980s, children in NFB society appear to be developing their own attitudes and expressing their own feelings on topics as complex and value laden as gender roles and relations, race and ethnicity, with very little adult guidance—but it is a cinematic illusion, of course. In reality, their social attitudes are being scripted or postproduced for them by cinematographers intent on the social reconstruction of the national character of Canadians through film. The socialization of NFB children becomes the prerogative of cinematographers. NFB kids become the subjects of a cinematic state—a progressive state without elected leaders—in which parents and teachers are quite literally written out of the script.

Epilogue

I have been cautious from the outset of this study to make a distinction between Canadian society and its cinematic portrayal by the NFB. But I would be remiss not to state what the significance of the transience of NFB social structures may be for that society, not to observe that, whether the boundaries surrounding traditional Canadian socializing structures have become equally less well-defined or not, there are no well defined boundaries surrounding the cinematic state.

Media anthropologist and journalist Joyce Nelson has analogized this concept of the unbounded cinematic state in her collection of short works, *Sign Crimes/Road Kill: From Mediascape to Landscape* (1992), in which she depicts Canada as a "Great White Screen": "not just any movie screen...but a Cinerama screen stretching its white expanse widely across our imaginations."[1]

Expanding the metaphor, Nelson argues that Canadian culture does not emerge "from a body of people and their experiences of a particular locale in human time and geographical space," but rather from their media experiences—which originate, primarily, from the United States:

> Here we see the full projection apparatus at work: the giant screen does in fact run from east to west, but the projecting line runs north-south, with images originating south of the border and playing across the national screen.[2]

———

Notes to chapter 8 are on p. 271.

Nelson's model for the Americanization of Canadian culture via cine-matic media has merit, but there is a historical dimension to be weighed into the model that has been overlooked by theorists such as herself—ie., that the implantation of American socializing structures into Canada in the 1940s and 1950s contributed to the likelihood of Canadian chil-dren being influenced by American cinematic media after the 1960s and even more so after the 1980s. Indeed, this study suggests that succeeding generations of Canadian socializing structures are now caught in a cycle that tends to reify disorganization within them, in which case they are less and less likely to ever regenerate stable traditional structures. The probability of future generations of families, schools, and communities being able to effectively counterbalance the cinematic socialization of children is thus in an ever-downward spiral. The flower will come, more and more, to depend on cinematic cultivation without the fruit.[3]

In the end, however, as Grierson instructed his documentarians, "no matter what the circumstances, hope is the last word."[4] Toward that end, knowing that the dynamics of the balance have been shifted may not be as important as knowing (in part at least) how the shift in the existing equilibrium began. This study suggests that the advent of family "independence training," as Margaret Mead described it, was inarguably the pivotal event in this regard.[5] It was introduced into the family, according to Steven Schlossman, because progressives, such as Frank, "saw the family as a more essential lever than the school for creating a more perfect social order."[6] But in NFB society at least, "levering" the family created disorder instead, which ultimately tipped the existing bal-ance in the socializing matrix.

Various explanations have been advanced as to why Canadian moth-ers adopted the psychologized, "modern" child-rearing practices typi-fied by Benjamin Spock's *Common Sense Book of Baby and Child Care* (1946). Among these, Katherine Arnup in her *Education for Motherhood* (1994) suggests that "women craved informed advice on rearing their young;" an opinion that echoes that of John Seeley in *Crestwood Heights* (1956): "mothers rejected their own experience in favour of some [expert] formula."[7] Cynthia Commachio, writing about child-rear-ing advice in general in her *Nations Are Built of Babies* (1993), notes the sway of "the force of popular opinion"—a sentiment shared by Spock, who credits the popular *I Love Lucy* television series, which featured his book in more than one episode, for maintaining his dominance over the advice literature market.[8] But it is the American psychiatrist, Hilde Bruch, in discussing postwar parenting in her *Don't Be Afraid of Your Child* (1952), who comes closest to capturing the essence of why many mothers in postwar NFB society adopt mental hygiene practices: "the fear that even the most innocent appearing act or a carelessly spoken word may harm a child or damage his future happiness [which] has become so widespread that one might almost categorize it as a phobia."[9]

In the early postwar years, mothers in NFB society are frequently worried by experts into altering their relationships with their children. In the widely distributed film *What's On Your Mind?* (1946), Dr. Blatz, the psychological consultant for the Dionne quintuplets, warns a mother that "nagging" her child could cause the boy's "nervous breakdown" in adulthood.[10] From the film *Know Your Baby* (1947), approved by the Mental Health Division of the Department of Health and Welfare, comes this haunting couplet for young mothers: "Damage the emotions and damage the body," as well as this preventative for the damage: "Respect his demands."[11] And Mrs. Smith, of course, whose son, Tommy, is so pale and wan in *Why Tommy Won't Eat* (1948) is made to see that it was she who made his dinners hellish by insisting that he should finish them: "Mrs. Smith. You are the problem, not the boy."[12]

Whatever their reasons—whether seeking informed advice, following popular trends, or fearing failure—a significant number of young mothers became, as Schlossman notes, "eager to buy what Rockefeller-funded researchers, practitioners, and popularizers were trying to sell."[13] Whether they bought Gesell and Ilg, Spock or Blatz, or the advice of their family doctor, likely the very foundation of what they received was the child-rearing philosophy of the RF—and, consequently, the uniform cultivation of "the child."

Unwittingly, however, they participated in a uniform restructuring of "the family" as well. "Democratizing" social relations in one generation of families in turn restructured the social organization of the next generation of families, a self-perpetuating process once begun—which in the first generation alone caused Seeley's *Crestwood Heights* team some trepidation:

> The rather unexpected and perhaps extraordinary spectacle presented
> by a community such as the one studied calls for a radical reconsidera-
> tion of the whole enterprise of mental health education.[14]

But no serious reconsideration of the enterprise was undertaken, not then nor ever after. The die was cast. In the late 1940s, parents in NFB society set out to put their relations with their children on a scientific and democratic foundation—not through a conscious ambition to nurture democracy but through an immediate concern for the emotional well-being of their offspring.[15]

Ultimately, at the heart of the emotional well-being of a developing individual, family, or community—at the heart of the development of a healthy national character—lies the relationship between the mother and her child. For every mother and child, at the outset of their relationship an age-old contestation over food develops, a symbolic first struggle of wills, best described by Gesell and Ilg: "the [feeding] schedule thus becomes at once symbol and a vehicle of cultural control."[16] Concerning this, Spock concluded,

> I don't think myself it's very important whether a baby is fed purely according to his own demand or whether the mother is working toward a regular schedule—if she is willing to be flexible and adjust to the baby's needs and happiness."[17]

Here, in part, lies the heart of the matter: the mother's needs and happiness.[18] Perhaps this is where to begin the remedy, with the symbolic re-assertion of the mother's will. But either some start is made—either families, schools, and communities regain their traditional control over the socialization of children—or this next century, to paraphrase Key, will be the century of the cinematic child: "There is no alternative."[19]

Appendix 1: 300 NFB Films with Significant Portrayals of Children and Youth, 1939-89

1939-49

Youth Is Tomorrow (1939)
The Children from Overseas (1940)
Hot Ice (1940)
Iceland on the Prairies (1941)
Defeat Diptheria (1941)
100,000 Cadets (1942)
Arctic Hunters (1943)
Before They Are Six (1943)
Eskimo Summer (1943)
Strength for Tomorrow (1943)
New Scotland (1943)
Thought for Food (1943)
The Vitamin Films (1943)
What Makes Us Grow (1943)
Children First (1944)
Friend for Supper (1944)
Lessons in Living (1944)
People of the Potlatch (1944)
Poland on the Prairies (1944)
Supper's Ready (1944)
Better Education—Better Canada (1945)
School Lunches (1945)
A City Sings (1945)

Early Start (1945)
Les Reportages #102 (1945)
Suffer Little Children (1945)
Conte de mon village (1946)
Ecole No. 8 (1946)
Farm Electrification (1946)
Out of the Ruins (1946)
Rural Health (1946)
Sixteen to Twenty-Six (1946)
Small Fry (1946)
What's On Your Mind? (1946)
Sports and Seasons (1946)
Feeling of Rejection (1947)
Johnny at the Fair (1947)
Know Your Baby (1947)
Mother and Her Child (1947)
Au Parc Lafontaine (1947)
Something to Chew On (1947)
Spring on a Quebec Farm (1947)
Tomorrow's Citizens (1947)
Arctic Jungle (1948)
The Feeling of Hostility (1948)
Fitness Is a Family Affair (1948)
Holiday Island (1948)
Hungry Minds (1948)

Out Beyond Town (1948)
Pennies from Canada (1948)
People with a Purpose (1948)
Champions in the Making (1948)
Why Won't Tommy Eat? (1948)
Canoe Country (1949)
Inside Newfoundland (1949)
He Acts His Age (1949)
Over-Dependency (1949)
Canadian Cruise (1949)
White Fortress (1949)
Children's Concert (1949)

1950-59

Cadet Holiday (1950)
Church of the Open Road (1950)
Feeling of Depression (1950)
Holiday in Manitoba (1950)
Friend at the Door (1950)
From Tee to Green (1950)
Our Town Is the World (1950)
Pied Piper of the 3 R's (1950)
Freedom Jamboree (1951)
Winter Morning (1951)
The Children's Own Hospital (1952)
Land of the Long Day (1952)
Angotee (1953)
Musician in the Family (1953)
Shyness (1953)
Story of Peter and the Potter (1953)
Ti-Jean Goes Lumbering (1953)
Winter in Canada (1953)
Farewell Oak Street (1953)
Food for Freddy (1953)
Frustrating Fours and Fascinating
    Fives (1953)
Here's Hockey (1953)
Moppet Models (1953)
Charwoman (1954)
Chinese Canadians (1954)
Columbia Adventure (1954)
From Sociable Six to Noisy Nine
    (1954)
Look Alert-Stay Unhurt (1954)
What Do You Think? (1954)
Child Guidance Clinic (1955)
The Pony (1955)
Borderline (1956)

Night Children (1956)
The Nativity Cycle (1956)
Bar Mitzvah (1957)
Being Different (1957)
Howard (1957)
Joe and Roxy (1957)
Making a Decision (1957)
First Adventure (1957)
Choosing a Leader (1957)
Off to School (1957)
Making a Decision in the Family
    (1957)
Popular Psychology (1957)
Putting It Straight (1957)
The Suspects (1957)
Who Is Sylvia? (1957)
The Teens (1957)
The Chairmaker and the Boys (1958)
Craftsmen Young and Old (1958)
A Foreign Language (1958)
Music for Children (1958)
One Day's Poison (1958)
A Day in June (1959)
Eternal Children (1959)
Four Families (1959)
The Gifted Ones (1959)
Pangnirtung (1959)
The Threshold (1959)
U.N. in the Classroom (1959)

1960-69

Beaver Dam (1960)
Thousand Island Summer (1960)
Books for Beaver River (1961)
Boy Meets Band (1961)
The New Baby (1961)
Northern Campus (1961)
The Saddlemaker (1961)
The Test (1961)
The Boy Next Door (1962)
Kindergarten (1962)
The Living Machine (1962)
The Rink (1962)
September 5 at Saint-Henri (1962)
Strangers for the Day (1962)
The Teacher—Authority or Automa-
    ton (1962)
Willie Catches On (1962)

The Hutterites (1963)
Pipers and A (1963)
2½ (1964)
"All About Kids" Screen Magazine
    #40 (1964)
Because They Are Different (1964)
Child of the Future: How He Might
    Learn (1964)
The End of Summer (1964)
Joey (1964)
Northern Dialogue (1964)
People Might Laugh at Us (1964)
Phoebe (1964)
The Splendid Domain (1964)
Newfoundland Trailer Trip (1964)
Animal Stories (1964)
Stay in School (1964)
Trail Ride (1964)
Centennial Travellers (1965)
A Trumpet for the Combo (1965)
The Game (1966)
Inmate Training (1966)
The Merry-Go-Round (1966)
No Reason to Stay (1966)
Once Upon a Prime Time (1966)
A Search for Learning (1966)
The Shattered Silence (1966)
The Things I Cannot Change (1966)
Tuktu and His Eskimo Dogs (1966)
The World of Three (1966)
Camp-Sights Holiday (1966)
This Is No Time for Romance (1966)
The Summer We Moved to Elm
    Street (1966)
Flowers on a One-way Street (1967)
We're Gonna Have Recess (1967)
Origami (1967)
Invention of the Adolescent (1967)
King Size (1968)
Sir! Sir! (1968)
Children of Fogo Island (1968)
Mrs. Ryan's Drama Class (1969)
The Devil's Toy (1969)
Wow (1969)
Danny and Nicky (1969)
Unstructured for a Summer (1969)
Bing Bang Boom (1969)

1970-79

The Wish (1970)
Almost Everyone Does (1970)
Hiroko Ikoko (1970)
Loops to Learn By (1970)
The Burden They Carry (1970)
One/Two/Many/World (1970)
Out of Silence (1971)
Paper Boy (1971)
Christmas at Moose Factory (1971)
People of the Seal (1971)
A Time to Consider (1972)
Cold Pizza (1972)
Dans la vie (1972)
More Common than Measles and
    Mumps (1972)
Gore Road (1972)
The Huntsman (1972)
The Netsilik Eskimo Today (1972)
Jamie, Ethan and Keir (1973)
Summer Centre (1973)
Brian at 17 (1973)
The Binkly and Doinkel Safety Show
    (1973)
Purposes of Family Planning (1973)
Bye Bye Blues (1973)
Cree Hunters of Mistassini (1974)
Branche et Branche (1974)
Would I Ever Like to Work (1974)
Piece of Cake (1974)
Play to Learn (1974)
The New Boys (1974)
Bon Amis (1974)
VD—Kids Get It Too (1974)
David and Bert (1975)
My Friends Call Me Tony (1975)
Beautiful Lennard Island (1975)
And They Lived Happily Ever After
    (1975)
Ready When You Are (1975)
Pen-Hi Grad (1975)
Gurdeep Singh Bains (1976)
The Street (1976)
Kevin Alec (1976)
I Wasn't Scared (1977)
Nunatsiaq (1977)
I'll Find a Way (1977)
Rock a Bye Baby (1977)

Happiness Is Loving Your Teacher (1977)
Challenging the Future (1977)
School Safety Patrols (1977)
Daycare—The Newest Tradition (1978)
Teach Me to Dance (1978)
Wandering Spirit Survival School (1978)
4 Years to 6 Years (1978)
Family Down the Fraser (1978)
Horizons Unlimited (1978)
Bubbles (1978)
Let's Get a Move On (1978)
Growing Up at Paradise (1978)
Children - Enfants - Ninos (1979)
Ida Makes a Movie (1979)
This Is Me (1979)
Sexual Abuse of Children: A Time for Caring (1979)

1980-89

Being Male (1980)
Girls Fitting In (1980)
Two Dreams of a Nation (1980)
An Unexplained Injury (1980)
Julie O'Brien (1981)
Magic in the Sky (1981)
The Boy Who Turned Off (1981)
The Followers (1981)
Child Sex Abuse (1982)
The Way It Is (1982)
No More Secrets (1982)
It's Just Better (1982)
Our Land, Our Truth (1983)
An Instant of Time (1983)
Body Talking (1983)
Sequence and Story (1983)
Thanks for the Ride (1983)
Feeling Yes, Feeling No: Pt. 1 (1984)
Feeling Yes, Feeling No: The Adult Film (1984)

Gifted Kids (1984)
Children of Alcohol (1984)
Snow Angels (1984)
This Is Only a Test (1984)
School Bus Collision Tests (1984)
Nicholas (1984)
Starbreaker (1984)
Discussion in Bioethics (1985)
Left Out (1985)
The Magic Quilt (1985)
Dad's House, Mom's House (1985)
Blueline (1985)
The Umpire (1985)
The Hospital (1985)
The Recovery Series—Delia (1985)
Silence Upstairs (1985)
Street Kids (1985)
Coming Apart (1985)
The Movie Movie (1986)
No Longer Silent (1986)
Sitting in Limbo (1986)
Courage to Change (1986)
Acid Rain (1986)
The Children of War (1986)
Thin Dreams (1986)
Richard Cardinal (1986)
School in the Bush (1986)
Differences (1986)
Hayley's Home Movies (1987)
Wednesday's Children: Vicky (1987)
Trouble with the Law (1987)
Crown Prince (1988)
Rendezvous Canada, 1606 (1988)
The Old Believers (1988)
Bombs Away (1988)
Canada's Capital: Behind the Scenes (1989)
Head Full of Questions (1989)
The Dig (1989)
Nicholas (1989)
Shattered Dreams (1989)
Canadian Portraits (1989)

Appendix 2: A Note Concerning the Process of Film Selection

How were films chosen for this study? Could the selection process have influenced the results? Would the conclusions reached have been different had the four hundred films not selected for screening been the sample? Were any films systematically excluded from the study, and if so why? How many of the films screened were actually used in the study? How were the films analyzed? The internal validity and reliability of a study such as this one are dependent upon the answers to such questions of methodology. In this short essay, I will detail the process by which I selected and studied the cinematic portrayals of children and youth produced by the NFB—a review which may assist others who take up the study of cinematic societies as an academic pursuit.

When I began selecting films to screen, my foremost concern was that each film should contain a significant portrayal of a child or children: i.e., based upon NFB catalogue synopses, I chose films in which children were likely to figure prominently in the footage. A second concern was that the selection of films to be screened for any decade should be roughly representative of the entire body of children described in the catalogue synopses for that decade. Categories for this determination included gender, class, regional, and cultural backgrounds. No film with a significant portrayal of children was systematically excluded by this criterion. Core themes of films varied from decade to decade in the catalogues, but films containing major recurring themes—education, civics, recreation, health, early childhood, and adolescence for example—were most often selected. Even so, obscure themes were also given a roughly representational place in the data base; indeed, I was occasionally drawn to a film by a catchy title. In retrospect, my assessment of the initial body of 250 films I screened is, as a data base, that they are a fair, (i.e., unbiased) representation of the entire body of portrayals of children produced by the NFB from 1939-1989. Indeed, so representative was this sample that I soon encountered a major analytical problem in working with it.

The central problem in analyzing a massive collection of films representative of an even greater body of films is the difficulty of making any historical sense of the representation as a whole. Having spent more than one hundred hours in screening rooms taking field notes on the films, I was determined to use as much of the sample as was possible, but I could not see an internally generated narrative involving the children's images that was applicable to the entire sample, nor even to any large part of it. Without an internally coherent narrative, a massive body of films cannot be described coherently. Without an internally coherent narrative, each film is so disjoint from so many others in the collection that a description of the whole becomes a filmography of little historical value. This has been the great failing of large bodies of films as a historical resource to date— and it is why, at best, they have been sparsely used to support historical arguments derived elsewhere and for little else.

The breakthrough in my work came while writing a paper for a doctoral seminar in which families in Canada had been a focus. For the first time, I overcame the block of thinking that NFB images of children belonged solely to the conceptual category or theme by which they had been selected and, instead, I chronologically arranged family scenes with children no matter what the topic of the film. My essay, "Reel Families," influenced my thinking in three ways. In the first place, I now saw how the sample could be utilized almost in its entirety by grouping the images of children within three social scenarios: family, school, and community. Secondly, as I was juxtaposing my descriptions of family scenes, I noticed for the first time the shifting power relations between cinematic children and their parents. And thirdly, I observed the ironic connection between the advice of Dr. Blatz to NFB parents and these changing power relations. Secondary literature on Blatz advanced my interest in the American mental hygiene movement and American progressivism on the whole.

I returned to the film catalogues with an intent to select films that would broaden my sample in regard to scenes of children in families, schools, and community contexts. I also mined an exceptionally rich collection of psychiatric films extant in the NFB archives, a body of films produced for the most part from the late 1940s through the 1950s. These final forays into the archives raised my data base of films by thirty titles. Following the narrative thread imposed by the changing social relations of cinematic children, supplemented by the narratives imposed by the institutional history of the NFB and by Canadian social history more generally, I was able to include approximately 230 of 280, or 80 percent, of films screened in the final text of this study.

Films were excluded for a number of reasons, but not for presenting contradictions to the narrative. In fact, contradictions, especially in the schools of NFB society, underscored both the unevenness and hegemony of the progressive transitions taking place. Films were excluded when, despite NFB catalogue descriptions, portrayals of children were of minimal significance, when adolescents were clearly older than high school leaving age, when the children being portrayed were neither Canadian born nor immigrants to Canada, where the films were merely longer or shorter versions of previous titles, or where films were largely animated. Some films that might have been included in the text were not, simply because they would have lengthened the study unduly. Examples of this latter category include *One Day's Poison* (1958), about the types of accidental poisonings treated daily at Toronto's Hospital for Sick Children, *Stay in School* (1964) in which a small group of high school students from Victoria, BC, tour Royal Roads College, *Cold Pizza* (1972) a comedy about the misadventures of two pizza delivery boys in Montreal, and *Snow Angels* (1984) in which two young Manitoba girls playing in a snowcave are nearly killed by a snowplough. There was no particular reason to exclude films such as these; but neither was there any strong reason to include them.

Were a different sample of 250 films to be selected for the study, I have little doubt that, given the same selection procedures, the same social patterns would again become widely evident, as long as the films selected were arranged by family, school, and community scenarios and juxtaposed diachronically. "Truth brings beauty to any edifice," the young Grierson once remarked, and his test of beauty was, "whether or not the thing [would] roll down a hill without pieces breaking off." The beauty of this study is that the historical meta-narrative it develops is generated by the body of films itself, rather than being brought to the films by a historian. Its truth—its internal validity and reliability—lies in its internal coherency, in the simple fact that so many films fit together in a narrative so well. At the bottom of any hill it might be rolled down, NFB society as presented in this study would remain intact, I believe, due to the internal fit of its pieces.

Notes

Chapter 1: Children in a Cinematic Society

1 My research utilizes the English-language films of the NFB archival collection, including independently produced films commissioned for, or adopted by, the National Film Board of Canada under its mandate: "to interpret Canada to Canadians." Concerning the problem this poses in regard to the English/French dichotomy as it relates to the portrayals of children by the NFB, for the purposes of this study—i.e., to describe "NFB Society"—the solution is surprisingly simple. The Québec wing of the institution has from its inception in 1939 been known as the ONF: L'Office national du film du Canada. I include no films from the ONF in my description of NFB Society, except those which have been "versioned" into English by the NFB.

2 Exceptions to this include Barbara Halpern Martineau, "Before the Guerillières: Women's Films at the NFB During World War II," in *The Canadian Film Reader*, ed. Seth Feldman and Joyce Nelson (Toronto: Peter Martin, 1977), pp. 58-67; Yvonne Mathews-Klein, "How They Saw Us: Images of Women in National Film Board Films of the 1940s and 1950s," *Atlantis: A Women's Studies Journal* 4, 2 (1979): 20-38; and H. Clifford Chadderton *Hanging a Legend: The NFB's Shameful Attempt to Discredit Billy Bishop* (Ottawa: The War Amps of Canada, 1986).

3 In order to replicate the "presence" experience of a film spectator, I employ the historical present tense whenever describing the events of a film narrative.

4 For the purposes of this study, I employ Susan Houston's concept of a twentieth century "school-aged childhood," setting the parameters of the term "child" between infancy and school-leaving age.

5 In the 1940s, there are far more portrayals of boys than of girls. This imbalance is not fully addressed until the mid-1970s.

6 For some instances when "Canadian sensibilities" were piqued by National Film Board productions, see Gary Evans, *John Grierson and the National Film Board: The Politics of Wartime Propaganda* (Toronto: University of Toronto Press, 1984), pp. 207-15; and Gary Evans, *In the National Interest: A Chronicle of the National Film Board of Canada from 1949 to 1989* (Toronto: University of Toronto Press, 1991), pp. 179-89, 295-98.

7 From 1939 to 1950, the mandate of the NFB read somewhat differently: "to help Canadians in all parts of Canada to understand the ways of living and the problems of Canadians in other parts."

8 The first known reference to the phrase is in Ellen Key's *The Century of the Child* (New York: Knickerbocker Press, 1909), an argument for the emancipation of women through the rearing of children.

9 Exceptions to this include work by Kathy Jackson (1986) who has provided a "sociocultural analysis" of the themes of childhood in selected American feature films; Marjorie Keller (1986) who has analyzed childhood through the filter of Freud in the surrealist films of Cocteau, Cornell, and Brakhage; Andrea Darvi (1983) who has analyzed her own childhood as a Hollywood child actress; David Considine (1985) who has explored recurring narrative themes in popular films featuring adolescents; and Neil Sinyard (1992) who has celebrated artistry in motion-picture portrayals of childhood.

10 Indeed, among the earliest Lumière "movies" of the late 1890s, there are several featuring children. Most notably, the infant child of Louis Lumière, who appears in an outdoor breakfast scene in the short film *Le Repas de bébé* (1896), a scene that has been duplicated countless times by later generations of parents with their own 8mm or video equipment.

11 To be historically credible, a "non-fictional" film must meet the criteria set by the Zapruder account of the Kennedy assassination: that is, an unplanned, continuous recording of an event left in its original context. Good accounts of the use of film as a historical resource include V.M. Magidov, "Film Documentation: Problems of Source Analysis and Use in Historical Research," *Historical Journal of Film, Radio, and Television* 9, 2 (1989): 151-63; Raymond Fielding, "Newsfilm as a Scholarly Resource," *Historical Journal of Film, Radio, and Television* 7, 1 (1987): 47-54; John E. O'Connor, ed., *Image as Artifact: The Historical Analysis of Film and Television* (Malabar, FL: Robert E. Krieger, 1990); and Paul Smith, ed., *The Historian and Film* (Cambridge: Cambridge University Press, 1976).

12 A full discussion of the temporal dimensions of historical and social concepts may be found in E.P. Thompson, *The Making of the English Working Class* (Harmondsworth: Penguin, 1968).

13 John Grierson, cited in Dorothy Livesay, *Radio Talk on the Topic of* Lessons in Living, 9:30 C.B.R. Western and Prairie Networks, Thursday, November 16, 1944.

14 Theresa Richardson, *The Century of the Child: The Mental Hygiene Movement and Social Policy in the United States and Canada* (New York: SUNY, 1989).

15 Ibid., p. 3.

16 Ibid.

17 Lawrence K. Frank, "Childhood and Youth," *Recent Social Trends in the United States: Report of the President's Research Committee on Social Trends,* (New York: McGraw-Hill, 1933), 2: 753.

18 Ibid., p. 794.

19 Ibid., p. 754, 800.

20 Ibid., p. 753.

21 Ibid., p. 794.

22 Ibid., p. 753.

23 Ibid., p. 790. As observed by Joel Spring in *Images of American Life: A History of Ideological Management in Schools, Movies, Radio, and Television* (New York: SUNY, 1992), p. 59, the direct educative potential of film, as revealed in studies undertaken in the 1930s, could only have been perceived as promising. Another of the studies found that children retained information from movies over long periods of time. A group of second and third graders remembered at the end of six weeks 90 percent of what they remembered from a movie on the day they saw it.

24 Spring, *Images of American Life,* p. 96.

25 An exception to this is the recent contemplation of the effects of the 1933 Payne Fund Studies publications by Garth Jowett, Ian Jarvie, and Kathryn Fuller in *Children and the Movies: Media Influence and the Payne Fund Controversy* (Cambridge: Cambridge University Press, 1996).

26 Soundtrack from *Life with Baby,* 18 min., 16mm, sound, b&w film, Time/Life, New York, 1946.

27 Ibid.

28 Ibid.

29 Ibid.

30 Ibid.

31 This subtle transition is an illustration of what film historian Wolfgang Ernst has described as "the very force of [a] film working on the visual senses [to] overturn a viewer's contemplative stance." The rapid and irreversible movement of the film narrative impels the viewer's thought processes forward with equal rapidity, pass the transgressions without pause, the cinematic equivalent of a sleight of hand trick.

32 Soundtrack from *Life with Baby.*

33 Ibid. In his *Infant and Child in the Culture of Today* (1946), a popular child-rearing manual that resulted from the Yale Clinic of Child Development studies, Dr. Gesell acknowledged the substantial funding of the clinic by philanthropic foundations: "We are fundamentally indebted to the Rockefeller Foundation, which over a period of years has given generous long range support to systematic investigations which underly the present work. The more recent and extremely timely support of the Carnegie Corporation of New York has made the completion of this work possible," Arnold Gesell, Frances Ilg, inter alia, *Infant and Child in the Culture of Today: The Guidance of Development in Home and Nursery School* (New York: Harper and Brothers, 1943), p. xi.

34 John Grierson quoted in Evans, *John Grierson and the National Film Board: The Politics of Wartime Propaganda* (Toronto: University of Toronto Press, 1984), p. 32. The nascent documentary film movement itself had ties to Rockefeller philanthropy. The documentary idea germinated in John

Grierson's mind while he held a Laura Spelman Rockefeller memorial (LSRM) fellowship, fifteen years before his career as the government film commissioner for Canada began.

35 Geoff Eley, "Reading Gramsci in English: Observations on the Reception of Antonio Gramsci in the English-Speaking World, 1957-82," *European History Quarterly* 14 (October 1984), cited in Esteve Morera, *Gramsci's Historicism: A Realist Interpretation* (London: Routledge, 1990), p. 194.

36 Marjory McKay, "The Motion Picture: A Mirror of Time," *NFB Annual Report, 1958-1959* (Ottawa: National Film Board of Canada, 1959), p. 22.

37 See my Appendix 2, "A Note Concerning the Process of Film Selection," for a detailed description and rationale of the film selection process.

38 See bibliography for full citations of all secondary materials referred to in this study.

39 This dualism is consistent with Grierson's belief in the possibility of being "totalitarian for the good." John Grierson quoted in Evans, *John Grierson and the National Film Board*, p.14.

40 An inconsistency between NFB society and Canadian society is the absence of empirical evidence of Benjamin Spock's influence upon NFB parents. The *Ages and Stages* series of advice films produced from the late 1940s through the 1950s were heavily influenced by Gesell and Frances Ilg's *Infant and Child in the Culture of Today* (1943), and their guide, *The Child from Five to Ten* (1946) is literally opened for reference by a child-rearing expert in the film *He Acts His Age* (1949). Similarly, in the film *Mother and Her Child* (1947), an NFB mother seeks advice from Ernest Couture's *The Canadian Mother and Child* (1940), but not once within the films surveyed for this study does Spock's *Baby and Child Care* appear. Various explanations may be generated for the absence, but I am swayed to the opinion that the omission highlights Spock's role in the late 1940s as but one apostle of the gospel of the "parent education movement," the mental hygienist approach to child rearing funded by the LSRM after 1920, including Gesell's work and the immensely popular *Parents' Magazine*. It seems oddly ironic in regard to Spock's invisibility in NFB society that, in the Cardinal edition of his *Baby and Child Care* (1946), Spock acknowledges the contributions of many of his contemporaries (Dr. Ilg among them) but omits Gesell. With the omission, Spock inadvertently smudged the intellectual links of his own child-rearing "gospel" to Gesell's Yale Clinic and consequently to Rockefeller philanthropy. See Steven Schlossman, "Philanthropy and the Gospel of Child Development, *History of Education Quarterly* 21 (Fall 1981): 275-99.

41 The circumstances find theoretical unity in at least one critical analysis of Benjamin Spock and *Baby and Child Care*. See Michael Zuckerman, "Dr. Spock: The Confidence Man," from his *Almost Chosen People* (Berkeley: University of California Press, 1993), pp. 260-87.

42 "New Society" (Société Nouvelle) was the ONF equivalent to the NFB's "Challenge for Change" program.

43 For a media-oriented analysis of a similar phenomenon in North American society, see Joshua Meyrowitz, *No Sense of Place: The Impact of Electronic Media on Social Behavior* (New York: Oxford University Press, 1985).

44 Anna Torti, *The Glass of Form: Mirroring Structures from Chaucer to Skelton* (Cambridge: D.S. Brewer, 1991), pp. 1-2.

Chapter 2: Early NFB Society: The Eyes of Democracy

1 David B. Jones, *Movies and Memoranda: An Interpretative History of the National Film Board of Canada* (Ottawa: Canadian Film Institute, 1981), p. 30.

2 An energetic, hardy, law-abiding, and loyal people were the attributes of the Canadian national character from the mid-nineteenth century through the early-twentieth century, according to Carl Berger in "The Canadian Character," in *The Sense of Power: Studies in the Ideas of Canadian Imperialism, 1867-1914* (Toronto: University of Toronto Press, 1970), pp. 128-52. In addition, most English Canadians remained "British" in their outlook at least until the end of World War II. Indeed, not only did the Union Jack fly over the inside front cover of the *New Canadian Readers* (Toronto: W.J. Gage, 1929) but, to judge from NFB films from 1939-46, over most Canadian cities, towns, and villages as well.

3 Nicholas Pronay, "John Grierson and the Documentary—60 years on," *Historical Journal of Film, Radio and Television*, 9 3 (1989): 238.

4 John Grierson, *Eyes of Democracy* (Stirling: University of Stirling Press, 1990), pp. 130-31, 133.

5 Ibid., p. 105.

6 Ibid., p. 136.

7 Ian Aitken, *Film and Reform: John Grierson and the Documentary Film Movement* (London: Routledge, 1990), p. 19.

8 Ibid., p. 25.

9 Ibid.

10 Walter Lippmann, *Public Opinion* (New York: Macmillan, 1922), p. 29.

11 Ibid., p. 222.

12 Ibid., p. 369.

13 Ibid., pp. 378, 386.

14 Ibid., p. 92.

15 Ibid., pp. 91, 165.

16 Ian Jarvie and Robert L. MacMillan, "John Grierson on Hollywood's Success, 1927," in *Historical Journal of Film, Radio, and Television* 9, 3 (1989): 314.

17 John Grierson quoted in Jarvie and MacMillan, "John Grierson on Hollywood's Success, 1927," p. 313.

18 Ibid., p. 309, 313.

19 Ibid., p. 313.

20 Ibid., p. 310.

21 Ibid., p. 315.

22 John Grierson quoted in The John Grierson Project, McGill University, *John Grierson and the NFB* (Montreal: ECW Press, 1984), p. vii.

23 John Grierson quoted in Gary Evans, *John Grierson and the National Film Board: The Politics of Wartime Propaganda* (Toronto: University of Toronto Press, 1984), p. 94.

24 Soundtrack from *100,000 Cadets*, 17 min., 16mm, sound, b&w film, National Film Board of Canada, Montreal, QC, Canada, 1942.

25 John Grierson quoted in Evans, *John Grierson and the National Film Board*, p. 95.

26 "Final Commentary for *Lessons in Living*," Production No. 6034, Recorded October 26, 1944. National Film Board Archives, Montreal, QC, Canada.

27 Soundtrack from *Before They Are Six*, 19 min., 16mm, sound, b&w film, National Film Board of Canada, Montreal, QC, Canada, 1943.

28 Ibid.

29 John Grierson quoted in Dennis Forman and Gus MacDonald, *The John Grierson Archive* (Stirling: University of Stirling Press, 1978), p. 18.

30 C.W. Gray, "Movies for the People: The Story of the National Film Board's Unique Distribution System," unpublished major paper (Ottawa: National Film Board of Canada, 1973), p. 92.

31 Soundtrack from *Small Fry*, 10 min., 16mm, sound, b&w film, National Film Board of Canada, Montreal, QC, Canada, 1946. Ironically, although Grierson pressed his cooperative philosophy at the Film Board, underscoring his policy of filmmaking as a cooperative effort by imposing a policy of no credit titles on "prestige" films, in his own work he demonstrated "a brazen independence from others." See Evans, *John Grierson and the National Film Board*, p. 214; see Joyce Nelson, *The Colonized Eye: Rethinking the Grierson Legend* (Toronto: Between the Lines Press, 1988), p. 29.

32 Evans, *John Grierson and the National Film Board*, p. 170.

33 Tom Daly quoted in Evans, *John Grierson and the National Film Board*, p. 120. Grierson described Lorne Greene's voice as "having a built-in cello."

34 Soundtrack from *Tomorrow's Citizens*, 10 min., 16mm, sound, b&w film, National Film Board of Canada, Montreal, QC, Canada, 1947.

35 John Grierson quoted in Nelson, *The Colonized Eye*, p. 80.

36 Soundtrack from *Suffer Little Children*, 10 min., 16mm, sound, b&w film, National Film Board of Canada, Montreal, QC, Canada, 1945.

37 Outside of Québec, the second largest market for the wartime films of L'Office national du film was Ciné France.

38 James Beveridge, *John Grierson, Film Master* (New York: MacMillan, 1978), p. 127.

39 Paul Theriault, quoted in Beveridge, *John Grierson, Film Master*, p. 207.

40 The use of technicolour in National Film Board films of this era is unique to the filmed portrayals of the Indians and the Inuit, for tourism films, and for the animated films of Norman McLaren.

41 Basil Wright, "An Innocent in Canada," in The John Grierson Project, *John Grierson and the NFB*, p. 133.

42 Family Allowance Act, 1944, 8 & 9 George V, ch. 40, 11 (d): "provide that in the case of Indians and Eskimaux payment of the allowance shall be made to a person authorized by the Governor in Council to receive and apply the same."

43 John Grierson, "Searchlight on Democracy," in Forsyth Hardy, ed., *Grierson on Documentary* (London: Faber and Faber, 1966), p. 233. Although unique for the scope and scale of the system, in fact a similar system of distribution had been put in place in Nazi Germany to bring propaganda films to the most remote regions of that nation in the 1930s. See Martin Loiperdinger and David Culbert, "Leni Riefenstahl, the SA, and the Nazi Party Rally Films, Nuremberg 1933-1934: *Sieg des Glaubens* and *Triumph des Willens*," *Historical Journal of Film, Radio and Television* 8, 1 (1988): 12.

44 Forsyth Hardy, *John Grierson: A Documentary Biography* (London: Faber and Faber, 1979), p. 48.

45 Evans, *John Grierson and the National Film Board*, p. 122.

46 C.W. Gray, "Movies for the People," p. 7. Gray's work is an entertaining first-hand account of the early showmen and NFB projectionists.

47 Ibid., p. 40.

48 Evans, *John Grierson and the National Film Board*, p. 162.

49 Ibid., p. 148.

50 Gray, "Movies for the People," p. 38.

51 Ibid., p. 48.

52 Evans, *John Grierson and the National Film Board*, p. 150. Audience attendance averaged from provincial figures provided by Evans.

53 Gray, "Movies for the People," p. 56.

54 Evans, *John Grierson and the National Film Board*, p. 162. Audience numbers are a summation of figures provided by Evans.

55 Ibid.

56 Government of Canada, *The Canada Year Book* (Ottawa: Dominion Bureau of Statistics, Department of Trade and Commerce, 1946), p. 94. Even if NFB attendance figures are halved to allow for a tendency toward exaggeration, the scope and size of the national audience is impressive.

57 The John Grierson Project, *John Grierson and the NFB*, p. 33.

58 B.T. Richardson, "Our Films and Critics," *Victoria Daily Times*, 6 April 1944, p. 4. A.R. Adamson quoted in Evans, *John Grierson and the National Film Board*, p. 207.

59 Evans, *John Grierson and the National Film Board*, p. 215.

60 Grierson's reputation was a casualty of what Reg Whitaker and Gary Marcuse have described as the "national insecurity state" that followed Gouzenko's defection from the Soviet Embassy. The documents handed over to the RCMP by Gouzenko implicating the Film Board in a Soviet spy ring included a hastily jotted note by a Lieutenant Colonel Motinov: "Professor. Research Council—report on organization and work. Freda to the Professor through Grierson." The intent was to have Freda Linton, Grierson's secretary, transferred from the Film Board to the National Research Council through Grierson's office. See Reg Whitaker and Gary Marcuse, *Cold War Canada: The Making of a National Insecurity State, 1945-1957* (Toronto: University of Toronto Press, 1994).

61 According to Nelson, following Grierson's first appearance before the Taschereau-Kellock Commission in April 1946, J. Edgar Hoover was so convinced that Grierson was a communist sympathizer that he sent out Grierson's dossier to various senior bureaucrats in Washington and did his utmost to cause problems and delays in Grierson's securing of an immigration visa, which was eventually revoked in February 1947. Nelson, *The Colonized Eye*, pp. 154-58; Hardy, *John Grierson*, pp. 162-63.

62 Grierson, *Eyes of Democracy*, p. 136. Emphasis his.

Chapter 3: Lessons in Living: "Deconstruction" of a Rural Community in Early NFB Society

1 Ruth Anderson, Armand Caillet, Yvonne Ruggles, Arnold Tjorhom, and Wilma Tjorhom, private interview with child actors from *Lessons in Living* (1944) recorded at Lantzville, BC, 2 November 1991.

2 Donald W. Bidd, ed., *The NFB Film Guide: The Productions of the National Film Board of Canada from 1939-1989* (Montreal: The National Film Board of Canada and The National Archives of Canada, 1991), pp. 915-16.

3 Forsyth Hardy, *John Grierson: A Documentary Biography* (London: Faber and Faber, 1979), p. 96.

4 Gary Evans, *John Grierson and the National Film Board: The Politics of Wartime Propaganda* (Toronto: University of Toronto Press, 1984), p. 1.

5 "Final Commentary for *Lessons in Living*," Reel #1, Production No. 6034, Recorded 26 October 1944. National Film Board Archives, Montreal, QC, Canada.

6 "Final Commentary for *Lessons in Living*," Reel #3, Production No. 6034, Recorded 26 October 1944. National Film Board Archives, Montreal, QC, Canada.

7 Progressivism in education is, as George Tomkins observed, "a loosely applied label, a complex reality that has both liberal and conservative dimensions." In British Columbia by the mid-1940s, progressive education had both a classroom component, "the reorganization of the curriculum into a succession of projects of purposeful activity...consistent with the child's interests...in a school environment nearly typical of life itself," and an administrative component, which "sought to centralize education under expert leadership in the interests of social efficiency and social control." See George S. Tomkins, *A Common Countenance: Stability and Change in the Canadian Curriculum* (Scarborough: Prentice-Hall, 1986), pp. 189-90.

8 Canada and Newfoundland Education Association. *Proceedings of the Twentieth Convention* (Toronto: University of Toronto Press, 1942), p. 51.

9 Ibid., p. 52.

10 Ibid., p. 53.

11 Ibid., p. 57.

12 Indeed, "Kindling New Fires in Smoky Lane" was printed in the appendix of the *Proceedings of the Twentieth Convention* in conjuction with another article, "The Role of Education in Post-War Reconstruction."

13 Letter, Dallas E. Jones to Dr. William A. Plenderleith, 3 January 1944, *Lessons in Living* File, National Film Board Archives, Montreal, QC, Canada.

14 *Proceedings of the Twentieth Convention*, p. 52.

15 Canada and Newfoundland Education Association. *Proceedings of the Nineteenth Convention* (Toronto: University of Toronto Press, 1941), p. 46.

16 Ibid., p. 24.

17 My thanks to Jane Gaskell for directing me towards the connection between the NFB and the delegates at the 1941 CNEA convention at Ottawa. The interest of the educational élite in the films of the nascent NFB may be explored in greater detail in the *Proceedings of the Nineteenth Convention* of the CNEA. For a succinct description of both the Matsqui-Sumas-Abbotsford

as well as the Nanaimo-Ladysmith consolidation experiments see Jean Mann, "G.M. Weir and H.B. King: Progressive Education or Education for the Progressive State?" in *Schooling and Society in Twentieth Century British Columbia*, J. Donald Wilson and David C. Jones, eds. (Calgary: Detselig, 1980), p. 108.

18 William A. Plenderleith, "The Peace River Larger Unit of Administration: A Report of an Experiment in the Reorganization and Administration of a Rural Inspectoral Unit in British Columbia" (D.Paed. dissertation, University of Toronto, 1936), p. 5.

19 Ibid., p. 11. For recent insights into the influence of a rural community over its teachers see Paul J. Stortz and J. Donald Wilson, "Education on the Frontier: Schools, Teachers and Community Influence in North Central British Columbia," in *Histoire Sociale-Social History* 26, 52 (November 1993): 265-90. For early, but similar, insights into the phenomenon see Bird T. Baldwin, et al., *Farm Children: An Investigation of Rural Child Life in Selected Areas of Iowa* (New York: D. Appleton & Co., 1930).

20 Plenderleith, p. 22.

21 Ibid., p. 22.

22 Unnamed Peace River resident quoted in Plenderleith, p. 65.

23 Ibid., p. 38.

24 Ibid., p. 24.

25 Ibid., p. 62.

26 Ibid., p. 67.

27 Ibid., p. 80.

28 Ibid., p. 75. Citation from "Public Education in Oklahoma," U.S. Bureau of Publications, 1922, p. 49.

29 Ibid., p. 96.

30 Ibid.

31 A.H. Child, "Herbert B. King, Administrative Idealist," cited in Jean Mann "G.M. Weir and H.B. King: Progressive Education or Education for the Progressive State?" in *Schooling and Society in 20th Century British Columbia*, J. Donald Wilson and David C. Jones, eds. (Calgary: Detselig, 1980), p. 108. It is interesting to note that the British Columbia Teacher's Federation (BCTF), which had favoured consolidation in the Peace River area, became convinced in the Matsqui-Abbotsford campaign that the government was more interested in economy than a better quality of education. See Mann, in *Schooling and Society in 20th Century British Columbia*, p. 108.

32 "Final Commentary for *Lessons in Living*," Reel #3, Production No. 6034, Recorded 26 October 1944. National Film Board Archives, Montreal, QC, Canada.

33 "Final Commentary for *Lessons in Living*," Reel #3, Production No. 6034, Recorded 26 October 1944. National Film Board Archives, Montreal, QC, Canada.

34 Letter, Dallas E. Jones to Dr. William A. Plenderleith, 23 December 1943, *Lessons in Living* File, National Film Board Archives, Montreal, QC, Canada.

35 Ibid.

36 Ibid.

37 Letter, Dallas E. Jones to Dr. William A. Plenderleith, 3 January 1944, *Lessons in Living* File, National Film Board Archives, Montreal, QC, Canada.
38 Evans, *John Grierson and the National Film Board*, p. 95.
39 John Grierson, quoted in Hardy, *John Grierson*, p. 126. The best description of John Grierson's ideological development is Ian Aitken, *Film and Reform: John Grierson and the Documentary Film Movement* (London: Routledge, 1990).
40 Letter, Dallas E. Jones to Dr. William A. Plenderleith, 3 January 1944, *Lessons in Living* File, National Film Board Archives, Montreal, QC, Canada.
41 "Final Commentary for *Lessons in Living*," Reel #1, Production No. 6034, Recorded 26 October 1944. National Film Board Archives, Montreal, QC, Canada.
42 Ibid.
43 Ibid.
44 Based upon instructions given by Dallas Jones to Mr. Caillet. Letter, Dallas E. Jones to Mr. Caillet, 29 December 1943, *Lessons in Living* File, National Film Board Archives, Montreal, QC, Canada.
45 Ruth Anderson, Armand Caillet, Yvonne Ruggles, Arnold Tjorhom, and Wilma Tjorhom, private interview with child actors from *Lessons in Living* (1944) recorded at Lantzville, BC, 2 November 1991.
46 Letter, Dallas E. Jones to Dr. William A. Plenderleith, 19 January 1944, *Lessons in Living* File, National Film Board Archives, Montreal, QC, Canada.
47 Ibid. The "other necessary materials," approximately $300 worth, were for paint, varnish, brushes, sandpaper, etc., to paint the school and build library bookcases and tables for the classroom.
48 Ibid. The working budget for *Lessons in Living* was $11,000.
49 Ruth Anderson et al.
50 Ibid.
51 Ibid.
52 After inspecting Catherine Mrus, Plenderleith wrote in November 1944: "She is obtaining the maximum cooperation from the members of the community in maintaining the high standards set at Lantzville during the past few years." See GR 456, "School Inspectors' Reports, 1940-1946," Box 16: Files 1-3, British Columbia Archives and Records Services, Victoria, BC.
53 Ruth Anderson et al. Plenderleith took responsibility for casting the teachers in the film, and he decided to replace the two teachers from Lantzville with Archie Mercer and Margo Fairbairn (née Margot Bate) both of Brechin School at Nanaimo.
54 "Final Commentary for *Lessons in Living*," Reel #2.
55 Ruth Anderson et al.
56 "Final Commentary for *Lessons in Living*," Reel #2.
57 Ruth Anderson et al., from field notes. Lantzville, BC, 2 November 1991.
58 One Lantzville child first learned of the film's appearance on the rural circuits when her grandmother telephoned from Port Alberni, BC, to tell her she had just seen the girl "in the movies." *Lessons in Living* was distributed both nationally and internationally. A projectionist report from Camden

Town, Ealing, and Acton in Britain recorded a total audience of 291, whose reaction to the film was "V. Good." A mystery related to the film was the lack of knowledge about the production at the lower levels of administration at the Department of Education. Indeed, a July 1944 letter from Dallas Jones, the producer, to Muriel MacKay, a research assistant in the Department of Education, suggests that with the exception of the Deputy Minister and Plenderleith, most of the Department was in the dark about the Lantzville project: "Regarding your suggestion that the Department of Education knows nothing about the film we prepared in Lantzville, I would like to call your attention to the fact that I consulted Dr. Willis before selecting the Lantzville location and Dr. Plenderleith kept him informed of our progress throughout the location production...Our Distribution Division will be pleased to send you a print [of the film] on loan or to sell you one if you would like to have one of your own."

59 "Nanaimo First to See Film Made in This School District," *Nanaimo Daily Free Press*, 13 November 1944.

60 Ibid.

61 Ruth Anderson et al.

62 "Information Sheet No. 51" issued by the National Film Board of Canada, November 1944, National Film Board Archives, Montreal, QC, Canada.

63 Thomas Prine, "Last Month on My Circuit," BC circuit report, August 1945, addressed to Helen Watson, Supervisor of Rural Distribution, National Film Board, Ottawa. National Film Board Archives, Montreal, QC, Canada.

64 Various respondents, "Special Report on LESSONS IN LIVING," July to August 1945, circuit reports addressed to Helen Watson, Supervisor of Rural Distribution, National Film Board, Ottawa. National Film Board Archives, Montreal, QC, Canada. "Pro-Rec" was a depression-era public program of physical recreation sponsored by the British Columbia provincial government. The program continued into the early 1950s. For a well-written historical account of the program see Phyllis Barbara Schrodt, "A History of Pro-Rec: The British Columbia Provincial Recreation Programme—1934 to 1953," (Ph.D. thesis, University of Alberta, 1979).

65 Betty Boyer, "Lessons in Living," typed essay by a grade 7 student from Miami, Manitoba, March, 1945. National Film Board Archives, Montreal, QC, Canada.

66 V. Poloway, "Special Report on LESSONS IN LIVING," July 1945 circuit report addressed to Helen Watson, Supervisor of Rural Distribution, National Film Board, Ottawa. National Film Board Archives, Montreal, QC, Canada.

67 Ibid.

68 J.C. Peck, "Special Report on LESSONS IN LIVING," July 1945 circuit report addressed to Helen Watson, Supervisor of Rural Distribution, National Film Board, Ottawa. National Film Board Archives, Montreal, QC, Canada.

69 M.J. Krewesky, "Special Report on LESSONS IN LIVING," 1945 circuit report addressed to Helen Watson, Supervisor of Rural Distribution, National Film Board, Ottawa. National Film Board Archives, Montreal, QC, Canada.

70 Elmer Brownell, "Special Report on LESSONS IN LIVING," 1945 circuit report addressed to Helen Watson, Supervisor of Rural Distribution, National Film Board, Ottawa. National Film Board Archives, Montreal, QC, Canada.

71 Pennsylvania College for Women, "Lessons in Living," evaluation no. 1949.502 prepared for the Educational Film Library Association, New York, 1949. National Film Board Archives, Montreal, QC, Canada.

72 Ruth Anderson et al., from field notes. The loss of community identity, of course, had been ironically foreshadowed at the "premiere" of the film, when the NFB decided "that since the *setting* was in *Nanaimo*...Nanaimo citizens should be given the first opportunity to obtain a preview of the film" [emphasis mine].

73 Fifty years following the first mass consolidation of school districts, British Columbia consolidated the remaining 75 districts to 46 in 1996, citing economic reasons. Despite considerable grumbling from some school boards, the public remained apathetic and no political party made school district consolidation an issue during the 1996 provincial election.

74 My thanks to Jan Clemson and Donald Haig of the NFB for pointing this out to me. Dr. Haig was able to discern this information from the header used on a 16mm print of the film.

75 Plenderleith, "The Peace River Larger Unit of Administration," p. 22. A final parallel between the "NFB community" of Lantzville and the actual educational history of the Vancouver Island community is instructive in regard to the progressive loss of community control over education. The Lantzville children who yearn at the beginning of *Lessons in Living* for "workshops with lots of tools and kitchens for the girls," the same as "those city kids" who "get everything" did, in fact, after consolidation, acquire these very things in real life. Not in Lantzville, however, but in the city of Nanaimo—a half-hour drive away on the consolidated school bus.

Chapter 4: Fields of Vision: Panoramas of Childhood in the Cinematic Society, 1947-1967

1 Ross McLean, *The National Film Board Annual Report, 1946-47* (Ottawa: Cloutier, King's Printer, 1947), p. 5.

2 Fertility rates among women of the 20-24 age group rose from 130/1000 in 1940 to 234/1000 by 1960. See John R. Miron, *Housing in Postwar Canada* (Kingston and Montreal: McGill-Queen's 1988), table 3, p. 35. Cited in Strong-Boag, "Home Dreams" in R. Douglas Francis and Donald B. Smith, *Readings in Canadian History: Post-Confederation* (Toronto: Harcourt Brace, 1994), p. 483.

3 Soundtrack from *Mother and Her Child*, 54 min., 16mm, sound, colour film, National Film Board of Canada, Montreal, QC, Canada, 1947.

4 Soundtrack from *Johnny at the Fair*, 12 min., 16mm, sound, b&w film, National Film Board of Canada, Montreal, QC, Canada 1947.

5 Soundtrack from *Out Beyond Town*, 11 min., 16mm, sound, b&w film, National Film Board of Canada, Montreal, QC, Canada, 1948.

6 Soundtrack from *Inside Newfoundland*, 11 min., 16mm, sound, b&w film, National Film Board of Canada, Montreal, QC, Canada, 1949.

7 Soundtrack from *Holiday Island*, 10 min., 16mm, sound, colour film, National Film Board of Canada, Montreal, QC, Canada, 1948.

8 Soundtrack from *From Tee to Green*, 12 min., 16mm, sound, colour film, National Film Board of Canada, Montreal, QC, Canada, 1950.

9 Illustrative of the caution NFB filmmakers exercised during the late 1940s is this quote attributed to Evelyn Cherry, speaking to her husband: "After one of these parties I said to Lawrence, 'Isn't it awful what's happened to us? We have nothing left to talk about except our children and our dogs.'" Evelyn Spice Cherry quoted in Reg Whitaker and Gary Marcuse, *Cold War Canada: The Making of a National Insecurity State, 1945-1957* (Toronto: University of Toronto Press, 1994), p. 258.

10 Marjory McKay, "History of the National Film Board of Canada," unpublished major paper (Ottawa: National Film Board, 1964), p. 73.

11 Gary Evans and Marjory McKay are both profuse in their praise of Irwin on these points. Even Grierson is said to have told Irwin, "You saved the Film Board." Grierson quoted in McKay, "History of the National Film Board," p. 89.

12 Gary Evans, *In the National Interest: A Chronicle of the National Film Board of Canada from 1949 to 1989* (Toronto: University of Toronto Press, 1991), p. 13.

13 W. Arthur Irwin, "The Canadian," *Maclean's: Canada's National Magazine*, 1 February 1950, p. 35.

14 Doug Owram, *Born at the Right Time: A History of the Baby-Boom Generation* (Toronto: University of Toronto Press, 1996), p. 52.

15 Soundtrack from *Cadet Holiday*, 12 min., 16mm, sound, colour film, National Film Board of Canada, Montreal, QC, Canada, 1950.

16 Soundtrack from *Our Town is the World*, 9 min., 16mm, sound, b&w film, National Film Board of Canada, Montreal, QC, Canada, 1950.

17 Soundtrack from "Pied Piper of the 3R's," in *Eyewitness #29*, 9 min., 16mm, sound, b&w film, National Film Board of Canada, Montreal, QC, Canada, 1950. More than 150 of the *Eyewitness Series* vignettes were produced by the Film Board between 1950 and 1953.

18 For a colourful description of the changing cult of the drive-in theatre in Canada in the 1950s see Owram, *Born at the Right Time*, pp. 151-52.

19 Soundtrack from "Church of the Open Road," in *Eyewitness #29*, 9 min., 16mm, sound, b&w film, National Film Board of Canada, Montreal, QC, Canada, 1950.

20 Joyce Nelson, *The Perfect Machine: TV in the Nuclear Age* (Toronto: Between the Lines Press, 1987), p. 25. Throughout the 1950s, while Canadian movie theatres for the most part were closed on Sundays by law, radio and television, which were from the outset an irresistable attraction to young people, circumvented the entertainment restrictions.

21 Evans, *In the National Interest*, p. 7.

22 *National Film Board Annual Report*, 1947, p. 222.

23 Evans, *In the National Interest*, p. 6.

24 The best history of the nascent CBC Television is Paul Rutherford, *When Television Was Young: Primetime Canada 1952-1967* (Toronto: University of Toronto Press, 1990). Good discussions of the cultural effects of early television include Nelson, *The Perfect Machine* and Joshua Meyrowitz, *No Sense of Place: The Impact of Electronic Media on Social Behaviour* (New York: Oxford University Press, 1985).

25 *Gallup Poll of Canada* (Toronto: Public Opinion News Service, 2 December 1953). Hereafter called CIPO-Gallup. The Gallup Poll, established in 1933 in the United States and founded in Canada in 1942, operated as the Canadian Institute of Public Opinion (CIPO). Every Wednesday and Saturday, CIPO-Gallup released opinion poll results about contemporary Canadian attitudes, behaviours, and opinions—a character sketch of the very public for whom postwar NFB films were being produced.

26 Evans, *In the National Interest*, p. 62.

27 Ibid., p. 31.

28 Ibid.

29 Although the largest audience was juvenile, the greatest number of films produced continued to be for adult groups.

30 Owram, *Born at the Right Time*, p. 111.

31 Evans, *In the National Interest*, p. 33.

32 Ibid., p. 64.

33 *Ti-Jean Goes Lumbering*, 16 min., 16mm, sound, colour film, National Film Board of Canada, Montreal, QC, Canada, 1953.

34 Soundtrack from *Story of Peter and the Potter*, 20 min., 16mm, sound, colour film, National Film Board of Canada, Montreal, QC, Canada, 1953.

35 Soundtrack from *Angotee: Story of an Eskimo Boy*, 28 min., 16mm, sound, colour film, National Film Board of Canada, Montreal, QC, Canada, 1953.

36 *Winter in Canada*, 14 min., 16mm, sound, b&w film, National Film Board of Canada, Montreal, QC, Canada, 1953.

37 Soundtrack from *Food For Freddy*, 18 min., 16mm, sound, colour film, National Film Board of Canada, Montreal, QC, Canada, 1953.

38 Soundtrack from *Look Alert - Stay Unhurt*, 15 min., 16mm, sound, b&w film, National Film Board of Canada, Montreal, QC, Canada, 1954.

39 Soundtrack from "Moppet Models" in *Eye Witness #52*, 10 min., 16mm, sound, b&w film, National Film Board of Canada, Montreal, QC, Canada, 1953.

40 Soundtrack from *Chinese Canadians*, 25 min., 16mm, sound, b&w film, National Film Board of Canada, Montreal, QC, Canada, 1954.

41 Soundtrack from *Farewell Oak Street*, 17 min., 16mm, sound, b&w film, National Film Board of Canada, Montreal, QC, Canada, 1953.

42 Evans, *In the National Interest*, p. 37.

43 Ibid., p. 38.

44 Ibid.

45 Ibid.

46 Soundtrack from *Night Children*, 30 min., 16mm, sound, b&w film, National Film Board of Canada, Montreal, QC, Canada, 1956.

47 Soundtrack from *The Suspects*, 28 min., 16mm, sound, b&w film, National Film Board of Canada, Montreal, QC, Canada, 1957.

48 *Having Your Say*, 7 min., 16mm, sound, b&w film, National Film Board of Canada, Montreal, QC, Canada, 1954.

49 CIPO-Gallup, 13 October 1954.

50 Soundtrack from *Joe and Roxy*, 30 min., 16mm, sound, b&w film, National Film Board of Canada, Montreal, QC, Canada, 1957.

51 Ibid.

52 Ibid.

53 Ibid. For an observation on the class implications of this film in relation to its construction of patterns of adolescent sexuality see Mary Louise Adams, *The Trouble with Normal: Postwar Youth and the Making of Heterosexuality* (Toronto: University of Toronto Press, 1997), pp. 90, 103-104.

54 Soundtrack from *Putting It Straight*, 14 min., 16mm, sound, b&w film, National Film Board of Canada, Montreal, QC, Canada, 1957. For a full discussion concerning what was perceived to be a new phenomenon in 1950s American society, "other-directedness," see David Riesman, *The Lonely Crowd: A Study of the Changing American Character* (New Haven: Yale University Press, 1950).

56 The religious makeup of NFB neighbourhoods is impossible to determine, since so few films of the 1940s and 1950s mention religion at all.

57 Soundtrack from "Bar Mitzvah," *Eye Witness #86*, 14 min., 16mm, sound, b&w film, National Film Board of Canada, Montreal, QC, Canada, 1957.

58 Soundtrack from *The Threshold: Immigrant Meets the School*, 23 min., 16mm, sound, b&w film, National Film Board of Canada, Montreal, QC, Canada, 1959.

59 The Mag family was not alone in its concern about school discipline. A majority of Canadians (57%) expressed this concern in 1959; in addition, 47 percent gave their approval for "paddling" as a means of maintaining school discipline. CIPO-Gallup, 20 June 1959.

60 Not all immigrants to Canada had adapted to the indigenous culture, of course.

61 Soundtrack from *A Foreign Language*, 29 min., 16mm, sound, b&w film, National Film Board of Canada, Montreal, QC, Canada, 1958.

62 George S. Tomkins, *A Common Countenance: Stability and Change in the Canadian Curriculum* (Scarborough: Prentice-Hall, 1986) p. 290.

63 Soundtrack from *The Gifted Ones*, 22 min., 16mm, sound, b&w film, National Film Board of Canada, Montreal, QC, Canada, 1959.

64 Ibid.

65 Ibid.

66 Soundtrack from *Eternal Children*, 30 min., 16mm, sound, b&w film, National Film Board of Canada, Montreal, QC, Canada, 1959.

67 According to Evans, following the appointment of Guy Roberge as Government Film Commissioner, "the [Québec] press campaign against the Film Board administration vanished, as if by magic." See Evans, *In the National Interest*, p. 46.

68 With the approaching death of Maurice Duplessis, Québec was on the threshold of its "Quiet Revolution."

69 Soundtrack from *A Day in June*, 25 min., 16mm, sound, colour film, National Film Board of Canada, Montreal, QC, Canada, 1959.

70 The predominance of Red Ensigns in the hands of the children is an intriguing image to contemplate. Just as English-Canadian women filmmakers would soon have an influence over the fashioning of feminism in English-Canada, Québecois filmmakers would come to have a significant impact upon the shaping of the "Quiet Revolution" and the nationalism that would follow. Indeed, according to Evans, that most famous of footage, Charles DeGaulle's 1967 "Vive le Québec libre!" was doctored at the ONF to add the tumultuous cheer when, in fact, there had been only stunned silence, as

was later confirmed by René Lévesque himself. (Evans, *In the National Interest*, p. 190).

71 Soundtrack from *The Chairmaker and the Boys*, 20 min., 16mm, sound, Colour film, National Film Board of Canada, Montreal, QC, Canada, 1958.

72 Soundtrack from *Beaver Dam*, 15 min., 16mm, sound, colour film, National Film Board of Canada, Montreal, QC, Canada, 1960.

73 Soundtrack from *The Saddlemaker*, 16 min., 16mm, sound, colour film, National Film Board of Canada, Montreal, QC, Canada, 1961.

74 Not all social issues introduced by the NFB in the early 1960s were addressed with the expediency that environmental and gender concerns proved to be. Indeed, some remain to be perceived as problems. A threat of science fiction proportions looms in the film *The Living Machine* (1962), an hour-long production made for television by the NFB, which contains a brief portrayal of the grandchildren of Professor Warren McCollar, an early artificial intelligence scientist. In the film, McCollar, dressed in canvas shorts and chain smoking, is certain that machines will eventually take over human society. He speaks of the coming end of humanity matter-of-factly while his grandchildren splash in the lake at his cottage. "Something else will come," he says. "If I can love my family, then a machine can too in time."

75 Soundtrack from *Thousand Island Summer*, 14 min., 16mm, sound, colour film, National Film Board of Canada, Montreal, QC, Canada, 1960.

76 *Boy Meets Band*, 11 min., 16mm, sound, b&w and colour film, National Film Board of Canada, Montreal, QC, Canada, 1961.

77 Soundtrack from *The Rink*, 10 min., 16mm, sound, colour film, National Film Board of Canada, Montreal, QC, Canada, 1962.

78 Soundtrack from *Northern Campus*, 21 min., 16mm, sound, b&w film, National Film Board of Canada, Montreal, QC, Canada, 1961.

79 Among the most enduring stereotypes in NFB films (and other Canadian curricular materials) is that of the innate mechanical ability of the Inuit.

80 Soundtrack from *Trail Ride*, 20 min., 16mm, sound, colour film, National Film Board of Canada, Montreal, Canada, QC, 1964.

81 Soundtrack from *Because They Are Different*, 29 min., 16mm, sound, b&w film, National Film Board of Canada, Montreal, QC, Canada, 1964.

82 *People Might Laugh At Us*, 9 min., 16mm, sound, colour film, National Film Board of Canada, Montreal, QC, Canada, 1964.

83 *September 5 at Saint-Henri*, 27 min., 16mm, sound, b&w film, National Film Board of Canada, Montreal, QC, Canada, 1962. Ironically, Evans notes in his *In the National Interest*, "it was alleged that the people of Saint-Henri were angered about being filmed by 'outsiders.'" (Evans, p. 84).

84 Evans, *In the National Interest*, p. 84.

85 Details concerning these commissions and related inquiries may be found in Hugh A. Stevenson, "Developing Public Education in Post-War Canada to 1960," in *Canadian Education: A History*, J. Donald Wilson et al., eds. (Scarborough: Prentice-Hall, 1970), pp. 399-402.

86 In Québec, the 1963 Parent Report led to a sixfold increase in kindergarten enrolment by 1968. In British Columbia, strong support for the principle of kindergarten education in the 1960 Chant Report led to an amendment of the Schools Act that very year to give any school board the right to establish kindergartens at its own discretion. See Tomkins, *A Common Countenance*,

p. 362; see Gillian Weiss, "An Essential Year for the Child: The Kindergarten in British Columbia," in J. Donald Wilson, ed., *Schooling and Society in Twentieth Century British Columbia* (Calgary: Detselig, 1980), p. 154.

87 Evans, *In the National Interest*, p. 90.

88 Soundtrack from *Kindergarten*, 22 min., 16mm, sound, b&w film, National Film Board of Canada, Montreal, QC, Canada, 1962.

89 Soundtrack from *The Test*, 29 min., 16mm, sound, colour film, National Film Board of Canada, Montreal, QC, Canada, 1961.

90 Ibid.

91 Soundtrack from *Child of the Future: How He Might Learn*, 58 min., 16mm, sound, b&w film, National Film Board of Canada, Montreal, QC, Canada, 1964.

92 To judge from the images presented in *Child of the Future*, a teacher in a "school of the future" would be of diminished stature in comparison to teachers of the past (such as Miss Fisher in *The Test*); i.e., the human teacher would be the "horseless carriage" in the McLuhan metaphor with technology as the "motor car."

93 Evans, *In the National Interest*, p. 113.

94 Ibid., p. 129.

95 Soundtrack from *Joe and Roxy*, 30 min., 16mm, sound, b&w film, National Film Board of Canada, Montreal, QC, Canada, 1957.

96 Soundtrack from *The Merry-Go-Round*, 23 min., 16mm, sound, b&w film, National Film Board of Canada, Montreal, QC, Canada, 1966. See my chapter 6 note concerning the uncomfortable roles of blacks in NFB society.

97 That is not to say that the phrase "sexual revolution" was inappropriate. The open portrayal of sexuality was certainly revolutionary.

98 Soundtrack from *The Game*, 28 min., 16mm, sound, b&w film, National Film Board of Canada, Montreal, QC, Canada, 1966.

99 Soundtrack from *The Shattered Silence*, 27 min., 16mm, sound, b&w film, National Film Board of Canada, Montreal, QC, Canada, 1966. As a crude rule of thumb in NFB films, whoever organizes a meeting to complain about something is generally found to be in the wrong.

100 For a full account of the Yorkville confrontation, see Owram, *Born at the Right Time*, pp. 210-15.

101 Soundtrack from *Invention of the Adolescent*, 28 min., 16mm, sound, b&w film, National Film Board of Canada, Montreal, QC, Canada, 1967. This film, as well as *The Shattered Silence*, may be seen as attempts to calm a rising "moral panic" in regard to the social turmoil of the late 1960s. See Mary Louise Adams, *The Trouble with Normal*, p. 56, for a discussion of the concept "moral panic."

102 Philippe Ariès, *Centuries of Childhood: A Social History of Family Life* (New York: Random House, 1962), p. 71.

103 Soundtrack from *Invention of the Adolescent*, 28 min., 16mm, sound, b&w film, National Film Board of Canada, Montreal, QC, Canada, 1967.

104 Owram reports "By 1954 the majority of fourteen- to seventeen-year-olds were in school; by the early 1960s, three out of four." Owram, *Born at the Right Time*, p. 140.

105 Ibid., p. 49.

106 Owram observes, as have others, that "Even the organization of [Spock's] book, with its age-specific references and comments, draws heavily on their [Gesell and Ilg's] precedent." Ibid.

107 By "controversial," Owram is referring to the inability to date to actually see the effect of the fourth "force"; i.e., changes in child-rearing practices over time. For him, it is a speculative postwar force. Ibid., xi. Perhaps prescient of the youth revolt to come in the late 1960s was a 1955 CIPO-Gallup poll in which Canadian adults were asked, "Do you think discipline in most homes today is too strict, about right, or not strict enough?" Only 2 percent replied "too strict"; 16 percent replied "about right"; but 78 percent replied "not strict enough." CIPO-Gallup, 30 March 1955.

Chapter 5: "The New Generation": Mental Hygiene and the Portrayals of Children by the National Film Board of Canada, 1946-1967

1 Sol Cohen, "The Mental Hygiene Movement, The Development of Personality and the School: The Medicalization of American Education," *History of Education Quarterly* 23, 2 (1983): 133.

2 Ibid. It is the invisibility of the impact, of course, which causes Owram in *Born at the Right Time* to qualify his "fourth factor" as controversial. See Doug Owram, *Born at the Right Time: A History of the Baby-Boom Generation* (Toronto: University of Toronto Press, 1996), pp. x-xi.

3 Theresa R. Richardson, *The Century of the Child: The Mental Hygiene Movement and Social Policy in the United States and Canada* (New York: State University of New York Press, 1989), p. 2.

4 Sol Cohen, "The School and Personality Development," in *Historical Inquiry in Education: A Research Agenda*, John H. Best, ed. (Washington: American Educational Research Association, 1983), p. 124. The American NCMH was founded in 1909 at Yale University. The CNCMH was founded in 1918 under Clarence Hincks. For a broad discussion of the various factions of the CNCMH see Angus McLaren, *Our Own Master Race: Eugenics in Canada, 1885-1945* (Toronto: McClelland and Stewart, 1990).

5 Cohen, "The School and Personality Development," p. 124.

6 The Commonwealth Fund was established in 1918 by the wife of Stephen Harkness, an early partner of John D. Rockefeller, Sr., in Standard Oil.

7 Cohen, "The School and Personality Development," p. 111.

8 Jessie Taft quoted in Cohen, "The School and Personality Development," p. 117.

9 William Healy quoted in Cohen, "The Mental Hygiene Movement, The Commonwealth Fund, and Public Education, 1921-1933," in *Private Philanthropy and Public Elementary and Secondary Education: Proceedings of the Rockefeller Archive Center Conference held on June 8, 1979*, Gerald Benjamin, ed. (New York: Rockefeller Archive Center, 1980), p. 46.

10 Sol Cohen, "Every School a Clinic: A Historical Perspective on Modern American Education," in *From the Campus: Perspectives on the School Reform Movement*, Sol Cohen and Lewis C. Solmon, eds. (New York:

Praeger, 1989), p. 27; Cohen, "The Mental Hygiene Movement, The Development of Personality and the School," p. 132.

11 Sol Cohen, "The Mental Hygiene Movement and the Development of Personality: Changing Conceptions of the American College and University, 1920-1940," in *History of Higher Education Annual*, 2 (1982): 65-101. See p. 72 especially. Cohen, "The Mental Hygiene Movement, the Development of Personality and the School," p. 131. The choice of the singular form of the term "personality" is Cohen's.

12 Cohen, "The Mental Hygiene Movement, the Development of Personality and the School," pp. 136-73.

13 Cohen, "The School and Personality Development," p. 122; Cohen, "Every School a Clinic," pp. 27, 28.

14 Cohen, "The Mental Hygiene Movement, the Development of Personality and the School," p. 137.

15 Ibid., pp. 137, 139.

16 See Richardson, p. 98, for a brief discussion of "mother blaming" in the 1920s.

17 Steven L. Schlossman, "Philanthropy and the Gospel of Child Development," in *History of Education Quarterly* 21 (Fall 1981): 279.

18 Lawrence K. Frank, "Childhood and Youth," in *Recent Social Trends in the United States: Report of the President's Research Committee on Social Trends*, (New York: McGraw-Hill, 1933), 2: 794.

19 Schlossman, p. 275.

20 Frank in *Recent Social Trends*, p. 793.

21 Frank in *Recent Social Trends*, p. 793; Schlossman, p. 294.

22 Schlossman, pp. 293-94.

23 Ibid., p. 283.

24 Cohen, "The Mental Hygiene Movement and the Development of Personality: Changing Conceptions of the American College and University, 1920-1940," p. 74.

25 Soundtrack from *Life With Baby*, 18 min., 16mm, sound, b&w film, Time/Life, New York, 1946.

26 Benjamin Spock, M.D., and Mary Morgan, *Spock on Spock: A Memoir of Growing Up with the Century* (New York: Pantheon Books, 1985), pp. 79-99.

27 Owram, *Born at the Right Time*, p. 48; Benjamin Spock, M.D., *The Pocket Book of Baby and Child Care* (New York: Pocket Books, 1946), pp. 260, 313.

28 Except of course in the sense that the "common sense" was being reshaped by Spock and other mental hygienists—such as the influential, Canadian child psychologists, William Blatz and Samuel Laycock. For a comparative discussion concerning the careers of Blatz and Laycock, see Mona Gleason, *Normalizing the Ideal: Psychology, Schooling, and the Family in Postwar Canada* (Toronto: University of Toronto Press, 1999).

29 Soundtrack from *Supper's Ready*, 8 min., 16mm, sound, b&w film, National Film Board of Canada, Montreal, QC, Canada, 1944.

30 Soundtrack from *A Friend for Supper*, 11 min., 16mm, sound, b&w film, National Film Board of Canada, Montreal, QC, Canada, 1944.

31 Soundtrack from *Tomorrow's Citizens*, 10 min., 16mm, sound, b&w film, National Film Board of Canada, Montreal, QC, Canada, 1947; *Lessons in Living*, 22 min., 16mm, sound, b&w film, National Film Board of Canada, Montreal, QC, Canada, 1944.

32 *The Children from Overseas*, 12 min., 16mm, sound, b&w film, National Film Board of Canada, Montreal, QC, Canada, 1940; *Out Beyond Town*, 11 min., 16mm, sound, b&w film, National Film Board of Canada, Montreal, QC, Canada, 1948. It is of interest to note that "formalist" educational practices are most often found in film productions in which the primary focus of the filmmaker is *not* education. In the film *The Children from Overseas*, for example, the school scene is incidental to the larger purpose of the documentary: i.e., to illustrate aspects of the lives of British refugee children. Likewise, in the rural production *Out Beyond Town* the object of the documentary is to persuade rural viewers toward improvements in social hygiene, rather than to persuade them toward changes in rural education. In both these films, in which pedagogical issues are of secondary importance, the classroom pedagogy is formalist. This formula holds true in other domestic films of this era as well: in particular, the educational scenes in films such as *What Makes Us Grow* (1943) and *A Friend for Supper*.

33 To judge from work by Neil Sutherland and others, this was not strictly the case with adult-child relations in Canadian society. However, in Vancouver during this era, Sutherland writes that "most parents continued to exert a very considerable measure of control over their children's social relations" and that "children...moved easily from the control of their families into the control of the school." Neil Sutherland, " 'Everyone seemed happy in those days': The Culture of Childhood in Vancouver Between the 1920s and the 1960s," in Jean Barman, Neil Sutherland, and J. Donald Wilson, eds., *Children, Teachers & Schools in the History of British Columbia* (Calgary: Detselig, 1995), pp. 82, 86.

34 Soundtrack from *Four Families*, 59 min., 16mm, sound, b&w film, National Film Board of Canada, Montreal, QC, Canada, 1959 MacNeil was likely referring to Philip Wylie's *Generation of Vipers* (New York: Rinehart, 1955).

35 Soundtrack from *The Pony*, 29 min., 16mm, sound, b&w film, National Film Board of Canada, Montreal, QC, Canada, 1955.

36 The best account of William Blatz's career may be found in Jocelyn Raymond, *The Nursery World of Dr. Blatz* (Toronto: University of Toronto Press, 1991). It is noteworthy that the Institute of Child Study, which was under the directorship of Blatz, received substantial Rockefeller Foundation funding through the Laura Spelman Rockefeller Fund (LSRM), as did the Canadian National Committee on Mental Hygiene, where Samuel Laycock was salaried as Director of Education.

37 Soundtrack from *What's On Your Mind?*, 10 min., 16mm, sound, b&w film, National Film Board of Canada, Montreal, QC, Canada, 1946. Laycock, unlike Blatz, never appears in NFB society.

38 Ibid.

39 Soundtrack from *The Feeling of Rejection*, 21 min., 16mm, sound, b&w film, National Film Board of Canada, Montreal, QC, Canada, 1947.

40 Soundtrack from *The Feeling of Hostility*, 31 min., 16mm, sound, b&w film, National Film Board of Canada, Montreal, QC, Canada, 1948.

41 Soundtrack from *Over-Dependency*, 31 min., 16mm, sound, b&w film, National Film Board of Canada, Montreal, QC, Canada, 1949.

42 Soundtrack from *Know Your Baby*, 9 min., 16mm, sound, b&w film, National Film Board of Canada, Montreal, QC, Canada, 1947.

43 Arnold Gesell, Frances Ilg, Louise Ames and Janet Learned, *Infant and Child in the Culture of Today: The Guidance of Development in Home and Nursery School* (New York: Harper and Brothers, 1943).

44 Gesell et al., *Infant and Child in the Culture of Today*, pp. 9-10.

45 Ibid., p. 10.

46 Ibid., p. 14.

47 Ibid., p. 10.

48 Ibid., p. 57.

49 Ibid., p. 48.

50 Ibid., p. 49. Emphases theirs.

51 Ibid.

52 Soundtrack from *Why Won't Tommy Eat?*, 17 min., 16mm, sound, colour film, National Film Board of Canada, Montreal, QC, Canada, 1948.

53 Soundtrack from *The Feeling of Hostility*, 31 min., 16mm, sound, b&w film, National Film Board of Canada, Montreal, QC, Canada, 1948.

54 Soundtrack from *He Acts His Age*, 14 min., 16mm, sound, colour film, National Film Board of Canada, Montreal, QC, Canada, 1949.

55 Soundtrack from *Frustrating Fours and Fascinating Fives*, 21 min., 16mm, sound, b&w film, National Film Board of Canada, Montreal, QC, Canada, 1953.

56 Ibid.

57 Cynthia R. Comacchio, *"Nations Are Built of Babies": Saving Ontario's Mothers and Children, 1900-1940* (Montreal and Kingston: McGill-Queen's University Press, 1993), p. 211.

58 John R. Seeley, R. Alexander Sim, and Elizabeth W. Loosley, et al., *Crestwood Heights* (Toronto: University of Toronto Press, 1956), p. 13. John Seeley's career is deserving of more careful scrutiny by Canadian social historians. He was involved in several projects on the behalf of the mental hygiene movement in Canada, including *Crestwood Heights* and NFB film productions of the early 1950s. Less conspicuously, he received acknowledgement from David Riesman as a consultant for his landmark work, *The Lonely Crowd* (1950), which links Seeley to that bastion of the mental hygienists—Yale University—at a particularly heady time for the movement.

59 Ibid., p. 382

60 Ibid., p. x.

61 Ibid., p. 359.

62 Ibid., p. 387.

63 Ibid., p. 167.

64 Ibid., p. 101.

65 Ibid., p. 270.

66 Ibid., p. 170.

67 Ibid., p. 207.

68 Ibid., p. 65.

69 Ibid., p. 70.

70 Ibid.

71 Ibid., p. 219. Here, Seeley seems to be referring to the phenomenon of "other-directedness" as conceptualized by Riesman in *The Lonely Crowd*.

72 Ibid., p. 416.

73 In *Crestwood Heights*, as in the films of the late 1940s and early 1950s, the term "mental hygiene" is gradually replaced by "mental health."

74 Seeley, *Crestwood Heights*, p. 113. It may be significant that, as sixteen to nineteen year olds, they would have been born prior to 1940, and thus prior to the introduction of mental hygiene in Crestwood Heights.

75 The industrial implications of the mental hygiene movement are discussed in Peter Miller and Nikolas Rose, "The Tavistock Programme: The Government of Subjectivity and Social Life, " in *Sociology* 22, 2 (May 1988): 171-92.

76 Hilde Bruch, *Don't Be Afraid of Your Child* (New York: Farrar, Straus and Young, 1952), p. 54.

77 Ibid., p. 49.

78 Ibid., pp. 7, 54, 69.

79 Ibid., p. 259.

80 Ibid., p. 81.

81 J.R. Seeley, quoted in Christopher Lasch, *The Culture of Narcissism: American Life in an Age of Diminishing Expectations* (New York: W.W. Norton, 1978), pp. 167-68.

82 Bruch, *Don't Be Afraid of Your Child*, p. 255.

83 Ibid.

84 Soundtrack from *Being Different*, 10 min., 16mm, sound, b&w film, National Film Board of Canada, Montreal, QC, Canada, 1957. The threat of being labelled "a girl" in this context is analogous to being accused of having homosexual tendencies and, as Mary Louise Adams observes in her *The Trouble with Normal: Postwar Youth and the Making of Heterosexuality* (Toronto: University of Toronto Press, 1997) was a powerful and ubiquitous means for shaping sexual roles in the 1950s.

85 Soundtrack from *Who Is Sylvia?*, 29 min., 16mm, sound, b&w film, National Film Board of Canada, Montreal, QC, Canada, 1957.

86 Soundtrack from *Shyness*, 22 min., 16mm, sound, b&w film, National Film Board of Canada, Montreal, QC, Canada, 1953.

87 Ibid.

88 Cohen, "The Mental Hygiene Movement and the Development of Personality: Changing Conceptions of the American College and University, 1920-1940," p. 65.

89 Cohen, "The School and Personality Development," p. 123.

90 Cohen, "The Mental Hygiene Movement, the Commonwealth Fund, and Public Education, 1921-1933," p. 42.

91 Cohen, "The School and Personality Development," p. 110.

92 Ibid., p. 120.

93 Cohen, "The Mental Hygiene Movement, the Development of Personality and the School," p. 131.

94 Cohen, "The School and Personality Development," p. 119.

95 Cohen, "The Mental Hygiene Movement, the Development of Personality," p. 132.

96 Soundtrack from *Child Guidance Clinic*, 28 min., 16mm, sound, b&w film, National Film Board of Canada, Montreal, QC, Canada, 1955.

97 Ibid.

98 J.D. Griffin and J.R. Seeley, "Education for Mental Health: An Experiment," in *Canadian Education* 7 (June 1952): 21.

99 Of all that failed to come to pass, perhaps most damning is the statistical rise in the number of children with mental health problems. The ratio of children with problems in the general population cited in *Child Guidance Clinic* (1956) is 1:10; a 1995 CBC Television public service advertisement placed the ratio at 1:5.

100 Soundtrack from *The Teacher—Authority or Automaton*, 28 min., 16mm, sound, b&w film, National Film Board of Canada, Montreal, QC, Canada, 1962; Soundtrack from *Child of the Future: How He Might Learn*, 58 min., 16mm, sound, b&w film, National Film Board of Canada, Montreal, QC, Canada, 1964.

101 Soundtrack from *The Test*, 29 min., 16mm, sound, colour film, National Film Board of Canada, Montreal, QC, Canada, 1961; *Child of the Future: How He Might Learn*, 58 min., 16mm, sound, b&w film, National Film Board of Canada, Montreal, QC, Canada, 1964.

102 Cohen, "The Mental Hygiene Movement, The Development of Personality," p. 142.

103 Ibid., p. 149.

104 Richardson, *Century of the Child*, p. 161.

105 Cohen, "The Mental Hygiene Movement, the Commonwealth Fund", p. 44. No matter that the hygienists' knowledge was "flimsy," this epistemological oversight was more than compensated for by the extraordinary popular support that the mental hygiene project garnered among the American public in the 1950s. In the postwar period, Cohen reports, the mental health point of view penetrated deeply into the zeitgeist of the United States as evidenced by *Life Magazine*'s 1950 survey of public attitudes toward education, in which 87% of those polled upheld personality development as a proper object of the schools' concern. However, by 1959 nearly 60 percent of adults reported to Canadian Gallup pollsters that "discipline in our schools is...not severe enough." *Canadian Institute of Public Opinion*, 20 June 1959.

106 Soundtrack from *Making a Decision in the Family*, 8 min., 16mm, sound, b&w film, National Film Board of Canada, Montreal, QC, Canada, 1957.

107 Another symbol of this fait accompli are the opening credits of *The New Baby*. In past films of this genre, the source of the child-rearing information contained within the film has been attributed to the "Mental Health Division" of National Health and Welfare. This reference is now dropped, and the origin of the advice is attributed to a more generic "Child and Maternal Health Division" of National Health and Welfare.

108 Soundtrack from *The World of Three*, 28 min., 16mm, sound, b&w film, National Film Board of Canada, Montreal, QC, Canada, 1966.

109 Soundtrack from *Phoebe*, 28 min., 16mm, sound, b&w film, National Film Board of Canada, Montreal, QC, Canada, 1964.

110 Soundtrack from *No Reason to Stay*, 28 min., 16mm, sound, b&w film, National Film Board of Canada, Montreal, QC, Canada, 1966.

111 Soundtrack from *Flowers on a One-way Street*, 57 min., 16mm, sound, b&w film, National Film Board of Canada, Montreal, QC, Canada, 1967. Somewhat ironic are the lyrics of a popular song that summer: "All the children are insane; all the children are insane, waiting for the summer rain, yeah." (The Doors, "The End" in *The Doors* ASCAP 1967.)

112 Seeley, *Crestwood Heights*, p. 219; Bruch, *Don't Be Afraid of Your Child*, p. 255.

113 Joshua Meyrowitz, *No Sense of Place: The Impact of Electronic Media on Social Behaviour* (New York: Oxford University Press, 1985), p. 3.

114 Ibid., p. 238.

115 Seeley, *Crestwood Heights*, p. 416.

116 Seeley, *Crestwood Heights*, p. 65.

Chapter 6: A Progressive State of Disequilibrium: Social Relations in the Cinematic Society, 1968-1989

1 Ellen Key, *The Century of the Child* (New York: G.P. Putnam's Sons, 1909), p. 198. Perhaps H. Clay Trumbull in his *Hints on Child Training* (Philadelphia: John D. Wattlers, 1896) comes closest in this regard with his admonition that "breaking a child's will is tantamount to destroying his powers of free choice." Cited in Glen Davis, *Childhood and History in America* (New York: The Psychohistory Press, 1976), p. 113.

2 As Linda Pollock observes upon reviewing the methodological difficulties in using this type of literature in her *Forgotten Children: Parent-Child Relations from 1500 to 1900* (1983), "Contemporary baby books are a rather poor indication of what actually happens in the home." Linda A. Pollock, *Forgotten Children: Parent-Child Relations from 1500 to 1900* (Cambridge: Cambridge University Press, 1983), p. 44.

3 Key, *The Century of the Child*, pp. 2-3; 100.

4 Ibid., p. 68.

5 Ibid., p. 101.

6 Havelock Ellis, foreword in Ellen Key, *Love and Marriage* (New York: Knickerbocker Press, 1911), p. vii.

7 Barbara Ehrenreich and Deirdre English, *For Her Own Good: 150 Years of the Expert's Advice to Women* (Garden City, NY: Doubleday, 1978), p. 172.

8 Ibid. Emphasis theirs.

9 Ibid.

10 Key, *The Century of the Child*, p. 175. In an anecdote illustrative of the potential harm done to the mother and child relationship by corporal punishment, Key recalls the prayers of a four year old who had received his first punishment of this kind ("happily it was his only one"): "Dear God, tear mamma's arms out so that she cannot beat me any more" (Key, p. 139).

11 Key, *The Century of the Child*, pp. 140-41. In contrast, Key believed that "children who strike back when punished have the most promising characters of all" (Key, p. 146). Robert E. Larzelere in his survey, "Moderate Spanking: Model or Deterrent of Children's Aggression in the Family?" suggests the psychological jury is still out on spanking, and that some research indicates that "moderate spanking can be part of a parenting style that is

beneficial for a child and increases prosocial aggression but not antisocial aggression." Robert E. Larzelere, in *Journal of Family Violence* 1, 1 (1986): 30.

12 Key, *The Century of the Child*, p. 124.

13 Ibid., p. 162.

14 Ibid., p. 206.

15 Ibid., p. 98.

16 Ibid., p. 183. Warned Key, "Either there must be such a transformation of the way in which modern society thinks and works that the majority of women will be restored to motherhood, or the disintegration of the home and the substitution of general institutions will inevitably result. There is no alternative" (Key, p. 99).

17 The best sources for child-rearing literature in nineteenth- and twentieth-century America are Glen Davis, *Childhood and History in America* (New York: The Psychohistory Press, 1976) and Ehrenreich and English, *For Her Own Good: 150 Years of the Expert's Advice to Women*.

18 For detailed descriptions of motherhood advice networks in early-twentieth-century Canada, see Katherine Arnup, *Education for Motherhood: Advice for Mothers in Twentieth-Century Canada* (Toronto: University of Toronto Press, 1994); Cynthia R. Comacchio, *"Nations Are Built of Babies": Saving Ontario's Mothers and Children, 1900-1940* (Montreal & Kingston: McGill-Queen's University Press, 1993); and the classic, Neil Sutherland, *Children in English-Canadian Society: Framing the Twentieth-Century Consensus* (Waterloo: Wilfrid Laurier University Press, [1976]). Parental discipline among the masses at the outset of the twentieth century ranged from the severely punitive, "breaking of will," to the less repressive, "bending of will," which was likewise designed to mold and shape the emerging personality and which was, according to Philip Greven in *The Protestant Temperament: Patterns of Child-rearing, Religious Experience, and the Self in Early America* (New York: New American Library, 1977), p. 152, "no less effective for being less direct and explicit." Greven notes that even "moderates" could be authoritarian in outlook. He observes that John Locke insisted that "children, when little, should look upon their parents as their lords, their absolute governors" (Greven, p. 160).

19 Lawrence K. Frank, "Childhood and Youth," in *Recent Social Trends in the United States: Report of the President's Research Committee on Social Trends*, (New York: McGraw-Hill, 1933), 2: 754 and 798.

20 Ibid., p. 753. There is a striking similarity between the phrasing of Ellen Key's principle of "holiness of generation" and Jeremy Bentham's principle of utility: "The greatest happiness of the greatest number is the foundation of morals and legislation." See Jeremy Bentham, *The Commonplace Book*, 266: 2, in *Works*, Vol. 10, 142.

21 Coincidentally, the same year that Ellen Key's *The Century of the Child* (1909) was published, a formal movement to create a science of mental hygiene originated in the United States.

22 Theodore Jacob, "Family Interaction in Disturbed and Normal Families: A Methodological and Substantive Review," *Psychological Bulletin* 82, 1 (1975): 33.

23 Ibid., pp. 48-49.

24 Anthony I. Schuham, "Power Relations in Emotionally Disturbed and Normal Family Triads," *Journal of Abnormal Psychology* 75, 1 (1970): 31.

25 Ibid., p. 36.

26 Stanley A. Murrell and James G. Stachowiak, "Consistency, Rigidity, and Power in the Interaction Patterns of Clinic and Non clinic Families," *Journal of Abnormal Psychology* 72, 3 (1967): 265, 270-71.

27 Schuham, "Power Relations in Emotionally Disturbed and Normal Family Triads," pp. 7, 36. Emphasis is mine.

28 In the affluent "Crestwood Heights" (Forest Hill), which was under study by Canadian psychologists in the late 1940s, early manifestations of a similar disequilibrium in Canadian society were being observed. See John Seeley, R. Alexander Sim, and E.W. Loosely, *Crestwood Heights: A Study of the Culture of Suburban Life* (Toronto: University of Toronto Press, 1956).

29 It can be argued that, within a single generation, the psychologists of the 1940s achieved exactly that which they claimed to abhor—a society shaped by scientifically unsound child-rearing practices.

30 For some ONF filmmakers, of course, "Société nouvelle" had a significance beyond that connoted by "Challenge for Change."

31 The best account of structural changes at the NFB is David B. Jones, *Movies and Memoranda: An Interpretive History of the National Film Board of Canada* (Ottawa: Canadian Film Institute, 1981).

32 My use of terms such as "modern families," "monolithic families," and "multi-dimensional family groupings" are derived from Margrit Eichler, *Families in Canada Today: Recent Changes and Their Policy Consequences*, 2nd ed. (Toronto: Gage Educational, 1988).

33 *Stalking Seal on the Spring Ice*, 28 min., 16mm, sound, colour film, National Film Board of Canada, Montreal, QC, Canada, 1968.

34 Wolfgang Ernst, "DIStory: Cinema and Historical Discourse," *Journal of Contemporary History* 18 (July 1983): 398.

35 *The Wish*, 28 min., 16mm, sound, colour film, National Film Board of Canada, Montreal, QC, Canada, 1970.

36 *Gore Road*, 8 min., 16mm, sound, colour film, National Film Board of Canada, Montreal, QC, Canada, 1972.

37 From Statistics Canada, *Vital Statistics*, Vol. II—Marriages and Divorces, 1979, cited in Eichler, *Families in Canada Today*, p. 58. A 1975 Statistics Canada table of divorces by sex and age group shows the modal age of those obtaining divorces in 1975 was twenty-five to twenty-nine years—i.e., members of the "new generation."

38 Margrit Eichler, *Families in Canada Today*, p. 72.

39 *Gallup Poll of Canada* (Toronto: Public Opinion News Service, 17/03/73). Hereinafter called *CIPO-Gallup*. 63 percent of Canadian adults (68% women) thought that, if this was the case, it was a "bad thing."

40 Gary Evans, *In the National Interest: A Chronicle of the National Film Board of Canada from 1949 to 1989* (Toronto: University of Toronto Press, 1991), p. 167. Stoney was a veteran American documentary filmmaker hired in New York City in 1968 by then Director of Production for the NFB, Frank Spiller.

41 Pierre Trudeau attending a conference on poverty in Canada was queried about the lack of any delegation of the poor at the conference. He shrugged

his shoulders and replied: "We had the film." Quoted in Evans, *In the National Interest*, p. 167.

42 Ibid., p. 170.

43 Ibid., p. 211.

44 Ibid., p. 212.

45 Soundtrack from *Sir! Sir!*, 20 min., 16mm, sound, b&w film, National Film Board of Canada, Montreal, QC, Canada, 1968.

46 Soundtrack from *Mrs. Ryan's Drama Class*, 35 min., 16mm, sound, b&w film, National Film Board of Canada, Montreal, QC, Canada, 1969.

47 *Loops to Learn By*, 25 min., 16mm, sound, Colour film, National Film Board of Canada, Montreal, QC, Canada, 1970.

48 Soundtrack from *The Burden They Carry*, 29 min., 16mm, sound, b&w film, National Film Board of Canada, Montreal, QC, Canada, 1970.

49 *Children of Fogo Island*, 18 min., 16mm, sound, b&w film, National Film Board of Canada, Montreal, QC, Canada, 1968.

50 Soundtrack from *The Devil's Toy*, 15 min., 16mm, sound, b&w film, National Film Board of Canada, Montreal, QC, Canada, 1969.

51 Doug Owram, *Born at the Right Time: A History of the Baby-Boom Generation* (Toronto: University of Toronto Press, 1996), p. 214.

52 Jon Ruddy quoted in Owram, *Born at the Right Time*, p. 199.

53 Soundtrack from *Wow*, 95 min., 16mm, sound, colour film, National Film Board of Canada, Montreal, QC, Canada, 1969.

54 *One/Two/Many/World*, 16 min., 3/4 inch videotape, sound, colour, National Film Board of Canada, Montreal, QC, Canada, 1970.

55 Christopher Lasch, *The Culture of Narcissism: American Life in an Age of Diminishing Expectations* (New York: W.W. Norton, 1978), p. 16.

56 Ibid., p. 16.

57 Both types among older youth in the late 1960s are likewise described by Owram in *Born at the Right Time*.

58 Soundtrack from *A Time to Consider—Ecology*, 11 min., 16mm, sound, Colour film, National Film Board of Canada, Montreal, QC, Canada, 1972.

59 National Film Board of Canada, *1971-1973 Catalogue of the National Film Board of Canada* (Montreal: National Film Board of Canada, 1973).

60 *Summer Centre*, 29 min., 16mm, sound, colour film, National Film Board of Canada, Montreal, QC, Canada, 1973.

61 J. Donald Wilson, "From the Swinging Sixties to the Sobering Seventies," in *Precepts, Policy and Process: Perspectives on Contemporary Canadian Education*, Hugh A. Stevenson and J. Donald Wilson, eds. (London, ON: Alexander Blake Associates, 1977), p. 34.

62 *CIPO-Gallup*, 15 October 1975.

63 Richard Farson, *Birthrights* (New York: MacMillan, 1974), pp. 3-4, 13, 16. The theme of childhood liberation was not uncommon in the early 1970s. See also Ivan Illich, *Deschooling Society* (New York: Harper and Row, 1971) and Harley S. Rothstein, "The New School, 1962-1977," (M.A. thesis, University of British Columbia, 1992).

64 The film won an Oscar at the Academy Awards Ceremony in 1977.

65 *I'll Find a Way*, 26 min., 16mm, sound, colour film, National Film Board of Canada, Montreal, QC, Canada, 1977.

66 For a synthesis of the debate over ethnicity and multiculturalism, see Karl Peter, "The Myth of Multiculturalism and Other Political Fables," in J.L. Granatstein, et al., eds., *Twentieth Century Canada: A Reader* (Toronto: McGraw-Hill Ryerson 1986), pp. 289-304. A materialist analysis of the ideological imperatives behind Canada's "search for identity" is found in Tony Wilden, *The Imaginary Canadian* (Vancouver: Pulp Press, 1980).

67 From 1972, Ottawa provided almost $2 million over five years to version NFB productions into languages other than French or English for domestic audiences and to make films about the contribution and problems of ethnic groups. See Evans, *In the National Interest*, pp. 208-10 for a fuller discussion of multiculturalism and the NFB.

68 *Gurdeep Singh Bains*, 12 min., 16mm, sound, colour film, National Film Board of Canada, Montreal, QC, Canada, 1976.

69 *Beautiful Lennard Island*, 24 min., 16mm, sound, colour film, National Film Board of Canada, Montreal, QC, Canada, 1977.

70 Evans, *In the National Interest*, p. 170.

71 Soundtrack from *Cree Hunters of Mistassini,* 58 min., 16mm, sound, colour film, National Film Board of Canada, Montreal, QC, Canada, 1974.

72 Soundtrack from *Would I Ever Like to Work*, 9 min., 16mm, sound, colour film, National Film Board of Canada, Montreal, QC, Canada, 1974.

73 It is interesting to note that only nine percent of children in daycare in any year in the decade 1975-1985 were actually served by licensed daycare facilities. See Eichler, *Families in Canada Today*, p. 318.

74 Soundtrack from *Day Care—The Newest Tradition*, 28 min., 16mm, sound, colour film, National Film Board of Canada, Montreal, QC, Canada, 1978.

75 Eichler, *Families in Canada Today*, p. 319. Eichler notes that the Department of Health and Welfare has suggested that about 50 percent of all daycare centres in Canada which were (then) presently licensed should not have been due to unsatisfactory standards of care.

76 In a 1976 Gallup Poll, commenting upon their own community, 44 percent of Canadian adults indicated that their opinion of public education had fallen during the previous five years. Only the opinion of 17 percent had risen. *CIPO-Gallup*, 26 June 1976. See Wilson, "From the Swinging Sixties to the Sobering Seventies," for a fuller discussion of public opinion of Canadian schools during this era.

77 *Pen-Hi Grad*, 27 min., 16mm, sound, colour film, National Film Board of Canada, Montreal, QC, Canada, 1975.

78 Soundtrack from *Happiness Is Loving Your Teacher*, 28 min., 16mm, sound, colour, National Film Board of Canada, Montreal, QC, Canada, 1977. The gender (female) of the main classroom troublemaker is itself an innovative aspect of the film.

79 Again, see Rothstein, "The New School," for the evolution of alternate schools through the 1960s and 1970s and their eventual absorption by the public school system.

80 Soundtrack from *Wandering Spirit Survival School*, 28 min., 16mm, sound, colour film, National Film Board of Canada, Montreal, QC, Canada, 1978.

81 *Let's Get a Move On*, 23 min., 16mm, sound, colour film, National Film Board of Canada, Montreal, QC, Canada, 1978.

82 *Challenging the Future*, 28 min., 16mm, sound, colour film, National Film Board of Canada, Montreal, QC, Canada, 1977.

83 *Teach Me to Dance*, 21 min., 16mm, sound, colour film, National Film Board of Canada, Montreal, QC, Canada, 1978. It is striking to contrast the sentiment of this film with earlier NFB films concerning immigrant cultures on the prairies, especially Laura Bolton's *Poland on the Prairies* (1944). In the 1944 production, Polish Canadian children are filmed performing their folk dances in public schools, while the narrator remarks "Unfortunately, some of their festivities are disappearing."

84 *Nunatsiaq—The Good Land*, 42 min., 16mm, sound, colour film, National Film Board of Canada, Montreal, QC, Canada, 1977.

85 Soundtrack from *Nunatsiaq—The Good Land*.

86 The time frame used by Postman closely corresponds, of course, with a similar "disappearance of childhood" in NFB society. In the model employed by this study, however, the influence of television over the lives of children depends upon cohesive peer groups—a cohesiveness enhanced as television entered the consumer market by changes in child-rearing practices created by the mental hygiene movement. Joshua Meyrowitz makes the same point as Postman in *No Sense of Place: The Impact of Electronic Media on Social Behavior* (New York: Oxford University Press, 1985), p. 226.

87 Neil Postman, *The Disappearance of Childhood*, p. 99.

88 Ibid., p. 123.

89 Ibid., p. 124.

90 Ibid., p. 126. Postman notes that between 1950 and 1979, the rate of serious crimes committed by American children increased 11,000 percent, while the rate of "non-serious crimes" (burglary, larceny, and auto theft) increased 8,300 percent. Also in 1979, according to Postman, there were 711,142 reported cases of child abuse in the United States. In Meyrowitz, *No Sense of Place*, p. 229, the author reports that in 1951, children under 15 comprised only 0.02 percent of those arrested for murder, only 0.04 percent of those arrested for robbery, and only 0.01 percent of those arrested for rape. In 1981, however, children under 15 comprised 1 percent of those arrested for murder (a 500% increase), 7 percent of those arrested for robbery (a 1,750% increase), and 4 percent of those arrested for rape (a 4,000% increase). These jumps would be less significant, notes Meyrowitz, if those under 15 formed a higher proportion of the population in 1981 than they did in 1951, but the reverse is true: the proportion of the population that was under 15 dropped from 28 percent to 23 percent during the same three decades.

91 Soundtrack from *Sexual Abuse of Children: A Time for Caring*, 27 min., 16mm, sound, colour film, Profile Films, Berkeley, California, USA, 1979.

92 The girls speak in the dark to protect their identities.

93 Soundtrack from *Child Sexual Abuse: The Untold Secret*, 27 min., 16mm, sound, colour film, National Film Board of Canada, Montreal, QC, Canada, 1982.

94 Soundtrack from *No More Secrets*, 13 min., 16mm, sound, colour film, National Film Board of Canada, Montreal, QC, Canada, 1982.

95 *Feeling Yes, Feeling No: The Adult Film*, 27 min., 16mm, sound, colour film, National Film Board of Canada, Montreal, QC, Canada, 1984. The large

number of films produced in the early 1980s to deal with the issue of child sexual abuse is suggestive of a "moral panic" in progress. Again, see Mary Louise Adams, *The Trouble With Normal* (Toronto: University of Toronto Press, 1997), for discussions on the concept of moral panic.

96 A comparative *CIPO-Gallup* survey of 20 September 1978 found a steady increase in the percentage of Canadian adults consuming alcohol, from 59 percent in 1943 to 78 percent in 1978.

97 Soundtrack from *Children of Alcohol*, 19 min., 16mm, sound, colour film, National Film Board of Canada, Montreal, QC, Canada, 1984.

98 Eichler, *Families in Canada Today*, p. 246.

99 Soundtrack from *It's Just Better*, 15 min., 16mm, sound, colour film, National Film Board of Canada, Montreal, QC, Canada, 1982.

100 Hare Krishna, according to the soundtrack of *The Followers*, was founded in 1963 in New York City.

101 At a rock and roll recruitment concert, however, (at which the Krishna band members wear long-haired wigs and fashionable styles) young men and women are shown dancing together, as are children.

102 *The Followers*, 79 min., 16mm, sound, colour film, National Film Board of Canada, Montreal, QC, Canada, 1981.

103 Soundtrack from *Julie O'Brien*, 19 min., 16mm, sound, colour film, National Film Board of Canada, Montreal, QC, Canada, 1981.

104 Soundtrack from *This Is Me*, 28 min., 16mm, sound, colour film, National Film Board of Canada, Montreal, QC, Canada, 1979.

105 The process of regionalization of production studios in the late 1970s through the 1980s was a corollary of the move to studios in the early 1970s and is discussed at length by both Evans in *In the National Interest* and by Jones in *Movies and Memoranda*.

106 Soundtrack from *Being Male*, 15 min., 16mm, sound, colour film, National Film Board of Canada, Montreal, QC, Canada, 1980.

107 Soundtrack from *Girls Fitting In*, 16 min., 16mm, sound, colour film, National Film Board of Canada, Montreal, QC, Canada, 1980. As with *Being Male*, this a production of the Vancouver region.

108 See for example *Sequence and Story*, 5 min., 16mm, sound, colour film, National Film Board of Canada, Montreal, QC, Canada, 1983.

109 Soundtrack from *Gifted Kids*, 25 min., 16mm, sound, colour film, National Film Board of Canada, Montreal, QC, Canada, 1984.

110 Postman, *The Disappearance of Childhood*, p. 90.

111 *Starbreaker*, 23 min., 16mm, sound, colour, National Film Board of Canada, Montreal, QC, Canada, 1984.

112 The occurrence of parental separation and divorce in mid-1980s Canadian society was six times greater than in the mid-1960s. See Eichler, *Families in Canada Today*, p. 58. See also Barbara Ehrenreich, *The Hearts of Men: American Dreams and the Flight from Commitment* (New York: Anchor Press, 1983), for her astute identification of a "male revolt" against traditional commitments that was impacting more covertly than, but conjointly with, second wave feminism on modern family systems, providing a logic for the form of family abandonment depicted by the film, *The Umpire* (1985).

113 *The Umpire*, 17 min., 16mm, sound, colour film, National Film Board of Canada, Montreal, QC, Canada, 1985. Robert S. Weiss, "Growing Up a Lit-

tle Faster: The Experience of Growing Up In a Single Parent Household,"
Journal of Social Issues 35, 4 (1979): 97-111. Cited in Eichler, *Families in Canada Today*, p. 247.

114 *Hayley's Home Movies*, 23 min., 16mm, sound, colour film, National Film Board of Canada, Montreal, QC, Canada, 1987.

115 Soundtrack from *Hayley's Home Movies*.

116 Soundtrack from *Wednesday's Children: Vicky*, 13 min., 16mm, sound, colour film, National Film Board of Canada, Montreal, QC, Canada, 1987.

117 Judith Stacey, *Brave New Families: Stories of Domestic Upheaval in Twentieth Century America* (New York: Basic Books, 1990), p. 258.

118 Soundtrack from *Left Out*, 25 min., 16mm, sound, colour film, National Film Board of Canada, Montreal, QC, Canada, 1985.

119 *The Silence Upstairs*, 13 min., 16mm, sound, colour film, National Film Board of Canada, Montreal, QC, 1985; *Differences*, 17 min., 16mm, sound, colour film, National Film Board of Canada, Montreal, QC, 1986; *Blueline*, 52 min., 16mm, sound, colour film, National Film Board of Canada, Montreal, QC, 1985; *The Movie Movie*, 8 min., 16mm, sound, colour film, National Film Board of Canada, Montreal, QC, Canada, 1986.

120 Arnold Gesell and Frances L. Ilg, in collaboration with Louise B. Ames and Janet Learned, *Infant and Child in the Culture of Today: The Guidance of Development in Home and Nursery School* (New York: Harper and Brothers, 1943), p. 10.

121 Soundtrack from *The Children of War*, 25 min., 16mm, sound, colour film, National Film Board of Canada, Montreal, QC, Canada, 1986.

122 Soundtrack from *Bombs Away*, 18 min., 16mm, sound, colour film, National Film Board of Canada, Montreal, QC, Canada, 1988.

123 Soundtrack from *Head Full of Questions*, 20 min., 16mm, sound, colour film, National Film Board of Canada, Montreal, QC, Canada, 1989. For the first time among the films surveyed for this study, homosexual relationships are presented to children as "normal," ending (albeit indirectly) a half-century exclusion of gay and lesbian youth from NFB society. Again, see Adams, *The Trouble with Normal* (1997), for a discussion of the normalization of heterosexuality in postwar English-Canada.

124 Remarkable changes in the approach to sex education had occurred since the first film of the genre was produced four decades earlier. In *Sixteen to Twenty-Six* (1946), a dour, male doctor dressed in a three-piece suit delivers a sombre warning to high school girls not to engage in premarital sexual activity. Using charts and graphs and cinematographic illustrations, the doctor warns that the likely outcome of premarital sex for women is venereal disease, since the sort of men who "pick up" women are often carriers themselves. The film ends with an unhappy woman watching from her bedroom window as healthy infants are pulled on sleighs past her house by happy mothers. The doctor intones, "All young women should understand the problem of venereal disease, because it leads to the tragedy of lives shadowed by illness and the despair of knowing you may never bear children like other happier women."

125 *The Dig*, 24 min., 16mm, sound, colour film, National Film Board of Canada, Montreal, QC, 1989.

126 Soundtrack from *Thin Dreams*, 21 min., 16mm, sound, colour film, National Film Board of Canada, Montreal, QC, Canada, 1986.

127 Soundtrack from *Canadian Portraits*, 30 min., sound, colour video, National Film Board of Canada, Montreal, QC, Canada, 1989.

128 Soundtrack from *The Magic Quilt*, 13 min., 16mm, sound, colour film, National Film Board of Canada, Montreal, QC, Canada, 1985. At the time, of course, Yugoslavia was a united country under communist rule.

129 Soundtrack from *Richard Cardinal—Cry from a Diary of a Métis Child*, 29 min., 16mm, sound, colour film, National Film Board of Canada, Montreal, QC, Canada, 1986.

130 For an in-depth discussion of the views of E. Franklin Frazier, Kenneth and Mamie Clark, and Daniel Patrick Moynihan on the social problems of African-Americans, see Ellen Herman, *The Romance of American Psychology: Political Culture in the Age of Experts* (Berkeley: University of California Press, 1995), pp. 188-207.

131 From the 1940s to the 1980s, with the possible exception of *Flowers on a One-way Street* (1967) in which young blacks are warmly embraced by white teenagers, whether in English or French productions, blacks have been most often depicted as being subtly out of place in Canadian society.

132 Soundtrack from *Sitting in Limbo*, 95 min., sound, colour video, National Film Board of Canada, Montreal, QC, Canada, 1986.

133 Soundtrack from *The Old Believers*, 57 min., 16mm, sound, colour film, National Film Board of Canada, Montreal, QC, Canada, 1988.

134 Veronica Strong-Boag, "Home Dreams: Women and the Suburban Experiment in Canada, 1945-60," *Canadian Historical Review* 82, 4 (1991): 476, 504.

135 Key, *The Century of the Child*, p. 61.

136 Soundtrack from *The Pony*, 29 min., 16mm, sound, b&w film, National Film Board of Canada, Montreal, QC, Canada, 1955.

137 Seeley, *Crestwood Heights*, p. 194.

138 Ibid., p. 385.

139 Ibid., p. 408; 491. Remarkably, here in *Crestwood Heights* an important piece of information was, in effect, buried. In regard to the emotional health of children reared and schooled for mental health (the goal to which the "Crestwood Heights" project was directed) Seeley wrote: "The only objective evidence on this point would seem to point towards no better mental health, or perhaps worse, among children in this community compared with some others elsewhere." In the endnotes for the book, Seeley revealed that Crestwood children ranked significantly worse in a normed psychological bank of tests in the following categories: "sense of personal freedom; feeling of belonging; freedom from withdrawing tendencies, and community relations." They ranked significantly better in no category at all. "This distribution," reported Seeley, "is almost the mirror image—i.e., reversal—of the community's picture of itself."

140 The effect upon Canadian society may be discerned in a *CIPO-Gallup* Poll of 15 August 1981. When asked whether a father should have the final say in a family, those of fifty years or more agreed 49 percent to 45 percent; those of thirty to forty-nine years disagreed 60 percent to 35 percent; and those of 18 to 29 years disagreed 70 percent to 25 percent. In other words, of those

under 30 years, i.e., both the "new" generation and the "next" generation, only 25 percent believed that a father should have the final say.

141 The concept is even more succinctly put by a lesbian character in a popular feature film, *French Twist* (1995): "He who leaves his place loses it."

Chapter 7: Conclusion: The Century of the Cinematic Child

1 Marjory McKay, "The Motion Picture: a Mirror of Time," in the *NFB Annual Report, 1958-59* (Ottawa: National Film Board of Canada, 1959), pp. 19-22.

2 John Grierson quoted by Dorothy Livesay, "Report of Radio Broadcast, Thursday, Nov. 16th/44, 9:30 C.B.R. Western and Prairie Networks," *Lessons in Living* File, National Film Board Archives, Montreal, QC, Canada, p. 4.

3 Ted Magder, *Canada's Hollywood: The Canadian State and Feature Films* (Toronto: University of Toronto Press, 1993), p. 156

4 Ellen Herman, *The Romance of American Psychology: Political Culture in the Age of Experts* (Berkeley: University of California Press, 1995), p. 15.

5 Lawrence K. Frank quoted in Herman, *The Romance of American Psychology*, p. 35.

6 As Ellen Key expressed it, "nothing will be different in the mass except in so far as human nature itself is transformed." Ellen Key, *The Century of the Child* (New York: G.P. Putnam's Sons, 1909), p. 2.

7 Arnold Gesell, Frances Ilg et al., *Infant and Child in the Culture of Today: The Guidance of Development in Home and Nursery School* (New York: Harper and Brothers, 1943), p. ix. The irony in the progressive exaltation of democratic ideals, as noted by Herman, was that even maverick sociologists, such as C. Wright Mills, who had "chastised members of his own intellectual generation for arrogant pretensions to power," believed that history itself was "warning that too much faith in the tenets of democratic theory could be a grave error." Herman, *The Romance of American Psychology*, pp. 6-7.

8 Henry Murray quoted in Herman, p. 177.

9 Lawrence K. Frank quoted in Theresa Richardson, *The Century of the Child: The Mental Hygiene Movement and Social Policy in the United States and Canada* (Albany: State University of New York, 1989), p. 190.

10 Richardson, *The Century of the Child*, p. 190.

11 Lawrence K. Frank, "Childhood and Youth," in *Recent Social Trends in the United States: Report of the President's Research Committee on Social Trends*, (New York: McGraw-Hill Book Company, 1933), 2: 790.

12 Ibid., pp. 753, 790.

13 For a complete account of the circus atmosphere that surrounded the release of the Payne Fund Studies (PFS), see Garth S. Jowett, Ian C. Jarvie, Kathryn H. Fuller, *Children and the Movies: Media Influence and the Payne Fund Controversy* (Cambridge: Cambridge University Press, 1996). For a brief account of the hoopla see Joel Spring, *Images of American Life: A History of Ideological Management in Schools, Movies, Radio, and Television* (Albany: State University of New York Press, 1992), pp. 58-60. While the instigator and promoter of the studies, the Rev. William Short, publicly expressed the

hope that the PFS would become the bane of the motion picture industry, in the mind of W.W. Charters, the academic chairperson of the research group of educators, psychologists, and sociologists who conducted the research, this was not at all the goal of the PFS: "My understanding is that it is not the purpose of these studies to throw bricks at the moving picture industry, but rather to make a study of what the possibilities of moving pictures are in our social life, and to present measures by which the influence of moving pictures may be gauged or scaled."

14 Jowett, Jarvie, Fuller, *Children and the Movies*, p. 5.

15 W.W. Charters, *Motion Pictures and Youth: A Summary* (New York: MacMillan, 1933), p. 9. No significant sex differences appeared in the study. Boys and girls remembered about equally well.

16 Ibid., pp. 9-10.

17 Specifically, the attitudes studied concerned the Chinese, "negroes," and peace.

18 Charters, p. 22.

19 Ibid., p. 17.

20 Jowett, Jarvie, Fuller, p. 219.

21 Paul Cressey quoted in Jowett, Jarvie, Fuller, p. 219. More than a half-century later, John B. Thompson, in his *Ideology and Modern Culture: Critical Social Theory in the Era of Mass Communication* (Cambridge: Polity Press, 1990) reaches a similar conclusion: "The deployment of technical media should be seen, not merely as the establishment of new channels of diffusion which exist alongside pre-existing social relations, but rather as potential reorganization of social relations themselves, in the sense that new media make possible new forms of action and interaction in the social world."

22 Herbert Blumer and Philip M. Hauser, *Movies, Delinquency, and Crime* (New York: MacMillan, 1933), p. 202.

23 Ibid.

24 As Donald Fisher observes in *Fundamental Development of the Social Sciences: Rockefeller Philanthropy and the United States Social Science Research Council*, the 1920s were heady times in America for social science academics and their students, as LSRM-funded SSRC programs produced opportunities for both "to conduct an experimental study of society." The catch, according to Fisher, was that "the relationships between the foundations and social scientists encouraged them to become servants of power and to become salespeople for the ruling class." In effect, "What brought the social scientists and the foundations together was the concept of 'social control' "—ie., the practical interest of foundations in increasing human welfare within the existing economic system by applying scientific programs of progressive reformation to current social systems. See Donald Fisher, *Fundamental Development of the Social Sciences: Rockefeller Philanthropy and the United States Social Science Research Council* (Ann Arbor: University of Michigan Press,1993), pp. 35, 58, 71.

25 Sol Cohen, *Progressives and Urban School Reform* (New York: Bureau of Publications, Teachers College, Columbia University, 1964), p. 126. The parallels between the events described by Cohen concerning the Little Red School House and those surrounding the production of *Lessons in Living* are quite remarkable, especially in regard to their use for propaganda purposes.

Though neither program was actually supported by their respective communities, both were exhibited as exemplary models of progressive education and utilized to entice other communities to adopt a pedagogy that was close to the heart of American progressives.

26 For an early urban perspective on traditional pedagogical practices see *The Children From Overseas*, 12 min., 16mm, sound, b&w film, National Film Board of Canada, Montreal, QC, Canada, 1940; and for a rural viewpoint see *A Friend for Supper*, 11 min., 16mm, sound, b&w film, National Film Board of Canada, Montreal, QC, Canada, 1944.

27 The only spanking a mother administers to a child in the 1940s is in a mental hygiene film: *Why Won't Tommy Eat?*, 17 min. 16mm, sound, Colour film, National Film Board of Canada, Montreal, QC, Canada, 1948.

28 This balance in the dynamics of parental relationships in the films corresponds to the results of a *CIPO-Gallup* Poll of 15/08/81. When asked whether a father should have the final say in a family, men and women born before World War II agreed 49% to 45%. The figures begin shifting dramatically among Canadian adults born after the war, so much so that those born between 1952 and 1963 disagreed 70% to 25%.

29 Soundtrack from *He Acts His Age*, 14 min., 16mm, sound, Colour film, National Film Board of Canada, Montreal, QC, Canada, 1949.

30 Soundtrack from *Child Guidance Clinic*, 28 min., 16mm, sound, b&w film, National Film Board of Canada, Montreal, QC, Canada, 1955.

31 John R. Seeley, R. Alexander Sim, Elizabeth W. Loosley, et al., *Crestwood Heights* (Toronto: University of Toronto Press, 1956), p. 241.

32 Soundtrack from *Popular Psychology*, 9 min., 16mm, sound, b&w film, National Film Board of Canada, Montreal, QC, Canada, 1957.

33 The semantic association between flowers and "hippies" in the late 1960s ("flower children," "flower power," "flowers in their hair," etc.) is a curious one given the "flower and fruit" analogy offered by L.K. Frank in 1925.

34 The first use (misuse) of the term "generational gap" in NFB society is made by DePoe in *Flowers on a One-way Street*. That cinematic adolescents by the mid-1960s exhibit a character that is different from that of their counterparts of the generation preceding them is perhaps not so surprising. What is surprising, however, is the abruptness of the rupture from one group personality to the other, since the demeanour of adolescents in films from the late 1960s is markedly different even from that of teenagers in late 1950s films such as *Joe and Roxy* (1957), *Making a Decision in the Family* (1957), *Who Is Sylvia?* (1957) and *The Teens* (1957). Generally, birthdate demarcates the boundary from one group personality to the other: teenagers in the above mentioned late 1950s films were born prior to 1945, thus prior to the introduction of mental hygiene practices into NFB homes and schools.

35 Soundtrack from *No Reason to Stay*, 28 min., 16mm, sound, b&w film, National Film Board of Canada, Montreal, QC, Canada, 1966.

36 Hilda Neatby, *So Little For the Mind* (Toronto: Clarke, Irwin & Company, 1953), p. 259. It may seem odd that Neatby's critique of progressive education never found its way onto film. However, it should be recalled that, from the outset, NFB society was a progressive society that brooked few criticisms.

37 Ironically, elementary education appears to lose direction in NFB society in this era precisely because it is advancing in so many directions, all the while, as in the production *We're Gonna Have Recess* (1967), seeming not to have moved at all. To paraphrase Stephen Leacock, the pedagogical structure of the elementary school in the 1960s appears to have "flung itself upon its horse and was riding madly off in all directions."

38 The children in *We're Gonna Have Recess* seem an anachronism for the era they represent in NFB society, yet, paradoxcially, the production itself is one of the most authentic depictions of school routines ever produced by the Film Board. In the film, children ranging in age from eight- to eleven-years-old race down the stairs of an older urban school on their way to the playground for recess. On the playground, they reveal a "culture of childhood" that is steeped in tradition. One mixed group of boys and girls is entirely engrossed in the singing game "In and Out the Window." A group of girls wait their turn to perform a skipping rope routine while singing the "Teddy Bear" skipping song. Boys "play-fight" or chase each other's shadows. Girls play hopscotch. Best buddies play practical jokes on each other. Recess ends when a teacher blows a whistle and the children line up to go inside.

39 *Child of the Future: How He Might Learn*, 58 min., 16mm, sound, b&w film, National Film Board of Canada, Montreal, QC, Canada, 1964.

40 The "flower connection" might also be said to include the 1948 daisy-filled mental hygiene production, *They Act Their Age*, as well as the carnation contemplated by DePoe in *Flowers on a One-way Street*.

41 Soundtrack from *Flowers on a One-way Street*, 57 min., 16mm, sound, b&w film, National Film Board of Canada, Montreal, QC, Canada, 1967.

42 Soundtrack from *Flowers on a One-way Street*, 57 min., 16mm, sound, b&w film, National Film Board of Canada, Montreal, QC, Canada, 1967.

43 Soundtrack from *The Teens*, 26 min., 16mm., sound, colour film, National Film Board of Canada, Montreal, QC, Canada, 1957.

44 Occasionally during the filming in the council chambers, members of the NFB film crew unintentionally become part of the scene. They are approximately the same age as those who are protesting, a possible explanation for the bias of the film as well as for the discomfort of the mayor with their presence.

45 Soundtrack from *Flowers on a One-way Street*, 57 min., 16mm, sound, b&w film, National Film Board of Canada, Montreal, QC, Canada, 1967. Indeed, the NFB was accused by the Toronto press of being the instigators of the "revolution" on Yorkville Street, perhaps of even staging it. See Gary Evans, *In the National Interest: A Chronicle of the National Film Board of Canada* (Toronto: University of Toronto Press, 1991), p. 153. The seemingly subconscious choice of the singular term "mind" in the remark made by councillor Lamport neatly captures the cohesive thinking of the protestors.

46 Soundtrack from *Flowers on a One-way Street*, 57 min., 16mm, sound, b&w film, National Film Board of Canada, Montreal, QC, Canada, 1967.

47 That is, Studio D rapidly gained hegemony over production of childhood images, especially after winning an Academy Award for best documentary production with *I'll Find a Way* (1977).

48 Christopher Lasch, *The Culture of Narcissism: American Life in an Age of Diminishing Expectations* (New York: W.W. Norton, 1978), p. 30.

49 Ibid.

50 Ibid., p. 48.

51 The exception to this is the Newfoundland family portrayed in the production of *Julie O'Brien*, 19 min., 16mm, sound, Colour film, National Film Board of Canada, Montreal, QC, Canada, 1981.

52 Soundtrack from *Day Care—The Newest Tradition*, 28 min., 16mm, sound, Colour film, National Film Board of Canada, Montreal, QC, Canada, 1978.

53 Soundtrack from *The Umpire*, 17 min., 16mm, sound, Colour film, National Film Board of Canada, Montreal, QC, Canada, 1985.

54 The social interactions between the local adult leaders of these groups and the children they coach or supervise—typically warm but demanding—are more resistant to democratization than any parallel interpersonal relationships in the NFB family or school, possibly one reason why, despite the clientele potential, extinction is the cinematic fate of many of these bodies.

55 No doubt these cinematographers have followed the Griersonian credo: "actions of great consequence in the profession of mindbending [have] to be considered *sub spatia* [i.e., in the light of eternal judgement.] John Grierson quoted in The John Grierson Project, McGill University, *John Grierson and the NFB*: (Toronto: ECW, 1984), p. 44.

Chapter 8: Epilogue

1 Joyce Nelson, *Sign Crimes/Road Kill: From Mediascape to Landscape* (Toronto: Between the Lines, 1992), p. 64.

2 Ibid. Nelson is not unmindful of the existence of Canadian projectors playing images across the national screen, the Canadian Broadcasting Corporation (CBC) Television Network in particular. But she notes the following "ghastly details" from a 1984 study of programming practices on English-language Canadian TV stations and networks: 1) only 28% of all English-language television is Canadian and 2) for every hour of Canadian drama on Canadian TV and cable, there are 45 hours of foreign drama (predominantly American).

3 This conclusion seems at odds with Neil Sutherland's contention in *Growing Up* (1997) that, in general over the "century of the child," most aspects of childhood have either improved or remained much as they were. Sutherland, however, allows that the subject is a contentious one, particularly in regard to children's mental health.

4 John Grierson quoted in Evans, *In the National Interest*, p. 214.

5 Soundtrack from *Four Families*, 59 min., 16mm, sound, b&w film, National Film Board of Canada, Montreal, QC, Canada, 1959. "Liberty," Gesell wrote, "is the life principle of democracy." Gesell and Ilg, *Infant and Child in the Culture of Today*, p. x.

6 Steven L. Schlossman, "Philanthropy and the Gospel of Child Development," in *History of Education Quarterly* (Fall 1981): 297.

7 Katherine Arnup, *Education for Motherhood: Advice for Mothers in Twentieth-Century Canada* (Toronto: University of Toronto Press, 1994), p. 40; Seeley et al., *Crestwood Heights*, p. x.

8 Cynthia R. Comacchio, *"Nations Are Built of Babies": Saving Ontario's Mothers and Children, 1900-1940* (Montreal and Kingston: McGill-Queen's University Press, 1993), p. 184.

9 Hilde Bruch, *Don't Be Afraid of Your Child* (New York: Farrar, Straus and Young, 1952), p. 7.

10 Soundtrack from *What's On Your Mind?*, 10 min., 16mm, sound, b&w film, National Film Board of Canada, Montreal, QC, Canada, 1946.

11 Soundtrack from *Know Your Baby* 9 min., 16mm, sound, b&w film, National Film Board of Canada, Montreal, QC, Canada, 1947.

12 Soundtrack from *Why Won't Tommy Eat?*, 17 min. 16mm, sound, Colour film, National Film Board of Canada, Montreal, QC, Canada, 1948.

13 Schlossman, "Philanthropy and the Gospel of Child Development," p. 295.

14 Seeley et al., *Crestwood Heights*, p. 410.

15 Why the NFB chose to cast its cinematic parents in the hygienist mould is readily apparent: the philosophy was ubiquitous in the immediate postwar period. Again, see Gleason, *Normalizing the Ideal* (1999) in this regard. That the Film Board specifically chose Gesell and Ilg's *Infant and Child in the Culture of Today* as the authoritative interpretation of the construct may be attributed to the ideological underpinnings of their work: "democracy" and "scientism." In postwar Canada, these concepts had heightened power as rationales for public policy. Of the latter, as Donald Fisher observes in his *Fundamental Development of the Social Sciences: Rockefeller Philanthropy and the United States Social Science Research Council* (1993), p. 14, "By the turn of the century, "science" and "scientist" had become the most legitimate knowledge labels in North American society. During this century, the primary route for increasing the power and raising the status of knowledge has been to make it scientific." Democratic child-rearing praxis, being the product (or so it seemed) of systematic research conducted under the auspices of the School of Medicine at Yale University, was a paradigm for parenting that transcended personal experience and common sense.

16 Gesell and Ilg, *Infant and Child in the Culture of Today*, p. 48.

17 Benjamin Spock, *The Pocket Book of Baby and Child Care* (New York: Pocket Books, 1946), p. 30.

18 Perhaps Spock's most famous maxim for moms is of particular relevance in this regard: "Trust yourself. You know more than you think you do"; Spock, *Baby and Child Care* p. 3.

19 Key, *The Century of the Child*, p. 99.

Bibliography

Adams, Mary Louise. *The Trouble with Normal: Postwar Youth and the Making of Heterosexuality*. Toronto: University of Toronto Press, 1997.

Aitken, Ian. *Film and Reform: John Grierson and the Documentary Film Movement*. London: Routledge, 1990.

Ariès, Philippe. *Centuries of Childhood: A Social History of Family Life*. New York: Random House, 1962.

Arnup, Katherine. *Education for Motherhood: Advice for Mothers in Twentieth-Century Canada*. Toronto: University of Toronto Press, 1994.

Barnouw, Erik. *Documentary: A History of the Non-Fiction Film*. Oxford: Oxford University Press, 1983.

Beinart, Jennifer. "Darkly Through a Lens: Changing Perceptions of the African Child in Sickness and Health, 1900-1945." In *In the Name of the Child: Health and Welfare, 1880-1940*, edited by Roger Cooter. London: Routledge, 1992

Beveridge, James. *John Grierson, Film Master*. New York: MacMillan, 1978.

Bidd, Donald W., ed. *The NFB Film Guide: The Productions of the National Film Board of Canada from 1939-1989*. Montreal: The National Film Board of Canada and The National Archives of Canada, 1991.

Blumer, Herbert and Philip M. Hauser. *Movies, Delinquency, and Crime*. New York: MacMillan, 1933.

Bruch, Hilde. *Don't Be Afraid of Your Child*. New York: Farrar, Straus and Young, 1952.

Bruner, Jerome. *The Process of Education*. Cambridge: Harvard University Press, 1960.

Charters, Werret W. *Motion Pictures and Youth: A Summary*. New York: MacMillan, 1933.

Cohen, Sol. "Every School a Clinic: A Historical Perspective on Modern American Education." In *From the Campus: Perspectives on the School Reform Movement*, edited by Sol Cohen and Lewis Solomon. New York: Praeger, 1989.

————. "The Mental Hygiene Movement, the Commonwealth Fund and Public Education, 1921-1933." In *Private Philanthropy: Proceedings of the Rockefeller Archive Center Conference*, edited by Gerald Benjamin. New York: Rockefeller Archive Publication, 1980.

————. "The Mental Hygiene Movement and the Development of Personality: Changing Conceptions of the American College and University." *History of Higher Education Annual* 2 (1982): 65-101.

————. "The Mental Hygiene Movement, The Development of the Personality and the School: The Medicalization of American Education." *History of Education Quarterly*, 23 (1983): 123-49.

————. *Progressives and Urban School Reform: the Public Education Association of New York City, 1895-1954*. New York: Teachers College Bureau of Publications, 1964.

————. "The School and Personality Development: Intellectual History." In *Historical Inquiry in Education: A Research Agenda*, edited by John Best. Washington, DC: A.E.R.A., 1983.

Comacchio, Cynthia R. *"Nations Are Built of Babies": Saving Ontario's Mothers and Children, 1900-1940*. Montreal and Kingston: McGill-Queen's University Press, 1993.

Considine, David M. *The Cinema of Adolescence*. Jefferson: McFarland, 1985.

Cripps, Thomas. "Film: The Historian's Dangerous Friend." *Film and History* 5 (December 1975): 6-9.

Darvi, Andrea. *Pretty Babies: An Insider's Look at the World of the Hollywood Child Star*. New York: McGraw-Hill, 1983.

Davis, Glenn. *Childhood and History in America*. New York: Psychohistory Press, 1976.

DeMause, Lloyd, ed. *The History of Childhood*. New York: Psychohistory Press, 1974.

Ehrenreich, Barbara. *The Hearts of Men: American Dreams and the Flight from Commitment*. New York: Anchor Press, 1983.

Ehrenreich, Barbara and Deirdre English. *For Her Own Good: 150 Years of the Experts' Advice to Women*. Garden City: Anchor Press, 1978.

Eichler, Margrit. *Families in Canada Today: Recent Changes and Their Policy Consequences*, 2nd ed. Toronto: Gage, 1988.

Ellis, Jack C. "The Young Grierson in America, 1924-1927." *Cinema Journal* 8 (Fall 1968): 12-21.

Evans, Gary. "John Grierson's Final Advice to the National Film Board of Canada, 1966-1971." *Historical Journal of Film, Radio, and Television* 9 (1989): 291-300.

————. *John Grierson and the National Film Board: The Politics of Wartime Propaganda*. Toronto: University of Toronto Press, 1984.

————. *In the National Interest: A Chronicle of the National Film Board of Canada from 1949 to 1989*. Toronto: University of Toronto Press, 1991.

Farson, Richard. *Birthrights*. New York: MacMillan, 1974.

Fielding, Raymond. "Newsfilm as a Scholarly Resource: Opportunities and Hazards." *Historical Journal of Film, Radio and Television* 7 (1987): 47-54.

Fisher, Donald. *Fundamental Development of the Social Sciences: Rockefeller Philanthropy and the United States Social Science Research Council*. Ann Arbor: University of Michigan Press, 1993.

Fledelius, Karsten. "Audio-visual History: The Development of a New Field of Research." *Historical Journal of Film, Radio and Television* 9 (1989): 151-63.

Frank, Lawrence. "Childhood and Youth." In *Recent Social Trends in the United States: Report of the President's Research Committee on Social Trends*. 2 vols. New York: McGraw-Hill, 1933.

Freeman, Frank N. *Visual Education: A Comparative Study of Motion Pictures and Other Methods of Instruction*. Chicago: The University of Chicago Press, 1924.

Gesell, Arnold and Frances Ilg. *The Child from Five to Ten: From the Former Clinic of Child Development School of Medicine at Yale University*. New York: Harper and Brothers, 1946.

————. *Infant and Child in the Culture of Today: The Guidance of Development in Home and Nursery School*. New York: Harper and Brothers, 1943.

Gleason, Mona. *Normalizing the Ideal: Psychology, Schooling, and the Family in Postwar Canada*. Toronto: University of Toronto Press, 1997.

Graham, C.G. *Canadian Film Technology: 1896-1986*. Toronto: Associated University Presses, 1989.

Gray, C.W. "Movies for the People: The Story of the National Film Board's Unique Distribution System." Ottawa: National Film Board of Canada, 1973.

Greven, Philip J. *The Protestant Temperament: Patterns of Child-rearing, Religious Experience, and the Self in Early America*. New York: Alfred A. Knopf, 1977.

————. *Spare the Child: The Religious Roots of Punishment and the Psychological Impact of Physical Abuse*. New York: Alfred A. Knopf, 1991.

Grierson. 58 min., 16mm, sound, colour film. National Film Board of Canada, Montreal, QC, 1973.

Grierson, John. *Eyes of Democracy*. Stirling: University of Stirling Press, 1990.

Griffin, J.D.M. and J.R. Seeley, "Education for Mental Health: An Experiment." *Canadian Education* 7 (June 1952): 15-25.

Hardy, Forsyth. *John Grierson: A Documentary Biography*. London: Faber and Faber, 1979.

Hardy, Forsyth, ed. *Grierson on Documentary*. London: Faber and Faber, 1946.

Harrison, Ross. *Bentham*. London: Routledge & Kegan Paul, 1983.

Herman, Ellen. *The Romance of American Psychology: Political Culture in the Age of Experts*. Berkeley: University of California Press, 1995.

Hoover, Dwight. *Middletown: The Making of a Documentary Film Series*. Philadelphia: Harwood Academic Publisher, 1992.

Jacob, Theodore. "Family Interaction in Disturbed and Normal Families: A Methodological and Substantive Review." *Psychological Bulletin* 82 (1975): 33-65.

Jackson, Kathy Merlock. *Images of Children in American Film: A Sociocultural Analysis*. Metuchen, NJ: The Scarecrow Press, 1986.

Jarvie, Ian and Robert L. MacMillan. "John Grierson on Hollywood's Success, 1927." *Historical Journal of Film, Radio, and Television* 9 (1989): 309-320.

Jones, David B. "Assessing the Film Board, Crediting Grierson." *Historical Journal of Film, Radio, and Television* 9 (1989): 301-308.

————. *Movies and Memoranda: An Interpretive History of the National Film Board of Canada*. Ottawa: Canadian Film Institute, 1981.

Jowett, Garth S., Ian C. Jarvie, and Kathryn H. Fuller. *Children and the Movies: Media Influence and the Payne Fund Controversy*. Cambridge: Cambridge University Press, 1996.

Keller, Marjorie. *The Untutored Eye: Childhood in the Films of Cocteau, Cornell, and Brakhage*. Rutherford, NJ: Faircleigh Dickinson University Press, 1986.

Key, Ellen. *The Century of the Child*. New York: G.P. Putnam's Sons, 1909.

Lasch, Christopher. *The Culture of Narcissism*. New York: Norton, 1979.

Lippmann, Walter. *The Phantom Public*. New York: MacMillan, 1926.

————. *Public Opinion*. New York: MacMillan, 1922.

Lynd, Robert S. and Helen Merrell Lynd. *Middletown: A Study in American Culture*. New York: Harcourt Brace Jovanovich, 1929.

McKay, Marjorie. *History of the National Film Board of Canada*. Ottawa: The National Film Board of Canada, 1964.

————. "The Motion Picture: a Mirror of Time," in the *NFB Annual Report, 1958-59* Ottawa: National Film Board of Canada, 1959.

McLuhan, Marshall. *The Gutenberg Galaxy: The Making of Typographic Man*. Toronto: University of Toronto Press, 1962.

————. *Understanding Media: The Extensions of Man*. New York: New American Library, 1964.

McLuhan, Marshall and Quentin Fiore. *The Medium is the Massage*. New York: Bantam Books, 1967.

Magder, Ted. *Canada's Hollywood: The Canadian State and Feature Films*. Toronto: University of Toronto Press, 1993.

Mann, Jean. "G.M. Weir and H.B. King: Progressive Education or Education for the Progressive State?" In *Schooling and Society in 20th Century British Columbia*, edited by J. Donald Wilson. Calgary: Detselig, 1980.

————. "Progressive Education and the Depression in British Columbia." Unpublished M.A. thesis, University of British Columbia, 1978.

May, Elaine Tyler. *Homeward Bound: American Families in the Cold War Era*. New York: Basic Books, 1988.

Morera, Esteve. *Gramsci's Historicism: A Realist Interpretation*. London: Routledge, 1990.

Morris, Peter. *NFB: The War Years*. Ottawa: The National Film Board of Canada, 1965.

Murrell, Stanley A. and James G. Stachowiak. "Consistency, Rigidity, and Power in the Interaction Patterns of Clinic and Non-clinic Families." *Journal of Abnormal Psychology* 72 (1967): 265-72.

Neatby, Hilda. *So Little for the Mind*. Toronto: Clarke, Irwin, 1953.

Nelson, Joyce. *The Colonized Eye: Rethinking the Grierson Legend*. Toronto: Between the Lines Press, 1988.

————. *The Perfect Machine: TV in the Nuclear Age*. Toronto: Between the Lines Press, 1987.

————. *Sign Crimes/Road Kill: From Mediascape to Landscape*. Toronto: Between the Lines Press, 1992.

Owram, Doug. *Born at the Right Time: A History of the Baby-Boom Generation*. Toronto: University of Toronto Press, 1996.

Phillips, C.E. *The Development of Education in Canada*. Toronto: W.J. Gage, 1957.

Postman, Neil. *The Disappearance of Childhood*. New York: Delacorte Press, 1982.

Pratley, Gerald. *Torn Sprockets: The Uncertain Projection of the Canadian Film*. Toronto: Associated University Presses, 1987.

Pronay, Nicholas. "John Grierson and the Documentary—60 Years On." *Historical Journal of Film, Radio, and Television* 9 (1989): 227-46.

————. "The 'Moving Picture' and Historical Research." *Journal of Contemporary History* 18 (July 1983): 365-96.

Raymond, Jocelyn M. *The Nursery World of Dr. Blatz*. Toronto: University of Toronto Press, 1991.

Retamar, Roberto. *Cuba: la fotografía de los años 60*. Havana: Fototeca de Cuba, 1988.

Richards, Jeffrey. "The British Board of Film Censors and Content Control in the 1930s: Images of Britain." *Historical Journal of Film, Radio, and Television* 1 (1981): 95-116.

Richardson, Theresa. *The Century of the Child: The Mental Hygiene Movement and Social Policy in the United States and Canada*, New York: State University of New York Press, 1989.

Riesman, David. *The Lonely Crowd: A Study of the Changing American Character*. New Haven: Yale University Press, 1950.

Rutherford, Paul. *When Television Was Young: Primetime Canada 1952-1967*. Toronto: University of Toronto Press, 1990.

Schlossman, Steven L. "Philanthropy and the Gospel of Child Development." *History of Education Quarterly* 21 (Fall 1981): 275-99.

Schuham, Anthony I. "Power Relations in Emotionally Disturbed and Normal Family Triads." *Journal of Abnormal Psychology* 75 (1970): 30-37.

Seeley, John, R., Alexander Sim, and Elizabeth W. Loosley, *Crestwood Heights: A Study of the Culture of Suburban Life*. Toronto: University of Toronto Press, 1956.

Sinyard, Neil. *Children in the Movies*. New York: St. Martin's Press, 1992.

Spock, Benjamin, M.D. *The Pocket Book of Baby and Child Care*. New York: Pocket Books, 1946.

————. *Spock on Spock: A Memoir of Growing Up with the Century*. New York: Pantheon Books, 1985.

Spring, Joel. *Images of American Life: A History of Ideological Management in Schools, Movies, Radio, and Television*. New York: SUNY, 1992.

Stacey, Judith. *Brave New Families: Upheaval in Late Twentieth Century America*. New York: Basic Books, 1990.

Stamp, Robert M. *The Schools of Ontario*. Toronto: University of Toronto Press, 1982.

Stead, Peter. "Hollywood's Message for the World: The British Response in the Nineteen Thirties." *Historical Journal of Film, Radio, and Television* 1 (1981): 19-32.

Strong-Boag, Veronica. "Home Dreams: Women and the Suburban Experiment in Canada, 1945-60." *Canadian Historical Review*, 82 (1991): 471-504.

Sussex, Elizabeth. *The Rise and Fall of British Documentary: The Story of the Film Movement Founded by John Grierson*. Berkeley: University of California Press, 1975.

Sutherland, Neil. *Children in English-Canadian Society: Framing the Twentieth-Century Consensus*. Waterloo: Wilfrid Laurier University Press, 2000.

————. *Growing Up: Childhood in English Canada from the Great War to the Age of Television*. Toronto: University of Toronto Press, 1997.

————. " 'The Triumph of Formalism': Elementary Schooling in Vancouver from the 1920's to the 1960's." In *Children, Teachers and Schools in the History of British Columbia*, edited by Jean Barman, Neil Sutherland, and J. Donald Wilson. Calgary: Detselig Enterprises, 1995.

Swann, Paul. "John Grierson and the GPO Film Unit 1933-1939." *Historical Journal of Film, Radio, and Television*, 3 (1983): 19-34.

Taylor, Philip M. "Techniques of Persuasion: basic ground rules of British propaganda during the Second World War." *Historical Journal of Film, Radio, and Television* 1 (1981): 57-66.

Thompson, E.P. *The Making of the English Working Class*. Harmondsworth: Penguin, 1968.

Thompson, John B. *Ideology and Modern Culture: Critical Social Theory in the Era of Mass Communication*. Cambridge: Polity Press, 1990.

Tomkins, George. *A Common Countenance: Stability and Change in the Canadian Curriculum*. Toronto: Prentice-Hall, 1986.

Torti, Anna. *The Glass of Form: Mirroring Structures from Chaucer to Skelton*. Cambridge: D.S. Brewer, 1991.

Weiss, Gillian. "An Essential Year for the Child: The Kindergarten in British Columbia," in *Schooling and Society in Twentieth Century British Columbia*, edited by J. Donald Wilson and David C. Jones. Calgary: Detselig Enterprises, 1980.

Weiss, Nancy. "Mother, the Invention of Necessity: Dr. Benjamin Spock's Baby and Child Care." *American Quarterly* 29 (Winter 1977): 519-46.

Whitaker, Reg and Gary Marcuse. *Cold War Canada: The Making of a National Insecurity State, 1945-1957*. Toronto: University of Toronto Press, 1994.

Wilson, J. Donald. "From the Swinging Sixties to the Sobering Seventies," in *Precepts, Policy and Process: Perspectives on Contemporary Canadian Education*, edited by Hugh A. Stevenson and J. Donald Wilson. London, ON: Alexander Blake Associates, 1977.

Wilson, J. Donald; Robert M. Stamp, and Louise-Phillipe Audet. *Canadian Education: A History*. Scarborough: Prentice-Hall, 1970.

Wood, Anne. *Idealism Transformed: The Making of a Progressive Educator*. Kingston: McGill-Queen's University Press, 1985.

Zelizer, Viviana. *Pricing the Priceless Child: The Changing Social Value of Children*. New York: Basic Books, 1985.

Zuckerman, Michael. "Dr. Spock: the Confidence Man," in *Almost Chosen People: Oblique Biographies in the American Grain*. Berkeley: University of California Press, 1993.

Index

Note—Book titles followed by author in parentheses; films followed by (film).